CLAIMING SCOTLAND

CLAIMING SCOTLAND

National Identity and Liberal Culture

JONATHAN HEARN

POLYGON
AT EDINBURGH

© Jonathan Hearn, 2000

Polygon at Edinburgh
An imprint of Edinburgh University Press Ltd
22 George Square, Edinburgh

Typeset in 11 on 13pt Goudy Old Style
by Hewer Text Ltd, Edinburgh, and
printed and bound in Great Britain by
The Cromwell Press, Trowbridge, Wilts

A CIP record for this book is available
from the British Library

ISBN 1 902930 16 9 (paperback)

Recipient of a University of Edinburgh Award
for Distinguished Scottish Scholarship.

There is a country, said he, in the world, called Fourli, no matter for its longitude or latitude, whose inhabitants have ways of thinking, in many things, particularly in morals, diametrically opposed to ours. When I came among them, I found that I must submit to double pains: first to learn the meaning of the terms in their language, and then to know the import of those terms, and the praise or blame attached to them.

David Hume, *A Dialogue*

Contents

Acknowledgements

My thanks go out to Polygon for allowing me to quote extensively from their publication of the *Claim of Right for Scotland* (Edwards 1989), and to Hamish Henderson for allowing me to include the text of his song *Freedom Come-All-Ye*. Parts of Chapter 10 appeared previously in *Scottish Affairs* as 'The Social Contract: Re-Framing Scottish Nationalism' (Hearn 1998).

Preface

For we ha'e faith
in Scotland's hidden poo'ers,
The present's theirs,
but a' the past and fut_re's oors.[1]
Hugh MacDiarmid

These words are from the Scottish nationalist poet Hugh MacDiarmid's
The Flyting of Dunbar and Kennedie. They can be found inscribed in a
plaque embedded in the base of a cairn that sits atop Calton Hill, a
scenic park of observatories and monuments that overlooks central
Edinburgh. Called the 'Democracy Cairn', it was erected late in 1993
by an informal campaigning group called Democracy for Scotland that
had held a constant vigil between 1992 and 1997 outside the Scottish
Office at the base of Calton Hill, in protest at the Tory government's
intractable resistance to the widespread desire in Scotland for constitutional change, either in the form of a devolved Scottish parliament, or
national independence.

The Vigil, as it was commonly called, has packed up and gone, because of
two remarkable events that took place in 1997. First, in the general election
of May of that year, after eighteen years in opposition, the Labour Party
regained power, under the adroit leadership of Tony Blair and the reformed
and centrist mantle of New Labour. Moreover, of the seventy-two parliamentary seats in Scotland, not a single one was captured or retained by the
Tories, who had already been reduced to a mere eleven seats in Scotland,
despite their majority in England. This 'wipe out' of the Tories in Scotland,
the occasion of much celebrating in Scotland after the election, is the end
point of a long secular trend, and is due in large part to that party's
recalcitrance in regard to the constitutional issue, which had alienated even
its normal base of support. The second event was the national referendum

on the establishment of a Scottish parliament held on 11 September 1997. Blair's Labour Party had pledged itself before the election to administer such a referendum, and this was an essential factor in consolidating Scottish support. Memories of the rejection of devolution in a similar referendum in 1979, and the cessation of campaigning out of regard for the untimely death of the Princess of Wales ten days before the 1997 referendum, led many to fear a repetition of 1979. Instead, the two-part referendum, which asked voters if they wanted a parliament, and if they wanted it to have certain limited tax raising powers, the latter seen as more controversial, was approved overwhelmingly on the first question, and solidly on the second. In referendum parlance, the people of Scotland voted 'Yes/Yes'. As a result Scotland saw the election of its first parliament in almost 300 years on 6 May 1999, and many suspect that complete independence will follow within a few decades.

Thus it would appear that Scotland's powers are no longer hidden, that the present has been delivered back into Scotland's hands. This book asks how this change, this new political situation, came about, attempting an answer by examining the language of nationalism in Scotland, its moral critique of the status quo, and ways of articulating political claims. It is a language that has tended to oppose neoliberal social policies and radical free market agendas, while defending the ideas of social democracy and the welfare state, and associating these values and stances with Scottish history, culture, and identity. This study tries to make sense of such critiques and claims by contextualising them within the dynamics of political mobilisation and social movement organisation, and within a deeper history of political institutions and discourses in Scotland. A core argument that emerges out of this approach is that the histories of nationalism and liberalism are deeply entwined in Scotland, and that both are equally cultural processes. Thus, while affirming the common characterisation of Scottish nationalism as of a 'civic' or 'liberal' variety, conventional distinctions between 'cultural' and 'political', or 'ethnic' and 'civic' forms of nationalism are also called into question.

MacDiarmid's words also suggest a fundamental tension between the real, pragmatic holding of power in the present, and a morally superior faith in a power invested in a remembered past, and an imagined future. He provides us with a poetic gloss on the key dilemma of all oppositional political movements, which is how to translate a politico-moral agenda about what should be, into what is – how to obtain effective power, while retaining moral legitimacy. By the conclusion of this book I hope to have shown that a careful consideration of the Scottish case can shed light on this more general, and paradoxical, political process.

As usual, numerous debts, material, intellectual, and moral, have been incurred in the making of this book. Both the research and writing were funded by the Wenner-Gren Foundation for Anthropological Research, and the writing was also supported by the City University of New York Graduate School and University Center. The departments of politics and sociology at the University of Edinburgh have provided a friendly and stimulating environment during the final period of revisions, and my editor at Edinburgh University Press, Nicola Carr, has been both helpful and encouraging. My thanks also to Ian Clark for his careful copy editing.

Jane Schneider supervised the doctoral dissertation on which this book is based, and has been a key source of inspiration in my efforts to explore the interconnections between moral discourses and political economies, as well as a mentor in the ways of scholarship. Through many stimulating discussions, David McCrone and Lindsay Paterson have generously guided my struggles to understand Scotland and nationalism. John Glassford, as the tireless interlocutor wielding the opposing pint, has done much to sharpen my arguments all around. Although he was never directly involved in this project, I would like to acknowledge the considerable intellectual influence that the late Eric Wolf had on me. All of the following contributed intellectually to this book's development, both directly and indirectly, at various stages: Christiana Bastos, Helio Belik, Alice Brown, Anthony Cohen, Vincent Crapanzano, Arlene Davila, Molly Doane, Nick Hopkins, Yvonne LaSalle, Neil MacCormick, Alasdair MacIntyre, Anthony Marcus, Kate McCaffrey, Eric McGuckin, Tom Nairn, Maureen O'Dougherty, Gerald Sider, and Ara Wilson. I have benefited greatly from the critical engagements of these friends, peers, colleagues and teachers, and whatever shortcomings this work may have despite their contributions are strictly of my own doing.

I am deeply grateful to the many people in Scotland that have shared their time and thoughts both in interviews and in more informal conversations. At a minimum, I would specifically like to thank Vernon Galloway, Murdo MacDonald, Bob McLean, Tim Porteous, Kevin Pringle, Marion Ralls, Stan Reeves, Michele Sharon, everyone at the Adult Learning Project, and everyone at Democracy for Scotland, for their generous help in facilitating my research, and making it a such rewarding experience.

Finally, making this book has taught me a lot about that anthropological mainstay, kinship. I have drawn much moral (not to mention material) support from my extended family of parents, siblings, in-laws and cousins, and am enduringly grateful to Elinor Hearn, Arnold and Tricia Hearn,

Steve and Diana Hearn, Tim and Carol Hearn, Kris and Jeff Kidder, Betsy Hearn and Drew Danielson, and Karen McLaughlin and Mark Schubin. My special thanks to Gale, who saw the beginning of this book, and then reappeared so mysteriously, with Chicken and Mig, at the end.

– NOTE –

1. poo'ers = powers; oors = ours.

Chronology

1742 Centenary of the Solemn League and Covenant observed by Associate Presbytery

1745 Jacobite uprising

1746 Defeat of Jacobites at battle of Culloden

1761 Second church secession establishes the Relief Church

1790–1830 Main period of the Highland Clearances

1792 Friends of the People Society established (Radical organisation)

1793 United Scotsmen established (Radical organisation)

1820 The 'Radical War'

1832 First Reform Act

1842 Second Claim of Right

1843 Kirk splits in the 'Great Disruption'

1868 Second Reform Act

1880–1914 Approximate period of the 'Kailyard' literature

1882 Highland Land League formed

1884 Third Reform Act

1885 Secretary for Scotland established

1885 Crofter's Party established

1886 Scottish Home Rule Association established

1886 Crofter's Holding Act

1887 Scottish Office established

1888 Scottish Labour Party established

1893 Independent Labour Party established

1906 Labour Party in Scotland established

1912 Conservative Party merges with break-away pro-union Liberals

1918 Scottish Home Rule Association re-established

1919 Peak of Red Clydeside labour unrest

1920 Communist Party of Great Britain established

1920 Scots National League established

1923 John MacLean campaigns as a Scottish Worker's Republican candidate

1924 Labour home rule bill put before parliament

1927 Labour home rule bill put before parliament

1928 National Party of Scotland established

1932 Scottish Self-Government Party established

1934 Scottish National Party founded out of earlier national parties

1935 Communist Party adopts popular front, rapprochement with home rule movement

1942 Beveridge Report signals growth of British welfare state

1942 Split in SNP over party versus movement strategies

1945 Robert MacIntyre wins Motherwell by-election for SNP

1947   Scottish National Assembly formed by John MacCormick
1949   National Covenant created
1949–66   New Towns established
1967   Winnie Ewing wins Hamilton by-election for SNP
1972   Assembly in Northern Ireland abolished
1973   Scottish Local Government reorganisation; COSLA established
1974   SNP sends eleven MPs to Westminster
1978   *Scottish Government Yearbook* established
1979   First devolution referendum
1979   '79 Group formed (within SNP)
1979   Campaign for a Scottish Assembly (later Parliament) established
1979   Margaret Thatcher and Conservatives win general election
1979   First version of Siol Nan Gaidheal formed
1983   General election
1983–91   Duration of magazine *Radical Scotland*
1985   Greater London Council abolished
1987   General election
1988   Third Claim of Right
1988   Scottish Labour Action formed (within Labour)
1988   Second version of Siol Nan Gaidheal formed
1989   Scottish Constitutional Convention established
1989   'Poll Tax' introduced in Scotland
1991   Democratic Left formed out of Communist Party
1992   General election (April); Tommy Sheridan gets 20% of vote
          running for Westminster while serving sentence for non-
          payment of Poll Tax.
1992   Common cause established in run-up to general election
1992   Democracy for Scotland formed in wake of general election
1992   Scotland United formed in wake of general election
1992   Democracy Declaration presented at the Scotland Demands
          Democracy Rally, on the occasion of the European Summit
          (December)
1993   Scottish Watch and Settler Watch begin appearing in the news
1993   Coalition for Scottish Democracy formed
1993   Rally to Recall Scotland's Parliament out of Adjournment
          (November)
1993   Campaign for a Scottish Parliament conducts mini-referendum
          in Falkirk
1993   *Scottish Affairs* replaces the *Scottish Government Yearbook*
1994   Labour Party Scotland changes name to Scottish Labour Party

1994 Consultative Conference on the establishment of a Scottish Senate (later the Scottish Civic Forum)
1994 Death of John Smith, Labour Party leader
1995–96 Scottish Local Government reorganisation
1995 Scottish Constitutional Convention publishes *Scotland's Parliament, Scotland's Right.*
1996 Tory government returns Stone of Destiny to Edinburgh
1997 Labour landslide in general election (May)
1997 Scotland FORward formed
1997 White paper on *Scotland's Parliament* published (July)
1997 Second devolution referendum (September)
1997 Scotland Bill put before parliament (December)
1999 First general election to the Scottish parliament on 6 May
1999 Scottish parliament officially opened on 1 July

Introduction

– CLAIMING SCOTLAND –

There's a lot of talk, made about national debts, though you may not have realised it, but Scotland has a massive national debt, and it's not measured in money. It's a debt to the generations of people, who out of hard and bitter lives, generated decency. And who learned, because they had nothing – 'I know what I'll do, I'll get as much as I can' – no – what they learned is 'I know what I'll do, I'll share, wi' those wi' as little as I have'. [applause/cheers] And I once said, if there was to be a Scottish motto, you'd have the saltire, and the lion rampant, and you wouldn't have across the bottom 'who daur meddle wi' me – take another step and I'll bash your head in' – no – I said you'd have a very simple motto: 'Hey wait a minute – that's no' fair!' [laughter/applause] Because Scottish history I think demonstrates constantly, a terrible desire for fairness . . .

These words were part of a speech given by the Scottish novelist William McIlvanney on 19 March 1994, at a rally held by the Scottish National Party (SNP) in Glasgow's George Square in preparation for the coming local government and Euro-parliamentary elections. McIlvanney's was one of a set of speeches from a familiar cast of party leaders and publicly supportive celebrities. The novelist is not a member of any party, but he voices his political views regularly in public speeches and writings, views at once ensconced in the Labour/socialist tradition, and passionate about Scottish self-determination. His message was designed for his audience, and antici-pates their expectations. The tone struck is representative of the language that permeates Scottish nationalism. McIlvanney invokes a national iden-tity historically rooted in egalitarian values, and opposed (implicitly here, explicitly elsewhere in the speech) to the values of the Conservative Party and the unbridled free market. This book tries to put utterances like this in context, by examining the larger social processes that generate them.

The first question we must ask is: what do we mean by nationalism? The concept of nationalism is prone to reification. A term best used to designate a complex and little understood web of social processes easily appears to refer to some unitary historical force, or innate disposition of the human heart and mind.[1] This study is critical of this tendency, and seeks to help correct it by treating Scottish nationalism as a particular variation of the more general process of making political claims. When discussing Scotland, the term nationalism must be understood broadly to include both the demand for full national independence, and the more limited demand, now realised, for a devolved parliament within the UK framework. A distinction is often made between 'Nationalists with a big N', i.e., members or supporters of the SNP, and 'nationalists with a small n', i.e., those who feel a certain cultural pride, and probably support devolution, or perhaps even independence, but not the SNP. There are many in Scotland who desire greater political autonomy, but are very uncomfortable with the language of nationalism, and avoid it, well aware of its negative connotations. For simplicity's sake I have chosen to use the most common term and specify its broad sense, although sometimes I will simply refer to nationalism in this broadest sense as 'the Scottish movement'.

The modern, party-based nationalist movement in Scotland first arose in the 1920s, and has become an increasingly significant factor in Scottish electoral politics in the last thirty-five years. This movement is complex and often contradictory in terms of politics understood along a left-right axis, but it has a long association with the Scottish labour movement, and with calls for Scottish and Irish home rule from around the turn of the century. In the middle of the twentieth century however, the Labour Party's increasing access to power at Westminster, the growth of the Keynesian welfare state, and the reinforcement of British identity resulting from the experiences of World War II, all served to marginalise the call for home rule. But the movement has been gradually revitalised – in the 1960s by rising economic expectations, in the 1970s by the vision of underwriting an independent Scotland with revenues from newly discovered North Sea oil, and in the 1980s and 1990s by a defensive stance in regard to the welfare state, seen as a cultural tradition under attack by Conservative governments elected by English constituencies. Between 1974 and 1997 support for independence grew from 21% to 26%, for a devolved parliament from 44% to 51%, and support for an unaltered union fell from 34% to 17% (Brown et al. 1998: 160). Correspondingly, support for the SNP has grown, with considerable highs and lows, support for Labour, converted to the devolution cause in the 1980s, has remained solid, and support for the Conservatives, implacable opponents of constitutional change for so many years, collapsed at the 1997 general election.[2]

Beyond a parliament or a separate state, what do nationalists want? What kinds of claims are being made and associated with this cause? We can begin by outlining three categories: constitutional structures, social policies and cultural valorisation. The Scottish movement dovetails with calls for constitutional reforms found on both sides of the Border, including a written constitution with entrenched powers (i.e., not revocable by a simple majority in parliament), a bill of rights, and a more decentralised, federal governmental structure employing such devices as proportional representation, and actively promoting greater gender balance among political representatives. Attending to these kinds of demands has been a major part of the Blair government's UK-wide agenda, which in addition to delivering parliaments or assemblies in Scotland, Wales and Northern Ireland, is also establishing a Mayor for London, planning reform of the House of Lords, investigating the possibilities for proportional representation, and legislating a Human Rights Bill incorporating the European Convention on Human Rights. These issues have been central to the political programme of the Liberal Democrats, who, while ranking fourth in electoral support in Scotland, have been crucially active in the Scottish movement.

Surveys suggest that people in Scotland are moderately more left-wing than those in the rest of Britain as a whole, being more inclined to support collectivist and redistributive policies on questions such as support for public education, nationalisation of industries, a minimum wage, and income redistribution. However, the differences here are not profound, and when compared more specifically with Wales and northern England, often minimal. What is distinctive is that these values in Scotland have become closely associated with national identity and support for constitutional change, and thus with the parties that have supported such change. The Scottish movement has provided a forum over the years through which these values and policy preferences have been articulated and rendered uniquely Scottish in the popular imagination, an option which simply has not been available in England (Brown et al. 1999: 71–121; Brown et al. 1998: 163–5).

Finally, issues of cultural valorisation, while difficult to pin down, are also important, although some place much more emphasis on this than others. Scots are used to living in the cultural shadow of England, having their history, language and culture measured against an English standard. For centuries Scots have been told that historical progress is a matter of following England's example. Getting ahead has often meant suppressing the Scots language and approximating to the norms of middle-class English speech – and even leaving Scotland all together. Scottish culture has tended to be crudely stereotyped, portrayed as quaint and romantic, a pastiche of kilts, clans and bagpipes, and somehow suspended in a distant past, no longer truly relevant. These images and attitudes have been created as much by the Scots, especially expatriates and the middle class, as by the English. But the result none the less has been a legacy of resentment, and many Scots believe that greater control over their own politics would foster a more confident and self-assured cultural identity (cf. Beveridge and Turnbull 1989; Nairn 1997: 183–93). This said, many years of mobilisation around the cause seem to have already stimulated considerable revaluation of Scottish culture.

While I analyse them here into separate parts, all these concerns blend into a larger, manifold nationalism. Different people emphasise different views, but no one agenda should be mistaken for the whole. Moreover, although issues of cultural valorisation are important, the political activism of the movement is more centred on ideas of constitutional and democratic reform, and ideas about social justice and good government, whether through devolution or independence. There is a strong sense, however, that these ideas and values are grounded in the specifics of Scottish culture and history. Thus as we will see throughout this book, the cultural and the political cannot be fully disarticulated.

Support for nationalism is not easily reduced to social structural factors. In the 1960s and 1970s support for the SNP appeared to be associated with detachment from a traditional social base due to upward mobility from working- to more middle-class forms of employment, and to relocation from decaying urban areas to 'New Towns' established from the 1950s onwards to attract new high-tech industries. By the 1980s however, as the party increasingly moved to the left, its support shifted from predominantly middle class to predominantly working class. In the 1990s the class profiles of support for the SNP and Labour have become very similar in terms of types of employment, housing tenure, and levels of education, with a marginally greater ratio of middle- to working-class support for the SNP than for Labour. More pronounced are the associations of support for both the Conservatives and the Liberal Democrats with salaried employment, home ownership, and higher levels of education, but despite this similarity, these two parties have held almost diametrically opposed views on constitutional change (Brown et al. 1999: 52–9). Catholics tend to be more supportive of devolution than Protestants, reflecting their historical connections to the Labour Party. Men are more inclined to support full independence than women, and both devolution and independence get stronger support from younger age groups, but none of these are powerful predictors of constitutional preferences (Brown et al. 1998: 159–61). There is a tendency for Labour and SNP supporters to privilege their 'Scottish' over their 'British' identities, and to identify as 'working class' regardless of their structural class position. This is particularly true for the SNP. Analysis of voting behaviour around the 1997 referendum on the parliament and its tax raising powers indicates that support was associated with a firm belief that it would be able to improve the general social welfare of people in Scotland (Brown et al. 1999: 113–37). But these factors do not so much explain political preferences as force us to ask why people identify in this way, how they come to believe in the efficacy of the parliament, which is part of the task of this book.

Social movements like this one are not just manifestations of social structural conditions, but perhaps more importantly, strategic responses to changing structures of political opportunity (cf. Tarrow 1994: 17–18; 81–99). Four interrelated processes have been particularly important here. First, the move away from centralised economic planning and management, informed by neoliberal economic theories, has had the effect of weakening one of the main integrating forces in modern Britain. Second, the steady growth of the European Union has both eaten into the sovereignty of the British state, and made the viability of small nations within the EU seem more plausible, and Scottish independence less isolationist. Third, during the years of Conservative government there developed a pronounced polarisation of electoral support, for the Tories in the south-east of England, and for Labour in Wales, the Midlands, and to the north on up to Scotland. Thus tensions over London control of Scottish government were reinforced by the geography of party support and their associated ideologies and values. Finally, there exists in Scotland a complex network of powerful institutions and the social groups that find their careers in those institutions, that is commonly referred to as 'civil society'. This includes churches, unions, campaigning bodies, voluntary organisations, media, the educational and legal systems, as well as the more explicitly political bodies of political parties and local government. As dissatisfaction with Westminster government has grown, demands for constitutional change have been orchestrated throughout this civil society network, not just in the field of party politics. This aspect should remind us that nationalism makes claims not just over territory, but just as crucially over the social institutions that organise people's lives (cf. Brubaker 1996). In connection with this last point, it should be noted that nationalism and social movements more generally, often draw an important part of their leaderships from middling classes of intellectuals, professionals, and careerists, and Scotland is no exception (Hroch 1985; Mann 1993: 546–96) Though no attempt has been made to quantify this aspect of the Scottish movement, I aim to provide an initial mapping of this process (especially in Chapter 4), and of how the ideas and activities of more middle-class and intellectual groups articulate political claims, and influence a broader public opinion.

This movement is not simply a matter of conflicts over power and self-determination between Scotland and the British state. In a larger frame, authority over decisions about economic, and therefore social investment, have been increasingly transferred from democratically elected governments to private sector firms and financial markets. This process is frequently, if somewhat inadequately glossed as 'globalisation' and the decline of the state in the face of the internationalisation of capital (cf. Mann 1996). In Scotland's case, since World War II there has been a trend toward economic dependence on inward investment and external ownership, making for a kind of branch-plant economy. Well over half of Scottish industry is owned outside of Scotland, controlled either by British conglomerates from London, or firms in other countries, especially the US. This external control prevails in the larger industries, much of it in electronics firms linked to the defence industry. Tourism, a major part of the Scottish economy which helps support an extensive service sector, also relies on transnational economic flows, though of a different sort (Brown et al. 1998: 70–96).[3] But we should be careful about regarding this process as the natural and inevitable unfolding of capitalism's logic. There have been conscious decisions and strategies at work in recent decades for transferring investment decisions from public to private hands, the states that house Wall Street and the City of London where many of these decisions get made, have been key agents, not passive by-standers in this process (Henwood 1998; Gray 1999). None the less, we need to realise that part of what is being claimed in Scotland, whether adequately or not, is a more general sense of power and self-determination amid this increasing uncertainty and siphoning-off of power.

– NATIONALISM AND LIBERALISM –

We view the past through the most recent past, and this is true of nationalism. In the post-World War II era, among both marxist-socialists and liberals, there was a strong tendency to see the European conflicts and fascism as the essence of nationalism – its inner core revealed. Its fate was to be supplanted by internationalism, whether of the proletariat or of global free markets (cf. Connor 1994: 4–66; Nairn 1997: 25–46). The horrors of national socialism in Germany meant that racist nationalism became the 'true face' of nationalism in much of the popular imagination of the West. But if we had lived in the middle of the nineteenth century, the picture would have looked much different. Nationalism would more likely be associated for us with the progressive ideals of the French Revolution, *liberté, egalité, fraternité*, with popular sovereignty, and with the overturning of, or breaking away from, absolutist monarchical regimes. From the late eighteenth to the late nineteenth centuries, nationalism and liberalism were closely identified (Hobsbawm 1992; Woolf 1996: 8–15). A core contention of this book is that we must attend to the entwined histories of nationalism and liberalism if we are to understand the Scottish movement.

Theorists of nationalism tend to divide into two types. One tendency is to emphasise the modern origins of nationalism and the nation-state, in the functional requirement for mobility and mass culture in industrial society (Gellner 1983), in the need to ideologically integrate an expanding civil society with the modern bureaucratic state (Breuilly 1993), in the density of new communication networks (Deutsch 1953), and in the convergent effects of literacy, print technology, and capitalism encountering vernacular languages (Anderson 1991). In various ways these approaches maintain that national identity is a by-product of specifically modern political economic processes. The other tendency is to emphasise ethnicity as a much older and more fundamental process that under certain conditions is transformed into nationhood (Armstrong 1982; Smith 1986). These theorists do not deny the importance of modern developments of state and economy for nationalism, but tend to see them as acting on, and mobilised by, some pre-given substrate of ethnic identity. In broad outline, these two approaches reflect a debate about whether nations and nationalism are a result of modern states creating new ethnicities to accompany them, or whether they are a result of usually pre-modern ethnicities pursuing statehood. Still others have tried to reject this dichotomy (Calhoun 1997: 20–3, McCrone 1998: 16). The present study also aims for a middle path, allowing that nations are processes that are constantly made and remade, in some sense invented (Hobsbawm and Ranger 1984), but also the outcomes of very real histories, parts of which can reach back beyond the modern period (cf. Llobera 1994).

A closely related dichotomy, regarding typology as much as origins, is also involved here. It has been common to make a distinction between 'ethnic' and 'civic' forms of nationalism, the former involving beliefs in biological and cultural essentialisms, the latter involving commitments to ideas of citizenship and the rule of law. Hans Kohn (1967) formulated an enduring distinction between the civic nationalisms of Western Europe and the ethnic nationalisms of Central and Eastern Europe, and in a similar vein Rogers Brubaker (1992) has explored the underlying principles of French territorially-based and German descent-based conceptions of national membership. Some have posited an interactive dynamic between ethnic and civic forms. Thus Clifford Geertz (1963) argued that postcolonial nationalisms simultaneously mobilise both primordial ethnic identities and desires for a modern, civic politics. Partha Chatterjee (1993) on the other hand argues that political (i.e., civic) nationalism in postcolonial India was prepared by an earlier phase of cultural (i.e., ethnic) nationalism within the colonial state. Regardless of the subtleties of such context specific analyses, there is a strong tendency in both popular and scholarly discussions to reduce this to an evaluative distinction between good/civic and evil/ethnic nationalisms (Ignatieff 1994). This book questions how far this grand division can be maintained, considering the complex interactions of culture and politics, of ethnicity and the state (cf. Yack 1996).

Scottish nationalism is commonly classified as an example of 'neo-nationalism', along with such cases as Québec and Catalunya (e.g., Keating 1996). Paradigmatically, neo-nationalism occurs in the industrially developed states of the west, and involves political aims that are often ambiguous, combining demands for greater regional autonomy with those for independent statehood. Given this ambivalence, its supporters learn to negotiate complex dual identifications within the incongruent nations and states to which they belong. Significantly, neo-nationalism tends to happen where there is already a well developed economic base and civil society infrastructure, that provides certain base-line conditions for organisation and mobilisation (McCrone 1998: 128–9). Such nationalisms have often been viewed as either retrogressive throwbacks based on primordial cultural romanticism, or as pseudo-nationalisms that bargain instrumentally for a better position within the modern state. But McCrone has argued that such characterisations fail to grasp the flexible and adaptable nature of nationalism as an ideology and mode of political mobilisation (ibid.: 148). One result of this flexibility is that neo-nationalism can often be difficult to place along a conventional left-right political spectrum, seeming to merge these into a less clearly defined progressivism. Nonetheless, liberal and social democratic strains have often predominated in recent decades, even if substantially compromised by an encompassing neoliberal/neoconservative political and economic context. Thus neo-nationalisms are increasingly viewed as exemplifying the more civic species of nationalism.

The crucial points here are that nationalism and liberalism, both as ideas and political-economic processes, have been interdependent, and equating nationalism with ideologies of ethnic essentialism obscures this connection. There has been a recent trend in the nationalism literature toward exploring precisely this relationship from the perspective of normative political theory.[4] Some have relied on an evaluative distinction between nationalism and patriotism. Thus Jürgen Habermas makes a plea for the emancipatory potential of a 'generalised political culture' built around 'constitutional patriotism' rather than nationalism (1996: 289–90), and from a different angle, Maurizio Viroli argues for the rejection of nationalism and the recovery of a republican tradition of patriotism and 'love of country', understood as 'love of common liberty and the institutions that sustain it' (1997: 12). Others, however, have sought to reinterpret nationalism itself in liberal terms. One line of argument is that national identity is one of the many collective identities that a tolerant, culturally pluralist liberalism should respect and support, and that old beliefs in the necessary congruence of nationalities and sovereign states are passé (MacCormick 1996; Tamir 1993; Kymlicka 1995). Another strain, somewhat at odds with this, argues that in practice liberal principles must be embedded in state-associated national communities which can realise the collective will of a liberal minded community (Miller 1995).[5] As Miller observes (ibid.: 193), debates about the relationship between liberalism and nationalism have much in common with those between liberal and communitarian political theorists regarding the grounding of political principles (see Sandel 1984). The former, inspired especially by the work of John Rawls (1971, 1996), have sought to reaffirm the progressive and egalitarian potential of liberal traditions of thought, justifying respect for individual autonomy through rationalist, universalising arguments. Communitarians on the other hand have criticised the liberal position for being too ahistorical and abstract, failing to grasp the socially embedded specificity of the production of norms, and to recognise and respect the considerable differences that divide normative traditions.[6] Despite these differences, the participants in these debates usually share a fair amount of common ground in terms of left-of-centre values, it is in their approaches to theorising that they diverge. I shall be arguing that the tensions between abstract principles and sociohistorical specificity that these debates articulate can also be found in the discourses of Scottish nationalism, with its liberal, civic bent, rooted in Scottish history and culture.

– CULTURE AND IDENTITY –

Culture and identity are slippery concepts, often drafted into service when the processes under consideration are poorly understood. They will be of more use to us if we examine their perplexities at the outset, to alert ourselves to their mercurial tendencies. Many people today are familiar with anthropology's holistic conception of culture as an integrated system of institutions, ideas and practices through which a social group interacts and makes sense of its world. Indeed, when students of nationalism make recourse to the concept of culture, it is to this version that they usually turn. But this is only half the story. Another tendency in anthropology, famously aphorised by Robert Lowie, has been to portray culture as a 'planless hodge-podge', a 'thing of shreds and patches' (1947: 441). The argument here is not that cultures are utterly random and chaotic, but that they are pieced together out of historical contingencies, rather than the result of some fine-tuned ecological adjustment, or some unfolding historical design. Lowie's version has long been out of fashion, and is easily parodied, but it is worth recalling as a useful corrective to more holistic conceptions of culture, that seem to be taken for granted in many discussions of culture's role in the process of nationalism. Better to think in terms of a dialectic of openness and closure in the ways that societies pursue coherence while remaining adaptable and capable of change. Cultures involve a certain density of institutions and interactions, but they are never discrete, bounded systems.

Another question when considering the role of culture in nationalism is how to distinguish culture from ideology. Here again, it is a question of degree, in which the mid-range between the concepts may not be amenable to any clear-cut distinction. As a general guide it is useful to think of ideology as a relatively explicit political analysis and agenda, and culture as a more loosely cohering set of assumptions and beliefs. The clearest examples of ideology are associated with tightly bound social groups with common social and political goals, while culture tends to create a diffuse sense of communality among people who often have quite different interests and perspectives on reality. Much of what we encounter in this study exists in a grey area between these two ideal concepts, but this is precisely the point. In order for ideas to mobilise people they generally need to draw on a recognisable repertoire of cultural forms, so it is the traffic between culture and ideology that must interest us, as much as one or the other (cf. Hearn 1996; Wolf 1999).

One of the most basic puzzles about nationalism is how individuals can come to identify with such a large abstraction. Contemplating the Scottish case, and what he calls 'personal nationalism', Anthony Cohen has argued that part of the explanation lies in the multivocalic nature of the nation as a symbol, its ability to mean different things to different people, while at the same time suggesting a unified identity. Moreover, Cohen stresses that the audiences for nationalist messages are active interpreters, altering those messages in the process in idiosyncratic ways (Cohen 1996). Despite this fissiparous tendency however, social action can and does coalesce around national identities, and certain general features of the process of identification are worth noting here at the outset. First, identities are multiple and situational. Scottish national identity hangs in a constellation of overlapping and interpenetrating identities – British, Celtic, European, Western, working class, to name just a few – which can be variously combined and emphasised according to the goals and demands of the moment. Not only is identity a 'pick-and-mix' business to a degree, but the choices shift over time. Identity is processual, what it means to be Scottish not only varies between individuals, but also historically, as do the larger bundles of identifications with which it becomes associated. Thus the conceptual connections between being Scottish and being British and Protestant (cf. Colley 1992) appear to have weakened over the twentieth century, while those between Scottishness and socialism and Europeanness have become stronger. It has frequently been noted that identities are often constructed in opposition to a particular significant other. Englishness undoubtedly plays that role in relation to Scottishness, a role arising out of a long and complex history of rivalry and interdependence. It would be a mistake however to try to reduce Scottish nationalism to a reactionary anti-Englishness. However polysemic and contentious, there is positive content to Scottish identity, Scotland is a real place with a real history particular to it, no matter how forcefully shaped by external relations with that southern nation. Finally, national identity, like biography, has a tendency to be imagined in narrative forms (McCrone 1998: 52–5). There is a powerful inclination, especially amongst avowed nationalists, to impose a telos on national history – a necessary unfolding toward some ultimate resolution. Scotland is no exception to this tendency.

This returns us to the subject of claim-making. One of the main aims of this book is to understand the ways in which calls for greater political autonomy in Scotland are grounded in the particularities of Scottish culture and history, thereby gaining rhetorical force and political legitimacy. But when we recall our earlier characterisation of Scottish nationalism as, by and large, a liberal nationalism, a certain cognitive dissonance creeps in, because if the claims for this liberal nationalism are culturally constructed, in what sense is it 'liberal'? We are accustomed to thinking of liberalism as, by definition, universalist and a-cultural – this is precisely the nub of the communitarian's critique. Likewise we tend to think of cultures as unique and irreducible to general principles (however much they may exemplify them). But this dichotomy is more a stumbling block than a rule of clarification. Part of what the study of Scottish nationalism can teach us is how liberalism itself arises out of a many stranded culture history from which it cannot be effectively disengaged. The Scottish case illustrates one of those strands, and shows us not only how liberalism has a concrete genealogy in particular national histories, but also how the very practice of making political claims entails the regrounding of universalising arguments in cultural particularity, because such arguments are never made from 'nowhere', even when they aim for some pan-human utopia. It is for this reason that I find the distinction between ethnic and civic nationalisms problematic. To the extent that we understand 'ethnic' as meaning 'cultural' (as opposed to biological or based on some symbolic extension of kinship) all nationalisms, even the most civic and liberal, are ethnic (cf. Nielsen 1999). It seems to me that the conventional use of this distinction confuses very real and important differences between the kinds of ideas, institutions and social relations through which nationalist causes can be advanced, with the presence or absence of culture as a determining factor, and culture is never absent. We will return to this criticism at the end of the book.

– ETHNOGRAPHIC DESIGN AND METHODS –

I am an anthropologist, and while I make no rigid distinctions between anthropology and other disciplines in the social sciences and humanities, and draw on these others freely, the approach taken here is primarily ethnographic and ethnohistorical. Nationalism is, by definition, not a local phenomenon. This is a study of a variegated social movement within a liberal democratic state with a highly modernised economy. The unit of analysis is not a relatively bounded village or cultural group, but rather a range of social organisations, the social milieu they occupy, and the discourses generated within this milieu. Such a unit of analysis is always difficult to define at the margins. Social movements are social forces which confront a spectrum of responses – support, sympathy, ambivalence, indifference, resistance – in their broader social context. Accordingly, caution should be exercised in extrapolating from the beliefs, views and attitudes examined in this study, which are representative of movement discourse, to the same in Scotland as a whole. The larger frame involves substantial variations along dimensions of geography, class, gender and culture that cannot be adequately encompassed within a single ethnographic study. Still, there is broad support (of varying degrees) in Scotland for the movement, and focusing primarily and closely on movement language and social organisation is an important and necessary part of understanding the larger whole.

This study is shaped by the fact that I lived in Edinburgh, and made most of my contacts among a predominantly urban, middle to working class, central belt (i.e., Edinburgh-Glasgow) population. The research is oriented toward movement activism in this region, by far the most populous part of

Scotland. None the less, I made an effort to check, if not balance, this bias. Toward the end I travelled and did interviews in more rural areas outside the central belt of Scotland, namely in the south-west (Dumfries), the north-east (Inverness), and in the Highlands (Assynt) and Islands (Lewis), where Gaelic language and culture are a more important issue. I also did interviews with members of the Conservative Party, some supporting moderate forms of home rule, and others strongly opposed, to provide further points of reference outside the core of the movement.

This study is also shaped by the historical moment of the primary research, September 1993–September 1994, in the wake of the failure of the 1992 general election to advance the constitutional question, and before the possibility of Labour's recapture of Westminster was clearly in view. With the help of follow-up research done in the Summer of 1998 the story is brought up to date, but my interpretation was largely formed during the initial fieldwork. This book characterises the years leading up to the establishment of the new parliament, while allowing that a new chapter in Scottish history has now begun, which is beyond its scope. The historical dimension of the study is intended to help put the ethnographic present in perspective.

The research was structured around a range of organisations, from the more formal to the informal, and the more explicitly to implicitly political in purpose. Part One attempts to explicate this social field, but I will outline the basic categories here to give an initial sense.

Political Parties: The four major parties are Labour, the SNP, the Conservatives and the Liberal Democrats. including internal sections and pressure groups, such as the Young Scottish Nationalists (SNP), Scottish Labour Action (Labour), and the Scottish Tory Reform Group (Conservatives).

Campaigning Groups: These are generally cross-party in membership (though some seem to have affinities with certain parties), aiming at mobilising a broader public and overcoming the fundamental conflicts that exist between the competing political parties. These groups can be seen as reflecting a polarisation between civic and ethnic forms of nationalism, bearing in mind the problems with this distinction discussed above. Important examples of the former are the Coalition for Scottish Democracy and the Campaign for a Scottish Parliament; the latter would include more politically marginal and ephemeral groups such as Siol Nan Gaidheal and Scottish Watch.

The Adult Learning Project (ALP): This organisation constitutes a unique category in the research. It is a community education project partly funded by Labour-controlled local government and based on the educational philosophy of Paulo Freire. In it adult students and staff organise study groups which meet regularly to explore topics of mutual interest. These include such things as writing and photography, Gaelic language, Scottish music and dance, and Scottish land use and reform. I worked closely with two groups – the History Group, which examined Scotland's present situation in light of its social history, and the Democracy Group, which considered Scotland's 'democratic deficit' and sought collectively to design a parliament for Scotland. While not an explicitly political organisation, ALP groups are frequently involved in politics, for instance, organising hustings prior to local elections. During my field work ALP helped to organise public campaigns against a Criminal Justice Bill that would have put new limitations on public access to land and legal public assembly, and against government plans to impose a new Value Added Tax on heating fuel, seen as an unfair burden on the poor and elderly in the colder north of the UK.

The Intelligentsia: I use this term loosely. There is a social sphere of artists, journalists and academics who participate in the movement and publicly promote its ideas. Many are affiliated with the parties or campaigning bodies listed above, but I tend to view them as a social category in their own right, being key shapers of the public discourse. In other words, I made contacts and conducted interviews with some of these figures not so much because of their organisational memberships, as because of their widely recognised public personas.

The research methods used were varied and somewhat eclectic. Participant observation was employed in a range of contexts. In some settings, such as rallies, marches and political meetings, I was primarily an observer. In others the level of participation was much higher. For instance at ALP I participated in classes, did presentations, and went on study trips. At one point I helped go door to door picking up ballots in a mini-referendum on constitutional change organised by the Campaign for a Scottish Parliament and conducted in the town of Falkirk.

One of the main bodies of data used in this study comes from over 100 interviews conducted with individuals from across the spectrum of organisations and categories discussed above. These interviews were semi-structured and (almost always) tape recorded, usually lasting between one and two hours. The flexible interview schedule began with biographical questions (family background, employment, education, political and religious orientation), moved to questions about motives for participation in the movement (since when, how, why), then asked the informant to discuss three key themes in the movement discourse: that Scots are more egalitarian than the English; that Scotland is a colony of England (see Hearn 1996);

and the notion that there is a peculiar tension between the head and heart, reason and passion, in Scottish culture. These questions were used as a way of generating discussions around Scottish history in relation to the movement. I have focused on responses to the first question in particular in Chapter 8. I closed the interview by asking the informant what kind of society and government they would wish to see in Scotland. Within this general frame I allowed myself room to pursue interesting avenues that arose in the course of the interview, and more informal, unrecorded, but relevant conversations often preceded and followed the interview proper. In this book I have used pseudonyms and otherwise obscured the identities of informants whose words I have excerpted from interviews. I have not tried to hide the identities of known public figures, or people speaking publicly at public events.

I also conducted two 'focus group' style interviews (also tape recorded) using the two ALP study groups I worked closely with. These were designed, in consultation with Vernon Galloway, one of the main co-ordinators at the project at the time, to follow a format called 'decoding' often used in ALP classes. In this procedure, an image, picture, or brief quotation is treated as the focal point of discussion, with the group leader or interviewer asking questions that move the group from more surface to deeper issues of interpretation (cf. Kirkwood and Kirkwood 1989: 10–12). I found this a very rich method for generating collective discussions and would consider using it again.

Library/archival research, primarily at the National Library in Edinburgh, helped to broaden my understanding of the movement. This included surveying major secondary sources on Scottish nationalism, and reading various primary sources – for example, pamphlets and documents published by the political parties and campaigning bodies. I also surveyed selected journals and periodicals that have been central to the movement, such as the *Scots Independent* (published since 1926), and *Radical Scotland*, a major journal of the 1980s and early 1990s. These sources helped develop my understanding of shifts in style and tone in movement discourse, as well as in concrete aims, over the years. Current newspapers, radio, and television, while not utilised in any methodical way, were another valuable source for gauging how the movement is presented in public discourse.

– A BRIEF OVERVIEW –

The book is divided into three main parts, each with its own short introduction. Here I will simply outline the larger structure. Part One (Movement) introduces the language of the Scottish movement, its moral discourse, and then lays out its recent history and social anatomy, in order to describe the dynamics of its social organisation and processes of mobilisation. The presumption here is that we need to begin with a fairly close description of the social process in question. Part Two (History) turns to a deeper, though relatively synoptic history of Scotland, in order to provide a fuller sense of the institutional forms and political and economic processes that have led to and still shape the present situation. These chapters also serve a secondary purpose of presenting in context various key figures and events that have become important in the modern discourses of Scottish nationalism, in order to facilitate subsequent discussion of those discourses as such. Part Three (Culture) is still very much concerned with history, but history as it gets told, rather than as what actually happened – history as culture. In particular it explores how the idea of egalitarianism, and the metaphor of the covenant, are used to create linkages between Scottish history and nationalist discourse, i.e., as ways of getting at how this particular form of liberal nationalism is culturally constructed. The Conclusion reviews the themes discussed above, re-examining the idea of liberal nationalism, and arguing that the Scottish case provides an important illustration of a fundamental tension between description and prescription politics.

– Notes –

1. On the difficulties of generating a comprehensive theory of nationalism see Breuilly (1993: 2), Calhoun (1997: 8), and McCrone (1998: 3).
2. For introductions to the history of Scottish nationalism see Brown et al. (1998: 1–26), Finlay (1997), Harvie (1998), Marr (1992), Mitchell (1997), and Paterson (1994).
3. Further helpful sources on the Scottish economy include: Aitken (1992), McCrone (1992: 121–2), and Payne (1997).
4. For overviews of this trend see Beiner (1999) and McKim and McMahan (1997). See also the commentaries on Miller (1995) in O'Leary (1996).
5. Interestingly, despite differences over the terms 'nationalism' and 'patriotism' Miller's argument here is similar to Viroli's – both reject Habermas's culturally thin notion of constitutional patriotism.
6. For other examples of such recent liberal political theories see Barry (1996), Dworkin (1978), and Gauthier (1985); regarding communitarianism, see MacIntyre (1984), Sandel (1982), Taylor (1989), and Walzer (1983).

Movement

The term 'liberal nationalism' might be contentious, but the core subject of this book is undoubtedly a social movement. Part One sets out to describe and discuss this movement, to provide a well-rounded introduction to its history, dynamics, social organisation and language. Chapter 1 offers an ethnographic account of a movement rally that took place in 1993 as a way of introducing key actors and organisations, their relations, and the discourse of moral critique that pervades the movement. Chapter 2 overviews the history of the home rule movement up to 1979, and Chapter 3 examines the crucial years of 1979–97, focusing on the interactions of political parties and campaigning groups and how these led from the failure of the 1979 referendum to the success of the 1997 referendum and the establishment of the new Scottish parliament. Chapter 4 takes a closer look at the public sphere of social discourse in which intellectuals, broadly defined, have played a critical role in articulating the sentiments and ideas of the movement.

The political mobilisation described in these chapters is often seen by scholarly observers as taking place in 'civil society', and indeed it is common for movement activists themselves to describe it in these terms. In this case, the language of the researcher and of those being studied is disconcertingly congruent. All the same, civil society is a contentious term that means different things to different people, so we should begin with a brief clarification.[1] For our purposes, we can think of civil society as designating the ensemble of social institutions, associations, and organisations, distinct from kinship and the state, through which values, desires and demands are articulated, and which often serves to channel these demands toward the state (cf. Bobbio 1989: 25–6). As straight-forward as it may seem, this definition is already at odds with other versions in common currency. The main areas of contention involve civil society's relationships to the state, the market and the moral order.

Scottish Enlightenment thinkers, such as Adam Ferguson (1966) and Adam Smith (1981), used the term to refer to a late, 'civilised' stage in the development of society, which featured institutions of markets and private property, but also included those of law and government. In the work of Hegel (1991) however, civil society was construed as a zone of public life and interaction, between the family and the state, and since then it has become normal to define civil society in opposition to the state. In the modern world with highly developed bureaucratic states it is useful to make this analytic distinction, but because political thought is so often freighted with hostility to the state as an oppressive power, this distinction easily slips into an attempt to define civil society primarily in terms of its autonomy from the state. But it is more useful to think of civil society as having a complex, almost symbiotic relationship to the state, because the state must win its legitimacy through the networks of civil society, and political projects that arise out of civil society usually aim at influencing the state. The problem of classifying political parties in terms of this distinction is instructive, precisely because the role of political parties is to perform both these functions, trafficking back and forth between state and civil society.

Another confusing area has been civil society's relationship to the marketplace. For the Enlightenment Scots and Hegel the market was a central part of how civil society facilitates the interactions of free, public individuals, and for Marx civil society was all but reduced to the market, understood as a realm of class domination and unfreedom.[2] Current discussions of civil society have been largely stimulated by the study of new (i.e., post 1960s) social movements in which association and organisation around politicised identities seeking to assert rights have been central. Because of this, the traditional market component of the concept has tended to fall by the way-side (cf. Bryant 1993: 339; Cohen and Arato 1994: 2). This is true of the Scottish movement as well, where parties and campaigning bodies have loomed large, and the business community has often been either aloof or hostile. While this reflects very real cleavages between social movements that are frequently left-leaning and non-economically oriented, and market actors that tend to the right of the political spectrum, it is more useful to understand this as a key tension within civil society, as part of what gives it its dynamic. Moreover, in both its market and non-market aspects, civil society can either provide a base for political mobilisation, or it can absorb and defray those same energies, sending mobilisation in various contrary directions.

The work of the Italian communist Antonio Gramsci (1971) has been particularly influential in the revival of the concept of civil society in recent years. Responding in the early decades of this century to what he saw as the overly economistic analysis of his marxist contemporaries, he argued that the project of proletarian revolution faced a very different struggle in the liberal democracies of the west, where popular consent to government was more institutionalised. He conceived of civil society as an array of institutions that surrounded and bolstered the state, and had to be conquered, like terrain in warfare. This struggle involved the use of civil society to cultivate 'hegemony', in other words, a dominant consensus around a particular world view and political program. Thus in Italy he saw the Catholic Church as an historically crucial part of civil society, and the problem of creating a socialist culture that could transcend divisions among rural and urban workers as central to the making of a new hegemony. Current conceptions of civil society that are strongly oppositional to the state and emphasise cultural resistance lodged in non-market institutions are heavily indebted to the revival of Gramsci's ideas on the left, precisely when conservatives and neoliberalism were attaining state power, the established institutions of the Labour movement were weakening, and the left was feeling increasingly marginalised. It is worth noting for our purposes that the recovery of Gramsci's thought has been highly influential on the British left, and particularly in Scotland.

Finally, the term civil society often carries an aura of 'goodness', of something better and set apart from the vulgarities of the state and the market. So often associated with mobilisation in the cause of liberation, it has strong connotations of social solidarity, and is easily seen as a key to harmonising the disparate demands thrown up by society (cf. Seligman 1992: x). This connection between civil society and moral order goes a long way back. Ferguson, Smith, David Hume, and their contemporaries, were deeply interested in the reciprocal relationships between social institutions and values, the way such things as property, law and government shaped the ethos and behaviour of a people. Their work reflects an acute concern with the ability of market-driven social relations to generate adequate social mores to replace those associated with the waning feudal order and its ethos based on more fixed, and often hereditary statuses. By the time we get to Gramsci this concern with the moral order generated by civil society has been displaced by the more pragmatic and tactical notion of hegemony within civil society. None the less, the older notion of civil society as a primary shaper of social values still clings to the concept, imbuing it with a moral tone, no matter how hard we try to treat it as a morally neutral social-analytic concept.

– NOTES –

1. For fuller discussions of the civil society concept and its historical development, see: Bobbio (1989: 22–43), Cohen and Arato (1994), Keane (1988), Kumar (1993), and Seligman (1992).
2. In effect, Marx substitutes the concept of capitalism for civil society in his later work.

CHAPTER 1

Moral Economy

This chapter introduces the range and style of popular political discourse that exists in and around the Scottish movement, and some of the key actors, organisations and institutions that have provided an infrastructure for the movement and helped shape its discourse. I do this through an account of the 'Rally to Recall Scotland's Parliament out of Adjournment', because many central issues and tensions in the movement were nicely encoded in the symbolism and dramas of that event. This account also provides a fuller sense of central themes of the movement's discourse – calls for democratic reform and self-determination, for social justice and wealth redistribution, and a conception of Scotland as a kind of moral community which is under attack. After describing this event I propose a general characterisation of the movement's discourse as involving a notion of a 'moral economy of the welfare state', in other words, a defence of a threatened system of social and political norms that once protected members of the political community (i.e. British citizens) against the vagaries and ravages of an unregulated market. Later chapters will expand on the structural and historical reasons why Scottish culture and politics have taken on this corporatist and defensive stance in the current political-economic environment. For now though, I simply want to suggest the tone of the movement, as well as the rifts and lines of tension that provide much of its dynamic.

– THE RECALL RALLY –

The Recall Rally took place on 27 November 1993, a little over two months after I had arrived in Edinburgh. It was a relatively minor, even disappointing event in the history of the movement as a whole, yet many of the fundamental dynamics of the movement were in evidence, perhaps even more clearly in this case than in more successful events, precisely because central antagonisms between key organisations were not overcome. I intend this first hand account to provide an initial point of entry, from which to work out toward broader discussions.

A leading role in the Rally's planning and promotion was taken by the highly informal group, Democracy for Scotland (DFS), also known as 'The Vigil'. The primary purpose of this group was to keep a constant vigil, in the name of the Scottish demand for a parliament, across the street from the Scottish Office, the seat of British government in Scotland. This site also stands next to the Old Royal High School building, which had been outfitted in 1979 to house an anticipated Scottish parliament which, however, never materialised, because the popular referendum on establishing a parliament in Scotland failed to pass in that year. Instead, Britain got Margaret Thatcher.

The Scottish Office and the Old Royal High School, imposing stone structures in a classical style, stand diagonally across from each other along Regent Road on the side of Calton Hill, which rises over the north-eastern end of central Edinburgh, starkly capped with stone monuments to Admiral Nelson and the Scottish dead of the Napoleonic Wars. During my field work my almost daily walk into the 'Old Town' to meet people and use the libraries took me along Regent Road, past the site of the Vigil, so I quickly got into the habit of stopping by to chat with whoever was around, standing around the brazier made from a rusted fifty-five gallon drum (often reverently referred to as 'the flame of democracy' by core members), having a cup of instant coffee. The smell of wood smoke that clung to one's clothes and hair was a sure sign of time recently spent at the Vigil. The furnishings were modest: the brazier, a few folding chairs and benches, wood piles that grew and shrank according to the resourcefulness of the group and the charity of the general public, and the construction site portakabin, about ten by five feet, and eight feet tall, painted white with blue trim. A saltire (the Scottish flag with the St Andrew's cross) was kept waving during the day on a free standing pole, there was also a table with literature and a can for donations in front of the portakabin, and a whimsical road sign pointing to other small but self-governing European countries such as Norway and Denmark. It was policy that in the spirit of a true vigil, someone should be at the site at all times, which meant taking turns spending the long winter nights bundled up inside the portakabin.

The membership at that time was an odd assortment, young and old, a fairly even mix of women and men, from working- to middle-class backgrounds. Few had a full four years of university, if any. There were students and unemployed young people, some on the dole, some drifting in and out. There was also a stable core of people with jobs or family members with jobs ranging from civil service and clerical work, to lab work, carpentry, bus driving, and building maintenance. Several core members, who had earlier been involved together in the short-lived Scottish Socialist Party, lived in a single large household made up of two extended families. Some of the more educated members were also involved in the Scottish Green Party, and seemed to view the Scottish movement as interdependent with that commitment.

A brief profile of a couple of core members will help give a sense of the group. Rosalind, in her mid-thirties, was a civil servant with a degree in Secretarial Studies. Her parents were middle-class Tories, her father a manager for a construction firm, her mother working briefly as an 'air hostess' before marrying and becoming a homemaker. She had not been politically active, but joined Labour about three months before the 1992 general election. Afterward, she became disillusioned, doubting whether Labour could ever come to power again, and deciding that the party had moved too far to the right. She got involved in the Vigil in the weeks following the general election defeat, and it gradually became a more important commitment. When I asked her in an interview 'do you have a sense of what kind of Scotland you'd like to see, what kind of government, what kind of society?' she responded:

> I'd like to see a more 'fair shares for all' Scotland . . . and the Tory government as you're well aware, they push this low tax thing which is not really happening because of VAT on fuel coming up,[1] changes in national insurance, things that have happened in the past. They're not really the party of low taxation, but they do project themselves as this. To me people that are in work are very lucky, there's a world-wide recession and we're never going to get back to full employment. I mean if Scotland got independence tomorrow, I don't think everybody in Scotland would have a job in five years time, times have moved on too far, there's new technology, one machine can do hundreds of men's jobs, so many industries have been decimated, things could be a lot better. You could make, you could bring in a lot more social . . . type jobs, you could have more nurses on the ward, you could have smaller classes, but we're never gonna get full employment, I accept that. So I think that work, like anything else, is a resource. People that have work are lucky, they should be willing to pay more tax, more direct taxation, partly to fund the jobs which aren't producing anything . . . [a few words unclear] . . . I've just spoken about, [e.g.] home helps, so that there's more money going into the central belt so that these jobs might be available, and also so that there could be a better welfare system . . . the welfare system to me is absolutely bloody horrendous. That Archbishop that spoke at St. Mary's Cathedral last week, I thought he had a splendid quote, all about 'target poverty, not the poor'. And that is what this government is doing just now . . . .

William was about fifty years old. His parents were radicals, trade unionists, and Labour voters. His mother's mother was a suffragette and trade union organiser at a rubber mill, a tradition William's mother carried on. His father was a 'Father of the Chapel' (a shop steward) in the printing and bookbinding trade, once a major industry in Edinburgh. He was raised in a working-class tenement. He worked in the bookbinding trade where he had his City and Guild certification, until the industry collapsed in the late 1960s. Since then he has worked in a university Stationery Department, as a bus driver, and as a manager/maintenance person of a church, despite being an agnostic. After a brief flirtation with nationalism in his teens, he became an active member of the Labour Party. Disillusioned, he left Labour a few years ago, however, and has since joined the SNP, where he is somewhat active in his local branch. Toward the end of an interview, I asked him about 'the whole question of socialism . . . what does that word mean to you today, considering all the changes that it's gone through?':

> Yeah . . . I don't think Scotland's been a particularly socialist nation. [sigh] I suppose as I've always believed, [I'm] just a socialist . . . I've never, I've never had any high flown creeds or 'isms' that I've pursued . . . I've always called myself a socialist 'cos it seems the only fair and reasonable style of government that I've seen. I never thought that the eastern bloc countries were socialist [by the] wildest stretch of the imagination, they were just dictatorships. Ahh . . . I guess it's just livin' in a society . . . I still believe in . . . the wealth created, should be owned by the people who create it. I suppose I have to call mysel' a socialist. I don't think we would run things badly at all . . .

I then remarked that 'for some people socialism and nationalism are really antithetical things. Is that something that you puzzle over?' He seemed to wrestle with this answer even more:

> No, not at all, I don't see any reason why they cannae go hand in hand, there's . . . it's . . . national . . . it depends on . . . there we go, 'what is nationalism?' it's . . . I see nothing wrong with that, a grouping of people that appear to, well, we've got a very definite geographical boundary . . . so we're slightly different, we're not in the middle of a large continent, we're a small group of people, surrounded by the sea . . . with a hugely strong Celtic background, and Nordic background, and then a hundred, two hundred miles away there's a huge Anglo-Saxon/Norman group of people. I see no reason why we shouldnae . . . we are different . . . both in our appearances and our language. And I see no reason why we shouldnae, now it were a necessity I think we should be separate. 'Cause I think we're just being dragged down the tube, with Britain as a whole, and . . . I don't particularly look upon myself as a nationalist. I would prefer to think that I was an internationalist that thought Scotland could contribute to international understanding. I think that we've got something to say here, I think that the way people vote says that they don't like what's been happening for the past fifteen years . . . I'm no' saying that all the changes that took place over the past fifteen

years or whatever, uh . . . necessarily wrong . . . eh . . . there's always a way of doing things, you know. You don't just kill one of your children cause the rest of 'em are going hungry, you find another way of feeding all the children.[2] That, in particular is why Scotland now wants to be separate . . . I mean, Thatcher created that.

The Vigil grew out of a demonstration that took place outside the gates of the Royal High School on the evening of Friday, 10 April, 1992, in response to the general election of the previous day, which had once again returned the Conservatives to power in Westminster. The Conservative Party was the only party in Scotland that opposed the idea of a Scottish parliament – 75 per cent of the Scottish electorate had voted for other parties (primarily Labour and the SNP). Prior to the election there had been high hopes in some quarters that the Tories would be swept from power, or at least reduced to such a rump in Scotland that a constitutional crisis would ensue. The realisation that there would be continued deadlock on the issue created an air of frustration, but also hardened resolve. In the first few weeks and months after the general election the Vigil provided a site for focusing a general spirit of protest in the form of various meetings, rallies and marches. By the time I encountered the group, things had become more routinised, with a fluctuating cast of around forty core participants, any regular Sunday night meeting drawing around twenty people. The enthusiasm had died down, and most people with a long term active commitment to the cause felt that their time and energies were better spent elsewhere. Such activists sometimes characterised the people who had stuck by the Vigil as admirable, endearing, but perhaps unrealistic in their commitment to DFS's political potential. In my view some members of DFS saw the Vigil as a symbolic gesture worth sustaining, and as a meaningful focus for their social life, while others did have somewhat exaggerated notions of its political efficacy.

The Recall Rally grew out of a seed planted in another, more important event, the 'Scotland Demands Democracy' march and rally which was held in Edinburgh on 12 December 1992, on the occasion of the European Summit, and which drew over 25,000 people. The idea was to use this event to draw the attention of Europe to Scotland's complaint. At that rally a statement called the Democracy Declaration of Scotland, drafted by members of Common Cause (discussed further in Chapter 3), was read and endorsed by all the opposition parties and various civic organisations such as churches, unions, and other voluntary organisations. A passage from that document provides a sense of its purpose and tone; speaking of the Conservative government, it argues:

This government now imposes its minority policies on Scotland through an executive Scottish Office with more civil servants than Brussels, yet with no Scottish legislature to examine or pass such policies. The people of Scotland face problems and opportunities which can best be dealt with by our own Scottish Parliament. We know of no other nation placed in such a predicament and you can surely understand why we are calling for a constitutional referendum to enable democratic renewal within our country.

Five months later, at a Vigil meeting in May 1993, it was decided to capitalise on the public commitment made to this statement by seizing upon a fairly literal reading of one rather rhetorical passage: 'Today, the majority in Scotland demand the recall of our own Parliament as a modern and democratic body empowering all our citizens.'

It was argued that all those endorsing the original statement, which included all the opposition parties, had made a public commitment to reconstituting the actual Scottish parliament, which in fact, had never been dissolved, but only 'adjourned' in 1707, when the new combined parliament of Great Britain was formed.

Based on this somewhat far-fetched reading, the event was planned and a Recall Committee formed, which included representatives from DFS, the SNP, the Scottish Liberal Democrats, and the Scottish Green Party. Despite attempts to both woo and shame them into participation, the Labour Party kept its distance, deeming the pretence of establishing an alternative Scottish government outside of the British constitutional process unacceptable for a party of its stature. In fact, it is doubtful whether anyone other than some members of DFS ever took the idea of actually forming a new parliament very seriously. Rather, I think most of those involved simply saw it as another symbolic event to help keep the issue in the public eye, during the time between general elections, which had, over the previous fifteen years come to be perceived as shadow referendums on the constitutional issue.

Furthermore, it must be understood that the major players in this scenario were Labour and the SNP; despite their initiative, DFS and the smaller parties were only the supporting cast. Labour is the dominant party in Scotland, the SNP seeks to capture votes where it can, and most of those to be captured belong to Labour. Thus these two parties, despite strong similarities in their middle of the road social democratic policies, are always in direct and heated competition. It had been the constant frustration of key activists in the movement (whether party members or not), that attempts to foster co-operation on the constitutional question between these two major players always seemed to lead to divisiveness and posturing – especially when general elections were pending and the competition became fiercer. In short, the Recall Rally, as a public drama of the home rule issue, was fundamentally shaped by the fact that these two parties publicly define themselves in opposition to each other, and cannot afford to share the same stage as equals. In practice, the Rally became the SNP's show – yet another opportunity to shame Labour and argue that Labour's claims to be committed to home rule are not genuine.

These tensions were in evidence at two events during the week leading up to the Rally, which was held on a Saturday. On the previous Wednesday, the Recall Committee held a press conference. Lined up behind a long table facing eight or so rows of sparsely occupied folding chairs, four representatives from DFS and the three parties each spoke briefly. Beyond offering general information about the event, their remarks offered praise for the folk at the Vigil and disparaged Labour for not participating (but noting the exception of the renegade Labour MP Dennis Canavan, whose strong commitment to devolution led him to buck party discipline and attend the event). The media's interest seemed tepid – no television cameras and only a handful of newspaper reporters, whose vaguely hostile questions revolved around the inability of the SNP and Labour to co-operate, and the anticipated turn-out. The organisers tried discretely to lower expectation about attendance, emphasising the symbolic importance of the Rally.

On the following Friday, the day before the Rally, there was a public meeting of the Scottish Constitutional Convention, a diverse civic body which had been formed in 1989 to help thrash out ideas about what a Scottish parliament would/could look like (discussed further in Chapter 3). After a lot of initial notoriety, and then the disappointment of the 1992 general election, the Convention faded from public view, although its various committees remained active, hammering out details of the plan. The purpose of this public meeting was to remind active supporters and the general public that the Convention was still alive and hard at work. It is important to know that while the SNP was initially involved in the Convention, it backed out early-on due to intra-party disagreements about whether the SNP, committed by its constitution to a program of national independence, could legitimately work with an organisation committed only to devolution. Many key activists in the broader movement (and some members of the SNP) saw this withdrawal as an unfortunate and counterproductive move. In the eyes of many of the pro-parliament intelligentsia the SNP had been seen as an uncooperative spoiler ever since. In this light, it becomes clear that the SNP's use of the Recall Rally to shame Labour was a kind of counter-move, an attempt to turn the tables in the ongoing argument about just who is failing to co-operate.

The meeting was held in the opulent surroundings of the Signet Library in

Parliament Square. The speakers included major figures from Labour, the Liberal Democrats, the Convention of Scottish Local Authorities (COSLA – the largely Labour controlled co-ordinating body of local government), the Scottish Trades Union Congress (STUC), the Church of Scotland, the Democratic Left (an offshoot of the more moderate ranks of the fragmented Communist Party), and the Campaign for a Scottish Parliament (CSP), the pivotal campaigning body that had provided the initial impetus behind the creation of the Convention. The speakers tried to convey a sense of the steady labours of the Convention, with several emphasising the familiar theme of Scotland's strong moral traditions, and how these were at odds with current Tory policies and their conception of morality (the Tories had recently held a party conference stressing the theme of 'back to basics' morality). During the speech by Labour's Shadow Scottish Secretary at the time, George Robertson,[3] two members of DFS who had quietly slipped in and taken front row seats, stood up and unfurled a banner promoting the Recall Rally in front of Robertson and in view of the television cameras. Some tried to yank the banner down, and voices of disapproval fell from the speakers platform. Campbell Christie, General Secretary of the STUC, and a key leader and broker between various groups in the movement, expressed dismay and said he now doubted whether he would attend the Rally. Robertson's stock retort to the rally organisers, offered on more than one occasion, was that he believed in looking forward for a parliament, not to the past.

Fortunately, it was not raining the day of the Rally, but it was cold and windy at the site where it was held, among the stone monuments on the grassy summit of Calton Hill. The plan was for an afternoon of music from noon on, with the ceremonies and speeches beginning around half past four in the afternoon. The day started off slowly. Police were present, but fairly inconspicuous. At the top of the hill there were three food wagons, a toilet wagon and a stage made of three flat bed trucks. As the bands played, some people listened, some danced, some wandered around the monuments and visited the Vigil site below. A couple of fellows who were friends of the Vigil folk showed up in full traditional highland garb – rough woven kilts, belts, buckles and pouches with silver-work with inlaid stones, their long frizzy red hair tied back. A familiar peripheral figure in this milieu was handing out copies of a Scottish Constitution he had illustrated and published himself (based on one drawn up by some activists back in the 1950s). He also seemed to have had a hand in bringing a replica of the Stone of Destiny,[4] and placing it on a stone slab located on the south side of the summit.

The newspapers put the attendance at around 2,000, which seems accurate taking the whole day into account. My estimate is that throughout the afternoon there were around 200–400 people coming and going on the hill, and that most showed up between 4 and 5 pm, when the number rose to well over 1,000. It is likely that an anti-racism rally in Glasgow that day, held on the last Saturday in November for the last four years, cut into attendance. Although people were putting a brave face on it, and had lowered their expectations in the final weeks, the sparse turn-out was a bit of a let down. Even so, the DFSers seemed happy and relieved to have pulled it off and covered costs, with perhaps a couple hundred pounds left over to help support the Vigil.

A little after 4 pm, several members of DFS and miscellaneous supporters met at Parliament Square in the Old Town. A small party of about fifty or sixty, with banners, bagpipes and a mounted police escort, marched down the High Street, across the North Bridge, and up to the top of Calton Hill. This took about thirty minutes. After circling through the crowd on top of the hill, the marchers doubled back to the south-eastern side of the summit to the site of the 'Democracy Cairn', to hold an official dedication before the speeches began on the flat bed trucks. The Cairn had been made by Vigil member Ian Thompson, a semi-retired carpenter from the Inverness area, who had been involved in anti-nuclear protests at the Dounreay plant prior to his involvement with DFS. It was a round stone pedestal about five feet in diameter at the base, about three feet at the top, and around six feet tall. Another fifty-five gallon drum brazier was perched on top (there were plans for a more decorative one to be added later, but in the end it was simply capped off in stone). The Cairn incorporated stones that had been brought to the site from the four corners of Scotland during the 'Destiny Marches', another movement event of the previous April.

By the time the marchers reached the Cairn it was passing dusk. An amorphous circle of perhaps 150 people gathered around it, a few holding torches, as plaintive tunes were piped. Vigil member Jackie Wilkes had been nominated by the rest of the group to draft and read a dedication. She stressed the 'democratic deficit' in Scotland, and how greater local control would empower women and allow a greater concern for the environment. These were all standard themes in the DFS milieu. She also threw in a call for the reinvigoration of socialism, and I noted that one leading figure at the Vigil with Green Party affiliations grumbled, feeling that this was too explicitly partisan for a supposedly non-party organisation like DFS. The dedication culminated in the lighting of the brazier ('the flame of democracy'), and was capped off by reading the inscription on the granite plaque set in at the base of the Cairn, the passage by the poet/nationalist Hugh MacDiarmid that opens this book:

> For we ha'e faith in Scotland's hidden poo'ers,
> The present's theirs, but a' the past and future's oors

Born in Middlesex in England, Jackie had only moved to Scotland with her daughters in 1989, and was somewhat self-conscious about her rendition of MacDiarmid in an English accent. So after she finished, she asked Ian Thompson to step in and repeat it in a good, growling Scots. After this, the circle around the Cairn slowly dissolved, and people wandered back to the flat bed trucks, joining the bulk of the crowd to hear the politicians speak. Judging from the banners I saw, the faces I recognised, and the audience response to the speakers, it seems clear that the swell in turn-out that began around dusk was largely due to SNP ranks turning out to cheer and support their party leader, Alex Salmond, as well as to the late arrival of some people who had just attended the anti-racism rally in Glasgow. Several speakers decrying Scotland's political and economic situation were heckled with shouts of 'if you don't like it then vote SNP', and the lone Labour MP Dennis Canavan was booed by a few. Some excerpts from the various speeches, where the rhetoric is undeniably in full tilt, provide a nice sampling of movement discourse.

The first speaker was Helen Allen who, like Thompson and Wilkes, was also a core member of the Vigil. She began by describing the formation of the Vigil/DFS, and concluded with an effort to drum up practical support. In between she stressed themes similar to those in Jackie's dedication of the Cairn:

> You know the last fifteen years, have seen a massive increase, in unemployment, poverty and homelessness. Scotland's industrial base has been decimated. We all remember Ravenscraig and Rosyth [a steel mill and shipyard, respectively, recently shut down], and who can ever forget the Poll Tax, and now the carve-up of local government. Sometimes I wonder how much more the Scottish people can take! [cheers/applause] . . .
>
> Another elderly friend . . . [words unclear] . . . in the Poll Tax fiasco, was too ashamed to share his problems with his family and friends, is again worrying about how he will manage to pay his fuel bills. He has trouble with high blood pressure, and he's in hospital at the moment. Last week he said to me, at least while I'm in here, I can keep warm, without having to worry about my bills. What an indictment! what a terrible indictment against the policies of this British government! . . .
>
> DFS does not want to see a replica of Westminster. We would like to see new forms of democratic representation, some form of alternative to the first-past-the-post system, with representation of women guaranteed . . . in Scotland. We would like representatives in the Scottish parliament to be representative of Scottish society as a whole, and not dominated by lawyers, accountants and businessmen, as Westminster is [cheers/applause] . . .

After her there was a woman from the Scottish Green Party, who stressed the themes of political decentralisation, ecologically sound economics, and the revitalisation of community:

It's our belief that there's an overwhelming consensus amongst the people of Scotland – a consensus for social justice, fairness and equality, a consensus of belief in the community. We look at what this government is doing on health, education, and welfare, to rail, to all of our industry, to all of our futures. VAT on fuel, on domestic fuel, in a country so rich in energy, instead of a proper program in energy efficiency and energy conservation. It's a waste and it's a tragedy . . . [cheers] . . . and that consensus, that consensus of the Scottish people, that's bound up with our view of 'society' – that thing that our government says doesn't exist[5] – but we believe in society, we believe in community, and our concept of sovereignty, Scottish sovereignty, the sovereignty of the people, it's not parliament that's sovereign, it's not the monarch, they get their power from us, from the people of Scotland . . . [cheers/applause]

The Communist speaker drew a long parallel between Scotland and Cuba (which did not play all that well with some of the audience). His point of departure was a response to a book review he had read that day which was critical of the idea of 'utopian thinking'. He began with a quote from the reviewer:

'. . . a once fertile country like Cuba, has been destroyed by economic basket-cases . . .' now Cuba, there's a number of similarities between Cuba and Scotland . . . [some derisive laughter in background] . . . A small country, wanting independence, a small country dominated by another country only a few miles away, much bigger economically, and politically, than they are. What we're arguing here for is the right of small countries, to determine their own future, without the interference of big countries in their affairs. Now to argue that Cuba, that the Cuban economy has failed – and that's open to debate – because of utopianism, without taking into consideration the fact, that the largest economic and military power in the world, has drawn a net round Cuba for the past thirty years, and attempted to strangle it, is a failure, is a failure to understand the situation . . . [more laughter and jeers] . . . in Scotland, we have a similar situation, dominated by a larger power, a net drawn around us . . . the . . . failure of us to break that stranglehold, and establish a right to our own affairs . . .

Alex Salmond, leader of the SNP, gave his usual skilful and charismatic performance. He thanked the members of DFS for their efforts and in the middle of his speech addressed the major campaign issues of the moment – reorganisation of local government (widely viewed as Tory gerrymandering), impending privatisation of water services, and VAT on domestic fuel – asserting that a Scottish parliament would take action on these issues. But a large portion of his speech was taken up with criticism of those who did not participate – namely Labour:

Now I've been listening to the radio and the television over the last few days, and I'm told of course, this recalled parliament business, is just, 'historical abstraction', a historical abstraction, is what's been said. It's no historical abstraction, it's about the modern reality of what's happening to Scotland – that's why we need a recalled parliament. [cheers] Because . . . the concept of 'recall', encapsulates the principle of Scottish sovereignty. Sovereignty in Scotland lies not in the palace of Westminster, but in the streets of Scotland . . . [cheers/applause; a few words drowned out] . . . a recall should have been a vehicle for unity in Scotland, it should have been the principle behind which political forces could have united, but political forces can only unite if political leaders accept their responsibility, to go forward with declarations that they endorsed just a year ago . . . [cheers/applause] . . .

In conclusion, Salmond took one last shot at Labour, and then reconnected the parliament recall issue to the choice of voting for the SNP rather than Labour:

I've got one last message for George Robertson [Labour's Shadow Scottish Secretary]. George is a very clever debater, in the Westminster parliament, and that's been recently recognised. But there is no point, no point whatsoever, in covering yourself in glory, in a debating chamber at Westminster, when the Tory government is covering the Scottish people in poverty, and that's the reality, of what's happening now . . . [cheers/applause] . . . Some people, have chosen to present themselves as an obstacle, a stumbling block to progress, towards self-government, towards self-determination, towards a recalled parliament. That's their choice. But let us say to them and present a warning this evening – that stumbling blocks and roadblocks can be removed, and there's a ballot box opportunity next year, to start that process. For one way or another, the Scottish Parliament is going to be recalled, the democracy declaration is going to be honoured, and Scotland's going to step forward, to freedom – thank you. [cheers/applause]

This was supposed to have been the final speech, but Dennis Canavan, the renegade Scottish Labour MP had shown up late from the anti-racism rally in Glasgow, and stepped up to say a few words, arguing for a more unified front on the home rule issue:

As Alex Salmond said previously, many people, thousands of people, marched through the streets of Glasgow this morning, for a good cause. They were people of different parties, different beliefs, some of them perhaps of no political party membership at all, and it was for a good cause, the campaign against racism. And the reason why we marched together was quite simple. It was because we all agreed that that campaign, stood a much greater chance of success, if the people of Scotland were as united as possible, irrespective of their party political persuasion. And so it's the same, its just the same, with the campaign for a Scottish parliament. There may be, there may be genuine differences of opinion about the composition and powers of a Scottish parliament, but surely it would . . . require somebody with no political nous [i.e., savvy] at all, who would fail to realise that by maximising the unity of the people of Scotland, they would've got a better chance of achieving that Scottish parliament . . .

After the speeches, the speakers representing the participating parties and DFS each signed the Recall Declaration:

We the undersigned, hereby declare our continued support for the Democracy Declaration of the 12th of December, 1992 and solemnly pledge ourselves to the Recall of Scotland's Parliament from adjournment as a modern and democratic body empowering all our citizens.

Leaflets with the above text on one side had been passed out, and the crowd collectively recited it after the signing. The crowd was led, phrase by phrase, by a speaker from the platform, giving the recitation the feel of a collective church confession. On the other side of the leaflet was the text of the song *Freedom Come-All-Ye* written by Hamish Henderson. Henderson, then in his mid-70s, and something of a cult icon in Scotland, is a poet, folklorist, critic, co-founder of the School of Scottish Studies at Edinburgh, Communist, and early translator of Gramsci. He was present and led the crowd in singing the song, which paints images of 1920s marxist-nationalist John Maclean leading the freedom loving Scottish people to throw off the racism and war-mongering of their capitalist masters. It is one of a few unofficial Scottish anthems, particularly popular with the younger, more Labour/left-leaning wing of the movement:

> Roch the wind in the clear days dawin'
>> Blaws the cloods heelster gowdy ow'r the bay
> But there's mair nor a roch wind blawin'
>> Through the great glen o' the warld the day
> It's a thocht that will gar oor rottans–
>> A' they rogues that gang gallus, fresh and gay–
> Tak' the road an' seek ither loanins
>> For their ill ploys tae spo't an' play.

> Nae mair will the bonnie callants
>> Mairch tae war, when ocr braggarts crousely craw
> Nor wee weans frae pit-heid an' clachan
>> Mourn the ships sailin' doon the Broomielaw
> Broken families in lands we've harriet
>> Will curse Scotland the Brave nae mair, nae mair
> Black an' white, ane til ither marriet
>> Mak' the vile barracks o' their maisters bare.

O come all ye at hame wi' freedom
　　Never heed whit the hoodies croak for doom;
In your hoose a' the bairns o' Adam
　　Can find breid, barley bree an' painted room
When Maclean meets wi's freens in Springburn
　　A' the roses an' geans will turn tae bloom,
And a black boy frae yont Nyanga
　　Dings the fell gallows o' the burghers doon.[6]

This concluded the formal event, and while there was an open mike afterwards for people to say whatever they felt, the crowd dispersed fairly quickly, leaving sound crews and vendors to break down their equipment with the help of Vigil folk and their friends. Later I went by the Ceilidh House, a popular pub, where I ran into various young SNP activists and members of other nationalist organisations, digesting the event over a few pints. Another act in the long, sometimes plodding drama of Scottish home rule was over.

To this account I would simply add a few more interpretative remarks. It struck me at the time, and I raised this in later conversations with people at the Vigil, some of whom seemed to agree, that it was as though there were two separate events. The march and the dedication of the Cairn, wholly organised by DFS, had a loose, spontaneous, and popular feel. The marchers wound their way through the streets, with no clear internal structure, ending up in an unorganised cluster around the Cairn and its flame. The speeches and the Declaration Signing, on the other hand, displayed the usual sense of hierarchy, between organisations on the platform, and between party/group leaders and followers in the crowd. This was primarily the SNP's showcase. In all, the event revealed many of the classic differences and tensions between informal, small, face to face social groups, and larger formal organisations. The tensions between the mobilisation of diffuse public sentiments, and organised political action, were inscribed in the day's events.

– THE MORAL ECONOMY OF THE WELFARE STATE –

Certain themes occur again and again in the preceding account, and in the home rule discourse more generally. They run along two main lines. On the one hand, there is a call for democratic reform, for more direct, grassroots participation in government, for the entrenchment of basic political rights, and for self-determination (an interestingly ambiguous term which casts polities as selves). On the other hand, there is a call for a more just distribution of social goods, for the publicly managed investment of resources in society as a whole. These two lines obviously intersect, in that distributive justice is widely seen as the business of democratic government. Furthermore, there is also a distinct tone to the discourse – one of righteous indignation, moral protest, at times highly defensive. And connected to all of this is a portrayal of Scotland as somehow exemplifying, even personifying, precisely those qualities and values which are being defended – democracy, egalitarianism, fairness, social concern, and even basic conviviality.

Let me propose a way of looking at this. The term 'moral economy' has become a commonplace in anthropology in recent years. It is implicated in the substantivist economic theories developed first by Karl Polanyi (1957), which, put broadly, argued that 'historically the provisioning of humans – the securing of their livelihood – was located in, or integrated through, non-economic institutions . . . before modernity, the securing of human livelihood had no separateness – no boundary line that marked it out as distinct from the enveloping society's institutions and values' (Booth 1994: 653). But the term moral economy itself arose out of more specific discussions of the responses of peasant communities to the encroachments of externally driven market economies. Thus when E. P. Thompson first coined the term (1971), he was attempting a finer analysis of eighteenth-century food riots in England, trying to show that beneath the dynamics of crowd behaviour lay a set of cultural assumptions about how in times of scarcity the subsistence needs of the local producing community should take precedence over the demands of laissez-faire markets. While this relatively simple formulation has been elaborated, most notably by James Scott (1976) who has emphasised the role of expectations built around local patron-client relations, it provides the crux of the idea of the moral economy.[7]

So what do the beliefs and behaviour of peasants confronting capitalism have to do with those of citizens of a modern democratic welfare state well into a transition from an economy driven by heavy industry and state managed investment to one driven by a combination of light industries, the service sector, and international finance? And how does this relate to a popular critique of neoliberal social policies intermixed with a quasi-nationalist call for greater political autonomy? If we consider the idea of the moral economy at a higher level of abstraction, I think the answer is – quite a lot. Beyond the specifics of peasants versus markets, there is a more fundamental argument involved here about interdependent conceptions of community, membership and provisioning, and what happens when these become threatened and unstable. Michael Walzer, playing loosely on the notion of a 'social contract' (examined further in Chapter 10), offers us a useful characterisation of this nexus of community, membership and provisioning in his *Spheres of Justice* (1983):

> Here, then, is a more precise account of the social contract: it is an agreement to redistribute the resources of the members in accordance with some shared understanding of their needs, subject to ongoing political determination in detail. The contract is a moral bond. It connects the strong and the weak, the lucky and the unlucky, the rich and the poor, creating a union that transcends all differences of interest, drawing its strength from history, culture, religion, language, and so on. Arguments about communal provision are, at the deepest level, interpretations of that union. (1983: 82–3)

It is also important to consider that when this social contract is threatened, whatever its historical specificities, an unstable, and ideologically (we might also say culturally) generative situation is reached, where assumed norms become visible, contested, and recast. I agree with Robert Wuthnow when he maintains that:

> [i]deologies always contain propositions about moral obligations – obligations of patrons to clients, of clients to patrons, of members to communities, of citizens to states and state representatives to citizens, of persons to one another in their basic dealings. . . . These propositions specify how social relations should be conducted and therefore affect how social resources may be distributed. Insofar as ideologies also require social resources in order to be maintained, any disturbance of social resources that results in uncertainties about the nature of moral obligations is likely to result in some modification at the level of ideology itself. In other words, disturbances in the moral order are likely to be a factor in the production of new ideological forms. (Wuthnow 1987: 154)

Under such conditions of contestation, one likely aspect of 'new ideological forms' is that they will involve re-definitions of the relevant dimensions of community and membership. In essence the moral economists say that people who view themselves as members of a community with common interests in mutual provision, are likely to raise a protest when the means of provisioning are threatened. And that is precisely the predicament that those committed to the idea of the Keynesian welfare state, with its centrally managed economy, have found themselves in, in a world where, since the 1970s, laissez-faire economics has found a new lease on life. In few places in Europe, the historical root of the modern welfare state, has this shift been more pronounced than in Britain under the governments of Margaret Thatcher and her successors. Thatcherism was a radical ideological movement, and a key part of its rhetoric in regard to Scotland has been to decry the effects of a paternalistic state (note the parallel to the paternalistic patron-client relations of peasant moral economies), arguing that a 'dependency culture' needed to be replaced by an 'enterprise culture' which would hearken back to the spirit of Adam Smith. Ironically Scottish nationalism, with its conceptual opposition of Scotland to England and Britain, is in many ways a conservative defence the classic mid-century conception of community, membership and provisioning at the British level.

So the UK is a nation-state that has, in response to global economic pressures, elected to reverse many of its commitments to collective provisioning from within. One result has been a political polarisation, made manifest in the north-south divide between the Labour and Tory constituencies that will be discussed further in Chapter 3. In this context Scottish people of a left/social democratic persuasion, arguably the majority, are confronted by two major options for conceptualising and mobilising the community whose principles of provisioning are under threat: on the one hand they can struggle for the heart and mind of Britain as a whole, where the neoliberal agenda, first in the radical version of the Thatcherites, and now in the moderated version of New Labour, holds sway. On the other hand they can struggle to at least partly disengage the Scottish political community, where there is (or at least appears to be) a much closer consensus around issues of provisioning, from the larger political community of Britain. Support for the Scottish movement has grown in recent years because a significant portion of those politically active have leaned toward the latter interpretation of the situation as the appropriate strategic response.

It is worth considering some of the criticisms that have been made of the moral economy literature in order to sharpen this attempt to transfer the concept from one domain to another. Desan has noted that:

> Thompson's concept of communal consensus . . . may at times suggest a more cohesive and united community than in fact existed . . . [and he] . . . does not seem to recognize that the 'moral economy' might have different meanings or levels of significance for various members of the community . . . (1989: 57, 59)

This certainly applies to the modern Scottish case. As we have seen, there is a range of interests and motives involved here. While a certain attitude of discontent and complaint pervades the movement, actors are differentially situated. Political careers are being made and unmade in the process. Members of the intelligentsia have an interest in treating Scotland as an object of concern, study and discussion. And, as comes out quite clearly in the account of the Recall Rally, there is a complex process of competition and alliance going on – between the political parties, between these and the civic activists involved in campaigning bodies – to claim the role of true representatives of the Scottish cause. And while the political norm in Scotland is to the left of that in England, there are diverse and diverging conceptions of what should be done – creating government support for small businesses; re-nationalising industries; strengthening unions; capturing North Sea oil revenues; eliminating nuclear energy and military forces; increasing the role of Gaelic, Scots, and Scottish history in education; decentralising government while at the same time making it a more active force in the economy. The list, not entirely incoherent, but encompassing contradictory tendencies, goes on.

William Roseberry has also addressed problems in the moral economy literature (1989: 55–9). Following Raymond Williams' critique, he notes that supposedly pre-market peasant economies were hardly 'natural' and involved their own forms of brutality and exploitation. But he observes that this does not undo the usefulness of the concept, because

> the 'moral economy' need not have existed in the past; it may be *perceived* in the past from the perspective of a disordered present. The images [sic] of a moral economy may be a *meaningful* image even if 'what actually happened' was less idyllic. (1989: 57; emphasis in original)

Forging a link between the moral economy literature and that on the 'invention of tradition' (cf. Hobsbawm and Ranger 1984), Roseberry suggests that the moral economy be viewed not so much as an actual historical formation, but as an active and creative interpretation of the past in present circumstances. He further suggests that rather than think in terms of an ordered social universe being displaced by a disordered one, we think in terms of one system of disorder being replaced by another.

Again, these observations are salutary for the Scottish movement. For while I have said it is a defence of the modern welfare state, it simultaneously idealises and criticises that social order. Criticisms of the welfare state, for instance from the perspectives of gender, race, economically and ecologically sustainable economies, and resistance to bureaucratic control of daily life (cf. Pierson 1991: 40–101), are not lost on movement activists. Still, the movement discourse involves a strange blend of resistance to state centralisation, a long-standing theme in Scottish nationalism since before the turn of the century, along with a yearning for a pre-Thatcherite past in which there was, supposedly, a strong sense of community and mutual support, underwritten by the centralised state. While the actual problem that confronts this movement is how to sustain old and create new standards of communal provisioning under radically altered political economic circumstances, the sheer radicalism of the neoliberal agenda has in some sense dictated a conservative, backward-looking stance in the Scottish movement, even while it contains its own alternate visions of Scotland's future. In my experience, the more perceptive movement activists are alive to (and somewhat bemused by) the contradictions involved here, caught between aspirations for a better and more just social order in Scotland, and the realities of the present political economic environment in which a small country has very limited control over its own destiny.

– Notes –

1. A major campaigning issue during my field work, 'VAT on fuel' refers to a proposed Tory policy to levy Value Added Tax on domestic fuel consumption. This was widely seen as discriminatory against those who lived in colder climates that required higher heating bills, i.e., Scotland, and as a real threat to old age pensioners on fixed income.

2. I believe this metaphor was directed against the laissez-faire system in general, and not meant to characterise Scotland in particular as a starving child.

3. In the British political system, the major opposition party forms a cabinet-in-waiting which parallels the Prime Minister's cabinet. These 'shadow' ministers make a political career of formulating alternate policies and critiquing the work of the minister they are hoping to replace.

4. The Stone of Destiny, traditionally associated with the coronation of Scottish kings at Scone, was taken by Edward I during the medieval wars with England. It was briefly liberated from its resting place in Westminster Abbey in 1951 by a plucky bunch of young Scottish nationalists, and ever after rumours abounded that the stone returned was a replica, and the real one was hiding in safe hands until the appropriate day. Three years after the Rally, in 1996, in an attempt to improve the Conservative Party's poor reputation in Scotland, and appease nationalist sentiments, the Stone was returned to Edinburgh Castle on St Andrews Day (30 November), with some fanfare, and a great deal of public indifference.

5. The reference here is to a remark made by Margaret Thatcher, which is often refered to in anti-Thatcherite discourse. In 1987 she is reported to have said: 'There is no such thing as society. There are individual men and women, and there are families' (see footnote in Mitchell 1990: 141).

6. The following is my own translation from the Scots, with some divergence from literal meanings to try to capture the gist of the song as a whole, and further connotations of words supplied in parentheses after the main meaning. I have not attempted to preserve the rhythm of the verse.

> Rough the wind in the clear day's dawning
>> Blows the clouds head over heels across the bay
> But there's more than a rough wind blowing
>> Through the Great Glen of the world today

It's a thought that will make (command) our rats (rascals)
    All those rogues that go bold (impetuously), fresh and gay (in splendour)
Take the road and seek other pastures (paths, places)
    for their evil schemes to sport (parade) and play (prosecute).

No more will the handsome fellows
    March to war when our braggarts arrogantly crow
Nor small children from pit-head and hamlet
    Mourn the ships sailing down the Broomielaw (the River Clyde
      in Glasgow)
Broken families in lands we've harried
    Will curse Scotland the Brave no more, no more
Black and white, one to the other married
    Make the vile barracks of their masters bare.

O come all you at home with freedom
    Never mind when the hooded crows croak for doom (call for judgement)
In your house all the children of Adam
    Can find bread, drink (alcoholic), and painted room
When (John) Maclean meets with his friends in Springburn
    All the roses and wild cherries will turn to bloom
And a black boy from far Nyanga
    Knocks (beats) the mighty (ruthless) gallows of the burgers
      (bourgeoisie) down.

7. See Thompson's *The Moral Economy Reviewed* (1993: 259–351) for his responses
to the many uses this term has been put to following his initial essay.

CHAPTER 2

Home Rule History

– INTRODUCTION –

This chapter briefly lays out the historical background of home rule politics in Scotland, leading up to the pivotal years of 1979–97, which are examined more closely in the next chapter. More than just context, it is meant to suggest the historical continuities and discontinuities involved, and to support the general argument that Scottish nationalism has long had an affinity with liberalism, and deep roots in civil society, however we choose to understand that term.

– ANTECEDENTS: JACOBITES, RADICALS AND LIBERALS –

Although the movement which is the object of our study is really a twentieth-century phenomenon, it is worth briefly considering some of it precursors, both because these play a role in the conceptualisation of nationalism in the current movement, and because they highlight, by contrast, the specificity of the movement in this century. Perhaps the most recognised icons of the Scottish nation are the Jacobites, those largely Highland nobles and their clan followers who remained loyal to the Stuart dynasty after it was deposed in 1689, organising ill-fated military uprisings to reinstall the Stuarts in 1715, 1719 and 1745. The last uprising was brutally defeated at the battle of Culloden, and followed by harsh legal and military suppression in the Highlands by the British government. Although the Jacobites are often taken as the ultimate symbol of Scottish nationalism, it is important to remember that they were strongly opposed by many Lowland Scots themselves, who rejected Stuart Catholicism, and supported the general shift in power away from the king and toward the parliament. The Jacobite rebellions were a reactionary attempt to return to something closer to the declining feudal order.

By the later eighteenth century a new wave of revolutionary republican-democratic ideas were in the air, leading up to and subsequently inspired by the French Revolution in 1789. In Scotland members of various groups such as The Friends of the People Society (1792–4) and the United Scotsman (1793–4), a secret society modelled on the United Irishmen, argued, agitated and organised around these ideas, including various forms of advocacy for a Scottish parliament as part of a program of democratic reform. By the turn of the century these groups and their members had been persecuted and disbanded by the government, and a repressive atmosphere was maintained throughout the war with France (1803–15) (McLean 1988a: 5–6).

In the middle of the nineteenth century radical reform energies were generally channelled through the developing political parties toward the British parliamentary system. During this period the Whigs, the political faction of the urban commercial elite, evolved into the Liberal Party, displacing the party of the landed aristocracy, the Tories, and becoming the hegemonic political force in nineteenth-century Scotland. Some take this as a period of quiescence in regard to nationalist issues, but as Graeme Morton has shown, many in the Scottish middle class saw Britain and the empire as vehicles for the expression of a kind of nationalism that was compatible with a larger British unionism, what Morton calls 'unionist nationalism'(1998). In this context middle-class nationalist sentiments tended to take the form of calls for institutional reforms and greater parliamentary representation within the British political system, demands expressed especially by the National Association for the Vindication of Scottish Rights (Morton 1996). It was this kind of pressure that eventually led to the establishment of the Scottish Office in 1887, as a separate department of government dedicated specifically to Scottish concerns (Paterson 1994: 62), a process which simultaneously both further integrated and distinguished Scotland as a part of the larger British political system (McCrone 1993).

By the last two decades of the nineteenth century a new mixture of political concerns had developed, including radical land reforms in the Highlands, the rise of socialism and the trade union movement in the Lowlands, and mutually reinforcing demands for home rule in both Ireland and Scotland. Attempting to appeal to all these constituencies, and particularly dependent on the Irish nationalists for support in parliament, the Liberal Prime Minister Gladstone proposed 'home rule all around', in other words, parliaments to be established in both Ireland and Scotland (and possibly Wales). However, encountering long-standing Protestant anti-Catholicism, this led to a massive departure from the Liberal Party by staunch Protestant unionists, thereby undermining the Liberal Party's power and ability to proceed on the issue. Out of these events came the Scottish Home Rule Association in 1886, which continued, with limited effect, to campaign for the cause.

– THE EARLY TWENTIETH CENTURY:
SOCIALISM AND HOME RULE –

The opening decades of the twentieth century were marked by loss of imperial markets, a flagging industrial economy, growing protectionism, high unemployment, and agitation among industrial workers. The brief economic stimulation created by World War I was followed by a steady decline. It was in this context that the labour, socialist, and nationalist movements, already nascent in the previous century, coalesced into their twentieth-century forms. In terms of party politics, the story of the decades around the turn of the century is one of the formation of the Labour Party and its eclipsing of the old Liberal Party (treated in more detail in Chapter 6). Various Scottish streams fed into the growth of Labour.[1] The Highland Land League of the 1880s was formed to provide better representation for the highland crofters. Key figures such as James Kier Hardie, for whom 'socialism . . . was the industrial expression of Christianity' (Checkland and Checkland 1989: 80), organised the founding of the Scottish Labour Party in 1888 and its merger with the Independent Labour Party in 1893. These fledgling parties took shape amid the growing disaffection of the radical wing of the Liberal Party, and the growth of the trade union movement. By 1906 the Labour Party in Scotland was established.

Between 1914 and 1922, in the years surrounding World War I, there was a series of industrial strikes in the heavy industries along the river Clyde in Glasgow, which became known as 'Red Clydeside'. In 1919, at the peak of these strikes, the government sent out troops and tanks to prevent what it saw as a possible Bolshevik uprising. In Scottish leftist lore, for which this event is central, Bolshevism was indeed on the threshold. In fact however, most of the major organisers had more limited goals around securing certain conditions for labour (wage levels, preventing 'dilution' from less skilled workers, and so on), and it was the somewhat better paid tradesmen, for example, engineers, who spearheaded the action (Harvie 1981: 15–23).

This event fed into the development of communism in Scotland. The Communist Party of Great Britain (CPGB) was formed in 1920, and by 1921, following Lenin's advice, Willie Gallacher, a leading communist organiser of Red Clydeside had convinced the bulk of the Clydeside workers to come into the CPGB. A minority of the Clydeside communists, led by John MacLean, had stronger nationalist sentiments, and demanded a separate Scottish Communist Party. As a result of this split nationalism was marginalised in communist circles up to the mid-1930s.

> MacLean, a figure of legendary stature in Scottish socialist folklore, had gained considerable support for his stand against the war, which had cost him his job as a school-teacher and several spells in prison. He now moved in an increasingly nationalist direction and, impressed by the example of Sinn Fein and the Celtic nationalism of Erskine of Mar, saw the ferment on the Clyde, the land agitation in the Highlands and the clamour for Home Rule as creating the conditions for the declaration of a Scottish Workers' Republic. (Keating and Bleiman 1979: 65–6)

MacLean campaigned as a Scottish Workers' Republican candidate in 1923, but he died during the campaign, physically depleted by the rigours of prison and politics. This passionate mixture of equally intense nationalism and socialism endures in Scotland to this day, and MacLean is a major icon of, and martyr to, the cause of socialist nationalism.

Regardless of the CPGB's strategic distancing of itself from the cause, during the first two decades of this century home rule was a central tenet of the larger Scottish labour/socialist movement. In 1918 Labour in Scotland fought the general election on a program of 'self-determination for the Scottish people', and in 1924 and 1927 Labour put home rule bills before parliament, but these were 'talked out' at their second readings – this frustration being one of the more immediate spurs to the formation of the National Party of Scotland in 1928. From that time Labour support for home rule began to wane.

The Scottish National Party's genealogy illustrates two tensions that have endured in the nationalist movement to the present, between those who envision a broad based movement versus those who advocate party politics as the main route to power, and between those who would accept a path to independence via a devolved parliament, often called 'gradualists', and those who demanded a direct move to independence, often called 'fundamentalists' (see Finlay 1994; Jones 1992a: 387).[2] The Scottish Home Rule Association (SHRA), which called for a parliament within the UK, went through two incarnations. The first, founded in 1886, had strong ties to the old Liberal Party; the second, founded in 1918 after the war, drew support from across the Liberal-Labour spectrum. In 1920 the Scots National League was founded, with a more radical program of Gaelic revival and national independence. This group, inclined toward a cultural essentialism characteristic of the period in Europe, attracted a strange mix including the poet Hugh MacDiarmid, the novelist Compton Mackenzie, and Erskine of Mar, with his dubious and romantic notions of a racially based 'Celtic communism'. They also argued that a political party had to be established in order to fight for the cause through electoral politics, and in 1928 the National Party of Scotland was formed for this purpose, bringing together elements from the SHRA, the Scots National League, and the Glasgow University Scottish Nationalist Association, led by the young and able John MacCormick, who came from an Independent Labour Party background. The National Party was an eclectic left-of-centre party, but in order to unify forces and garner financial support, MacCormick, who had quickly gravitated to a leadership position in the Party, negotiated a merger with the smaller right-of centre Scottish Self-Government Party (established in 1932), and thus the Scottish National Party (SNP) was finally born in 1934.

– MID-TWENTIETH CENTURY: THE CONSENSUS' YEARS –

In 1935 the Communist Party adopted a Popular Front policy which opened the doors to co-operation with the home rule movement. On May Day 1938, now numbering just under 3,000, 'the Communists paraded in tartan, carrying banners of Bruce and Wallace, Burns, Calgacus and (rather oddly, in view of his high toryism) R. L. Stevenson' (Harvie 1981: 102). Adamant anti-war beliefs shared by some nationalists and the communists further connected these strains. But this rapprochement on the nationalist left was paralleled by the growing strength of the Labour Party and the marginalisation of the home rule issue. Both the harsh realities of the Depression and the strengthening of British level solidarity in World War II were major factors in this shift. In 1941 Churchill appointed long time Labour homeruler Tom Johnston to the post of Scottish Secretary of State. Under Johnston there was a substantial degree of administrative devolution to Scotland, which he used to guide war industries and infrastructural investment to Scotland. By the time of the 1945–51 Labour governments, the predominant view was that administration of the regions of the UK from a strong centre was the best way to rebuild after the war and lay the foundations for a modern welfare state.

During these years the policies of both Labour and the Conservatives tended to converge on a kind of technocratic managerialism. The Conservative Party of the nineteenth century had always had limited success in Scotland, and in 1912 it merged with the large break-away faction of the old Liberal Party that was fiercely opposed to Irish Home Rule. The party fared better in Scotland under its new unionist banner, capturing the Protestant, Orange Order portion of the working-class vote, and even managing to be the only party ever to attain a majority of the Scottish vote (50.1 per cent) in 1955.

By the 1950s the Communist Party (CP) had 10,000 members in Scotland, a quarter of the party's UK total despite Scotland only having a tenth of the UK's population (Harvie 1981: 109). During the middle of this century, when Labour was turning away from the idea of home rule, the CP carried the flame on the left. While its electoral success was largely limited to the Communist MP Willie Gallacher in the mining district of West Fife (1935–50), by the late 1950s and 1960s the CP had become important to the internal workings of the Labour movement through its influence on key industrial organisations, specifically the National Union of Mineworkers (NUM), the Transport and General Workers Union (TGWU), and to a lesser extent, the Scottish Trades Union Congress (STUC). Defections from the CP to Labour in the 1950s over Stalin and Hungary also influenced the general flow of ideas on the left. In 1964, the CP officially adopted support for home rule, and in 1969 it became part of the STUC's program. Thus, while the Labour Party in Scotland did not clearly turn toward support for a Scottish parliament until after the 1979 Referendum, the Communists early on played a key role in solidifying support for the cause within the institutional infrastructure of the Labour movement.[3]

Within the SNP John MacCormick, who favoured 'movement' and 'gradualist' approaches, had struggled to guide the young SNP along this path . Eventually however, factionalism led to an internal power struggle, and MacCormick and a handful of followers broke from the SNP in 1942. His next move was to form the Scottish Convention, which called a Scottish National Assembly in March of 1947, composed of some 400 delegates 'from churches, trade unions, chambers of commerce and co-operative societies. There was also a smattering of peers and MPs' (McLean 1988b: 5). The key objective of this campaigning group was to pressure the Labour government to take the home rule issue seriously. At its third meeting in 1949 the National Assembly launched a large scale public petition which came to be known the Scottish Covenant. The Covenant pledged its signatories 'in all loyalty to the Crown and within the framework of the United Kingdom, to do everything within our power to secure for Scotland a Parliament with adequate legislative authority in Scottish affairs.'

This finely crafted piece of broad-church politics attracted wide support: 50,000 signatures in the first week, and more than a million in six months. By 1952 the figure had reached two million, although it is suspected that this included repeat signatures and a few Micky Mouses and Winston Churchills. But strong Labour Party resistance to these pressures amid the growing concerns of the newly expanding post-war welfare state, meant that the Covenant failed effectively to advance the issue, and by the early 1950s it had lost its momentum (McLean 1988b: 5–11).

– 1970S: THE 'CONSENSUS' BREAKS DOWN –

The SNP's first electoral success came in 1945 when Robert MacIntyre won the Motherwell by-election, but that seat was subsequently lost in the next general election.[4] None the less it was a symbolic milestone, demonstrating that the party could capture a parliamentary seat. SNP support grew gradually in the 1950s and 1960s, membership reaching around16,000 in 1965, and peaking in another dramatic by-election victory for Winnie Ewing in Hamilton in 1967. Then, in the context of rising expectations generated by North Sea oil, support surged, and in two general elections in 1974 the SNP jumped from 22 per cent to 30 per cent of the vote, sending eleven MPs to Westminster. In terms of UK electoral politics, this was the SNP's high-water mark. In 1979 and through the 1980s the party was again marginalised by upheavals in British Labour politics, the temporary success of an alliance between the break-away Social Democratic Party and the Liberals, and an initial receptivity in some quarters for the neo-conservatism of Thatcher.

While there was always a pro-home rule minority within the Labour Party throughout the 'consensus' years, it was only with the rising fortunes of the SNP in the early 1970s that the party had to seriously address the issue again. During the weak minority Labour governments of 1974–9 there were strong splits within the party over the question of devolution. Unable to internally agree on the issue, the party created The Scotland and Wales Act in 1978, which called for the establishment of regional assemblies in those two countries, putting the Bill to the test of national referendums. Immediately, opposing factions formed rival campaigns: 'Labour Vote No' versus 'Labour Movement Yes'. Members of the 'No' contingent joined forces with Tories to append the infamous 40% Rule to the Bill, which required that in order for the Bill to be put into effect, those voting 'Yes' had to comprise at least 40% of the total Scottish/Wales electorates. In the event, 51.6% of those voting in Scotland said 'Yes' to a devolved assembly, but as turnout had been 63.8%, this was only 32.9% of the electorate, and so the Bill failed.

There are many reasons why the Bill failed, beyond dissension within the ranks of the Labour Party. For reasons of 'fundamentalism' versus 'gradualism' the SNP was also divided in its support. Those opposed in both the Labour and Tory parties stimulated strong fears of the costs of creating and supporting assemblies, and evoked the possibility that devolution would be the first step down a slippery slope to the break-up of the UK, for which there was much less popular support. Add to this the general vagueness of the plans for what the assembly would look like, and intimations by some Scottish Tories that if the Conservatives were to win power some form of assembly, more thoroughly thought through, would be on offer, and it is not surprising that many declined their support, either by voting 'no', or staying home. By the end, the devolution issue had absorbed much of Westminster's energies, to little effect. The election of Margaret Thatcher and the Tory Party in 1979 was partly a response of exasperation with the Labour governments of the 1970s. As it turned out, the UK as a whole opted for a radical move of a very different sort.

– NOTES –

1. Key sources for the history of the labour movement and home rule politics in Scotland include: Harvie (1981); Donnachie, Harvie and Wood (1989); Keating and Bleiman (1979); and McLean (1988a, 1988b).
2. For the history of the SNP see especially: Finlay (1994); Gallagher (1991); Harvie (1998); Kemp (1993); MacCormick (1955); and Marr (1992).
3. On the Communist Party and home rule in Scotland, see: Brotherstone (1993); Harvie (1981: 109–10); Jones (1992a: 384); and Marr (1992: 182–3).
4. By-elections are elections that take place between general elections due to the incidental vacancy of seats. Historically, voters are more likely to use them to express idiosyncratic preferences, coming back into the major party folds for general elections.

CHAPTER 3

The North-South Divide

This chapter focuses on the years between the first and second devolution referendums (1979–97), looking in more detail at how the movement evolved during this transformative period, and especially at the interactions between political parties and various campaigning groups. It does this under three main headings: political parties, the civic nationalist core, and the ethnic nationalist fringe. This gives us a rough breakdown of different sectors of civil society involved in this process and how they interact. It also allows us to look more closely at what the distinction between civic and ethnic forms of nationalism might mean in the Scottish context. I conclude with an overview of the final sequence of events, including the Labour victory at Westminster and the second referendum, leading up to the election of the new parliament on 6 May 1999.

– THE POLITICAL PARTIES –

As mentioned above, the years in question saw an increasing polarisation of electoral support for the two major UK parties, Labour and the Conservatives, into what came to be known as 'the north-south divide'. In short, the heartland of Tory support was in the south-east of England and the Home Counties, while support for Labour was concentrated in Wales and Scotland, and in England in the industrial midlands and the north. Thus estrangement from Tory government hardly fell along national lines, and it was actually northern England that often most strongly supported Labour. But the combination of national distinctiveness and this particular geography of party support meant that in Scotland, the north-south divide tended to easily map onto and ideologically reinforce political struggles construed in terms of Scotland versus England, or Scottish civil society versus Westminster government. As we shall see, this initial discussion of party politics in regard to nationalism can only fully be understood in relation to the dynamics of campaigning bodies in civil society that follows.

While there were flirtations in the Conservative Party with the idea of mild forms of devolution in the 1970s, philosophically in keeping with the neoliberal belief in smaller central government, the actual trend under the Tories was the opposite, toward a centralisation of political power in Westminster. A central tenet of Tory ideology is that true power, in the form of political sovereignty, is intrinsically indivisible. This idea is often summed up in the aphorism coined by Enoch Powell: 'power devolved is power retained', in other words, only an absolute power can grant provisional powers. Thus one of the most contentious points regarding the establishment of a parliament was always whether it would have entrenched powers that could not be later revoked by Westminster. Such an arrangement would be antithetical to the Tory philosophy, and in truth, not very compatible with ideas of democratic centralism still ingrained in the Labour Party, regardless of reforms. This unitary conception of power is evident in Westminster's frequent restructuring of local government, as well as the abolition of the Assembly in Northern Ireland (1972), and the Greater London Council (1985), which was a left-wing thorn in Thatcher's side. And in fact, the powers of the new Scottish parliament are not entrenched, despite the wishes of many in the pro-parliament movement.

In the political atmosphere of the 1980s and 1990s in Scotland, where the Conservatives increasingly stood as lone unionists pitted against all the leading parties and the vast majority of the electorate favouring some form of constitutional change, it was easy to miss the muted, pro-devolution voices among the Tories. The Scottish Tory Reform Group, a branch of the UK-wide Tory Reform Group which represents the left-wing of the party, was formed to help articulate a distinctively Scottish take on Conservatism and devise ways to counter further erosion of the party's Scottish base. I interviewed one leading member in 1994 who was not alone in advocating the creation of some form of assembly/parliament, believing that this would actually help revive Tory fortunes in Scotland by providing a Scottish context for the articulation of Conservative ideas and interests.

In the wilderness years of 1979–97 Labour, at least in Scotland, was gradually converted to the idea of a Scottish parliament for several reasons. Most basically, due to the north-south polarisation of Labour and Tory support since the 1950s, and especially during the period in question, Labour had become the de facto party of Scotland, and home rule had become a basic part of that mantle. As we shall see below, the party's participation in the Scottish Constitutional Convention in the 1990s was a key factor in effecting this transformation. This general situation combined with the strategic need to take the nationalist wind out of the SNP's sails by offering a firm programme of devolution. Another significant element in the party's conversion was the formation of the effective pro-parliament internal pressure group Scottish Labour Action (SLA) in 1988 under the skilled leadership of Bob McLean. One sign of this shift was SLA's success at the 1994 Labour Party Conference in Dundee in having the name of the party organisation in Scotland changed from Labour Party Scotland to the Scottish Labour Party, a name which has some bitter associations with the brief break-away Scottish Labour Party formed in 1976 and led by Labour devolutionist Jim Sillars, who later became a leading figure in the SNP in the early 1980s. Finally, it could be argued that the untimely death in 1994 of the party leader John Smith, who had shown a strong personal commitment to devolution since the first referendum, consolidated party identification with the cause. By the late 1990s, with the faltering of John Major's internally riven Conservative government and the new popularity in England of Tony Blair's modernised, business-friendly Labour Party, the conditions were ripe for the Labour victory of 1997, and the first referendum on a Scottish parliament in eighteen years.

Although a much smaller party, The Liberal Democrats have also played an important role. They grew out of the nineteenth-century Liberal Party which, as we have seen, had become politically marginalised around the turn of the century. In the 1960s their fortunes began to revive, and in 1987 the Liberals and the short-lived Social Democratic Party (SDP) formed an Alliance Party. The SDP, which broke away from Labour in 1981, has been described as 'a "quiche and claret" party of the London suburbs' (noted in Jones 1992a: 386). In 1988 these two merged to form the Liberal Democrats of today. The party has advocated federalism in the UK or 'home rule all around', since the days of Gladstone in the 1880s. But as Jones observes, '[t]he Scottish party is passionately committed to Scottish home rule . . . whereas the party in England has been rather more concerned with civil rights issues than with regional government for England' (ibid.).

By the 1983 general election support for the SNP had fallen to 11.7 per cent of the vote, but since then it has climbed back, reaching 22.1 per cent at the 1997 general election. By that time the party had four Westminster MPs and two members of the European Parliament (MEPs), and a substantial presence on many of the local government councils. The two central axes of strategy in the movement mentioned in the last chapter, between movement and party, and gradualism and fundamentalism, have shaped the dynamics and internal conflicts of the SNP during the last twenty years. Fundamentalists tended to view devolution as a device to block full independence and therefore to be resisted. Moreover, they saw the call for national independence as a primary issue that takes precedence over traditional left-right differences within the party. In the late 1960s there developed a new push in the SNP toward a party/fundamentalist approach, further stimulated by the defeated devolution referendum in 1979, which many in the SNP felt was undermined by Labour's ambivalent support, and false promises of 'a better plan' from the Tories. The party/fundamentalist combination entails certain contradictions however, in that a political party requires a more or less clearly defined position along a left-right spectrum, while fundamentalism treats these issues as secondary. The general result of a 'party' strategy that competes primarily with Labour has been a more clearly left-of-centre set of policies. Major pressure to move in this direction came from the left-wing '79 Group, formed in the wake of the referendum, which included some of the keenest thinkers and ablest politicians in the SNP.

Although briefly expelled from the party in 1982–3, many members of this group eventually reasserted themselves and became highly influential. The roles of two leading figures suggest its importance. Jim Sillars is a pro-European socialist who converted the SNP at the 1988 party conference to its present policy of 'Independence in Europe', thus helping to counter popular fears of nationalist isolationism. Sillars was a central charismatic figure in the party, presenting an unusual combination of extreme leftism with extreme fundamentalism, the latter being more often associated with the centre-right of the SNP. He has generally pulled back from the movement since the frustrating defeat of the 1992 general election. Alex Salmond is an economist by training and middle-of-the-road social democrat. As party leader since 1990, he has been skilful in negotiating between factions. Like many of the '79ers he is a gradualist at heart, and while he has often downplayed that position, he was clearly able to make the gradualist position prevail inside the party in regard to SNP participation in the 1997 Referendum. Now that the parliament has been achieved gradualism is less of an issue. The question becomes one of whether the SNP will become a domesticated national party, along the lines of the Convergençia i Unio in Catalunya, or whether the fundamentalist drive toward full independence will strengthen.

The SNP casts itself as the defender of Scotland, its political rhetoric full of indictments of what the 'unionist' parties, whether the Tories or Labour, have done to the Scottish economy. Thus in 1987, despite internal qualms, the SNP took a vocal stance against paying Thatcher's ill-conceived and abortive Poll Tax, which was introduced a year earlier in Scotland than in the rest of the UK. And in 1994 the SNP campaigned against a proposed Value Added Tax (VAT) on domestic heating fuel, seen as an unfair burden on the poor in the colder north of the UK. Party speeches and literature abound with images of the energy and economic potential that would be released upon independence. The SNP has been able to construct rather idealised manifestos describing it's goals and policies for Scotland, because the context in which these would have to be realised has been relatively remote, and difficult to determine very precisely in advance. The most hotly debated issues here are to what degree an independent Scotland would control North Sea oil revenues, and how substantial these might be, as well as whether or not Scotland has been a net source of economic loss or gain for UK revenues as a whole. Extreme arguments have been made on either side, with those opposed to independence often arguing that Scotland is not economically viable, and those in favour arguing that it would become an economic powerhouse. The truth is probably somewhere in between, and deeply complicated by the fact that modern national economies are interwoven and far from independent. If a Scottish government gained substantial control over the North Sea oil industry. it still could not control global oil markets.[1]

Political economic constraints today tend to inhibit mainline political parties from formulating unrealisable, let alone radical goals, thus muting the expression of more idealistic popular political desires. Because of their peculiarly hypothetical nature, SNP policies should be viewed as appealing to and articulating a generalised notion of how people in Scotland would like to see their country governed in the 'best of all possible worlds'. They are instructive for this reason, even if they bear only a loose relationship to any future Scotland. In broad outline, major SNP policies and proposals include:

1. A written constitution with a Bill of Rights at least as extensive as the European Convention on Human Rights. These would grant citizenship to everyone resident and/or born in Scotland (and others at the parliament's discretion), and legislate against discrimination on the basis of sex, race, ethnicity, sexual orientation and physical disability.[2]
2. Policies of job creation, including a target of full employment, infrastructural investments, and job training programs.
3. Retention and development of the National Health Service.
4. Increased investment in public housing stock.
5. A more progressive income tax regime.
6. Increases in unemployment and pension benefits.
7. Strong public investment in education, the arts, and the media.

In recent years, as devolution became more likely, SNP policies have shifted away from a more traditional social democratic agenda of centralised economic management to one more oriented toward attracting investment and appealing to business interests. Thus a comparison of manifestos and economic policy documents from 1992 and 1997 reveals various rephrasings: rather than 'policy', full employment will be 'aimed for'; rather than 'free', education will be 'well resourced'. Recent policy documents specify a business tax regime that would encourage growth, have abandoned the idea of re-nationalising the Scottish steel industry, and pay greater attention to social problems caused by drugs and crime. While the theme of protecting the environment and developing alternative energy sources (wind and wave power) continues, the goal of a pacifist and non-nuclear Scotland is less out front, and the plans for conventional defence forces more developed (cf. SNP 1992a; 1992b; 1997a; 1997b). Having said this, SNP policies can still be seen as reflecting a broad, left-of-centre consensus in Scotland, though perhaps increasingly caught in the gravitational pull of neoliberal political reality.

Despite this reflection of consensus, it is worth bearing in mind that the SNP itself remains a 'broad church' with a peculiar combination of rural, often more conservative support, and urban and more left-wing support. Research indicates that the party attracts defectors from other parties across the political spectrum (McCrone 1992: 164–9; Kellas 1989: 138–41). As might be expected, older Nationalists are often more conservative, younger ones more left and radical. Many involved in the movement believe that the SNP now attracts younger left-leaning activists who a generation earlier would have joined Labour, but are disillusioned with a modernising Labour Party, and more confident of the SNP's socialist credentials. Still, it is a party of strange bedfellows. I recall speaking in a pub during an SNP Party Conference with one group of fairly young members from a branch in Aberdeen, where no bones were made about the fact that under other conditions, while most would probably be Labour, at least one would have been a Conservative. More than once I was assured that after an initial transition to independence, many would defect to new parties reflecting the usual left-right spectrum, the SNP having served its purpose.

The Communists remained important to the movement through the 1980s and early 1990s, particularly by lending active support to the Scottish Constitutional Convention (see below). With the collapse of the Soviet Union came the fragmentation of the Communist Party. There are three major products of this convoluted story. First, a continuing Communist Party of Britain (the 'Great' seems to have been discreetly dropped), preserving the more hard-line, Stalinist tradition and still supporting a parliament, although wary of the European Union in some quarters (cf. Foster 1991). Second, the Democratic Left, formed in 1991 as a party, but reconfigured as an 'organisation' in 1993. This group has attracted a large portion of the support for the old CP in Scotland, and has a 'eurocommu-nist' orientation with a strong concern for new social movements and the importance of identities other than those based on class. And third, there is the small and young but active Communist Party of Scotland, formed in 1992, whose ideology is not hard line, but preserves the marxist primacy of class analysis, and includes strong support for a parliament in the old tradition.

It is worth noting the widespread reputation of the Communists in Scotland, which can almost be summed up in a word – respectable. With the exception of some of the hard right, across parties and classes, the Communists were widely viewed to have been exceptionally decent, disciplined and hardworking people, almost the paradigm of the Protestant ethic, though put to a different end. In keeping with this perception, they were often seen as the moral keel of the Labour movement – a stabiliser for the Labour Party and the unions which were prone to corruption and Labourism (i.e., 'old boy-ism') within their ranks. As a result their parti-cipation in the home rule movement is widely seen as giving it a stamp of respectability, not as marking it as a fringe endeavour. Another side of this respectable role in Scottish politics is that the CP tended to be 'bitterly hostile to Trotskyism and . . . ultra-leftism' (Marr 1992: 183), of the kind espoused by groups like Scottish Militant Labour, which I discuss next.

Scottish Militant Labour (SML), one of the more dramatic elements in recent Scottish politics, grew out of the Trotskyist, hard-left Militant Tendency which developed in the British Labour Party in the stormy 1970s. Under the charismatic leadership of Tommy Sheridan, SML had some striking successes in the impoverished public housing projects of Glasgow. Sheridan, who campaigned while serving a jail sentence for refusing to pay his Poll Tax, pulled 20 per cent of the vote when he stood for parliament in the 1992 general election, and in the mid-1990s SML held six local government seats, but by 1998 only Sheridan retained his seat. Their program of strong marxist socialism/anti-capitalism benefited stra-tegically from its militant opposition to the Poll Tax, which has been the springboard of their success. Just as the SNP's hypotheses about the prosperity of an independent Scotland are difficult to substantiate, SML's vision of a socialist Scotland tended to filter out the encompassing hostile capitalist context in which it would have to be realised. The party supported the idea of a Scottish parliament as an instrument of its socialist program, but parliamentary self-government was not central to its ideology. My sense from an interview with Sheridan in 1994 was that SML's position on the parliament was mainly a pragmatic embracing of the realities of politics in contemporary Scotland, where support for a such a body is overwhelming (cf. Wood 1989: 127–8). Despite its successes, SML showed little potential for expanding its base beyond a small fraction of intellectuals and the deeply disenfranchised urban poor in Glasgow, who feel abandoned by Labour. However, for the general election of the first Scottish parliament they reconfigured themselves as the Scottish Socialist Party, and Sheridan won a seat via proportional representation, due to strong support in their Glasgow heartland.

The Greens are relatively small with almost no electoral presence. But people in the Scottish movement generally want to defend Scotland's natural resources against exploitation and promote more ecologically sound forms of land and resource management and the development of wind and wave power technologies (reflected, for instance, in SNP manifestos). This is obviously compatible with the Green philosophy, as is the general idea of more decentralised forms of democracy and greater local control over production and consumption. As suggested in the discussion of Democracy for Scotland in Chapter 1, the Greens have naturally gravitated toward the movement, and it in turn has provided a platform for promoting the party's ideas. Here again, the Greens managed to obtain a seat in the first Scottish parliament via proportional representation.

Clearly, nationalist politics became pervasive in Scotland over the last thirty years, and are not simply the preserve of the SNP. The dynamic of electoral competition made it imperative for the parties to stake out positions on the issue of Scotland's constitutional future. The three major parties during this period took the three clearly contrasting positions in this field of arguments: the SNP for independence, Labour for a parliament within the UK, and the Conservatives for unionism. It is worth remembering that the SNP only has to take into account a Scottish constituency, while Labour and the Conservatives are ultimately UK-wide parties, although having unique forms and traditions of organisation at the Scottish level. Moreover, within each of these parties there are debates and members who dissent from their own party's official position.

Within this major frame the smaller parties take particular positions along the pro-parliament part of the spectrum, with the numerically small but venerable and respectable Liberal Democrats representing the desire for UK-wide federalism. The next section reviews the major pro-parliament campaigning bodies, and as we shall see, members of the smaller parties have been particularly active in this arena. The network of campaigning bodies provided a context in which experimental conceptions of democratic politics and potential parliaments can be articulated somewhat outside the direct pressures of party politics, and also provided a meeting ground for pro-parliament politicians and intellectuals who might otherwise keep their distance from party politics. The campaigning bodies served as a zone of negotiation (at times tenuous) between the parties, while at the same time substantiating the fact that nationalist politics and desires transcend the party system. It is to the evolution of the campaigning bodies that we now turn.

– THE CIVIC NATIONALIST CORE –

The Campaign for a Scottish Assembly (CSA) was formed in 1979 as a response to the demoralising failure of the referendum. In the 1990s it changed its name to the Campaign for a Scottish Parliament (CSP), the shift from 'Assembly' to 'Parliament' indicating the hardening demand for a legislature with substantial, entrenched powers. The CSP was a cross-party organisation whose membership included both individuals from across the party spectrum (although Liberal Democrats were disproportionately represented among its key activists), and organisations including local authorities (i.e., local government councils), trade unions, professional organisations and churches. It's day-to-day activities included such things as sponsoring public meetings on home rule related issues, running stalls at political events, and larger projects generating publicity – for example, organising a mini-referendum on the constitutional issue in Falkirk, an 'average' town in central Scotland, in December 1993.

A thumbnail biography of the last Convenor of the CSP is instructive concerning its inter-party function. Isobel Lindsay joined the SNP in the 1960s as a part of a new generation of young activists who, while politically to the left, were disenchanted with Labourism and attracted to the openness of the SNP's political agenda, as allowing a space for other concerns – she has a strong commitment to the peace and anti-nuclear movement. She originally participated in the CSA as a member of the SNP, having been the party's vice-president in charge of policy and publicity, but fell out with the SNP over its withdrawal from the Constitutional Convention (see below). After a few years of not being a member of any party and simply focusing on CSP work, she announced in July of 1994 that she was joining the Labour Party, believing that a Labour government had become the most likely vehicle for delivering a parliament. Among key activists in the movement, political biographies like this, in which people move in and out of, and tarry in between opposing parties, is not at all uncommon.

From the beginning however, the CSA's main purpose was to create a forum for promoting the home rule cause and to foster co-operation across often rancorous party lines. The founding membership included people from Labour, the SNP, the Communists, the Scottish civil service, the trade union movement, and professional academics. The early 1980s were a low period for the movement, and the CSA's work was modest and gradual, but the idea of organising some kind of Constitutional Convention early on became a central strategic goal. The CSA had some success in influencing the SNP, despite strong internal divisions, to take up the idea of an elected Convention as a way forward at the party's 1984 Conference. Late in 1987, two key CSA members – Jim Ross a former Under-Secretary from the Scottish Office under Labour in the 1970s, and Alan Lawson, editor of the political journal *Radical Scotland* – hit upon a plan:

> To explain what the Convention was for, and to rally support for it, there needed to be a report 'by a representative group of people who are not enslaved to political parties but who carry political weight' – or, in other words, the leadership-in-waiting of a civil political movement. (Marr 1992: 197)

Thus the Constitutional Steering Committee was formed, composed of eminent men, and some women, from the universities, the civil service, the churches and the voluntary sector. In 1988 this group issued *A Claim of Right for Scotland*, a widely publicised report to the CSA, which offered an analysis of Scotland's historical and political situation, and outlined the possibilities for an assembly, and how a Constitutional Convention could be organised to design such an assembly. The title of the document is an explicit reference, recognisable to historically literate Scots, to the Claims of Right of 1689 and 1842. The former had prohibited royal prerogative from overriding parliamentary law in Scotland, thus setting Scotland's terms for the accession of William and Mary. The latter was drawn up by the General Assembly of the Church of Scotland to voice objection to Westminster interference in Church matters, which had been nominally protected by the Treaty of Union in 1707. The 1988 document is lengthy, and provides one of the best available introductions to the issues involved (see Chapter 9). The prologue gives a sense of its mission:

> Twice previously Scots have acted against misgovernment by issuing a Claim of Right; in 1689 and 1842. Circumstances may now be thought less stark and dramatic than on these previous occasions. But they are none the less serious. Now, as then, vital questions arise about the constitution and powers of the state. Then it was clearly understood that constitution and powers were the issue. Now there is a danger that this will not be fully recognised; that symptoms, such as the Poll Tax, the Health Service, Education and the Economy, are mistaken for causes, which lie in the way in which Scotland is governed. It is for a larger body than ourselves to set out in full the constitutional rights Scotland expects within the United Kingdom. That would be the true equivalent of the Claims made in 1689 and 1842. But we hold ourselves fully justified in registering a general Claim

of Right on behalf of Scotland, namely that Scotland has the right to insist on articulating its own demands and grievances, rather than having them articulated for it by a Government utterly unrepresentative of Scots. (Constitutional Steering Committee 1989: 10)

In early 1989 a meeting was held to put the Steering Committee's proposals for a Convention before representatives of the parties and other interests. The Conservatives declined to participate and the SNP soon withdrew, responding to internal pressure from its fundamentalist wing, which maintained that participation would be at odds with the party's constitutional principles, compromising the cause of full independence. On 30 March, the Convention held its first meeting; its membership gives a sense of the project:

1. Elected officials: fifty-five Scottish MPs, seven Scottish MEPs, and fifty-nine representatives from local government councils across Scotland;
2. Party representatives from: the Labour Party, the Scottish Liberal Democrats (especially heavily represented), the Social Democratic Party (now defunct), the Co-operative Party, the Communist Party, the Scottish Green Party, and the Orkney and Shetland Movement (representing another regionalist movement specific to those Scottish islands);
3. Various institutional representatives from: the STUC, the Scottish Churches, the Scottish Council Development and Industry, the National Federation of Self-Employed and Small Business, the Committee of University Principals, the Scottish Convention of Women, Dundee and Tayside Chamber of Commerce, An Comunn Gaidhealach, Comunn Na Gaidhlig (both working for Gaelic cultural preservation and rejuvenation in the Highlands and Islands), and representatives from five ethnic minorities;
4. Three observers from the CSA.

The Convention 'unanimously adopted a Declaration acknowledging the sovereign right of the Scottish people to determine its own form of government and pledging the Convention to work toward the preparation of a scheme for an Assembly or Parliament for Scotland which would be put to the Scottish people for endorsement' (Scottish Constitutional Convention 1990: 4). After this august beginning the Convention occupied itself with refining its proposals, establishing working groups to hammer out thornier issues – such as what kind of system of proportional representation should be employed, and whether to require sex parity among parliamentary representatives in order to counter the strong male bias in Scottish political culture – with these groups reporting back to an Executive Committee. This produced several publications and meetings reporting on the Convention's progress, with the ultimate outcome being the Final

Report of the Scottish Constitutional Convention: *Scotland's Parliament, Scotland's Right* (1995), which served as the blueprint for the Labour government's 1997 white paper on Scottish devolution.

There is a general consensus that the Convention was crucially instrumental in effecting the Labour Party's shift toward strong support for home rule, and that this was a major strategic advance for the movement. The participation of the SNP would have given the Convention a much stronger popular mandate, and their withdrawal meant that many saw the Convention in much more partisan terms, as an instrument of Labour and the Liberal Democrats. It also led several formerly active members of the SNP to distance themselves from the party, and long term sympathisers in the broader movement to feel disenchanted with the SNP. None the less, it was well known that the situation most likely to deliver a parliament was one in which Labour maintained a clear public commitment, with an electorally strong SNP breathing down their neck in Scotland's Labour heartland in the central belt. In other words, the old SNP-Labour divisiveness, while often counter-productive to efforts to create movement solidarity, is also a part of a deeper logic of the movement in which the very antagonism between these parties has been central to its advance.

The 1992 general election came as blow to the movement. Many thought at the time, partly due to rather shallow opinion poll analysis in the Scottish press in the lead up to the election, that a Tory debacle was inevitable – either they would lose power in Westminster, or their electoral obliteration in Scotland would lead to a constitutional crisis. Instead, they not only won in England but gained one Scottish seat (from 10 to 11 out of 72). The constitutional stalemate continued. In the run up to and immediate wake of this event several new campaigning groups were formed. One of these was Democracy for Scotland, introduced in Chapter 1. Two others were Scotland United, and Common Cause.

Scotland United (SU) was also formed immediately after the 1992 general election in that brief period of inter-party co-operation between Labour and the SNP. In fact, it quickly became primarily a Labour party operation, as it and the STUC provided most of the organisation and resources. The central purpose of SU was to organise and run a new popular multi-option referendum (status quo versus parliament versus independence) throughout Scotland. This was an extremely costly and complicated task, and SU primarily dedicated itself to a fund-raising drive, which moved slowly. Moreover, the Labour Party was not interested in making a heavy investment in the project, preferring to focus its energies on winning the next general election. At the time many people felt that the Labour Party, the only institution in Scotland with sufficient resources to carry off such a massive project, had rendered it dead in the water, by commandeering the project, and then putting it on the back burner. When I left the field, there continued to be nominal participation by members of all parties, but initial enthusiasm had been much dampened. Few in the SNP seemed to take the project very seriously.

Common Cause (CC) defined themselves as 'a civic forum on the future of democracy in Scotland . . . founded to offer new ideas and initiatives to citizens calling for greater democracy through a Scottish Parliament' (Common Cause 1992: back cover). Its primary purpose has been to sponsor public meetings, forums, and debates on the constitutional issue. The list of Trustees includes many of the 'usual suspects' from the CSP orbit,[3] but with an unusual weighting in favour of writers, journalists and academics who have become associated with the movement over the years (e.g., Tom Nairn, Joyce MacMillan, Neal Ascherson, and William McIllvanney).

The group came together in the lead up to the 1992 election, out of conversations going on between the theologian/author the Rev. Will Storrar, and two lawyers, Allan Miller, Chair of the Scottish Council for Civil Liberties, and Bob McCreadie, one time vice-president of the Scottish Liberal Democrats. Their initial idea was that there needed to be some body to articulate arguments for a civic – as opposed to party – politics. Looking to the immediate future, they were concerned that if Labour won, there would need to be a voice arguing for innovative democratic reforms in a new parliament, not the same old politics as usual. If the Tories won, they would press for a new cross-party approach, to call for an autonomous politics outside the party system, including the organising of a referendum. As we have seen, this last initiative was quickly swallowed up by Scotland United and the Labour wing of the movement, and Common Cause ended up actually focusing its energies on organising public forums.

Common Cause played a key role in organising the Scotland Demands Democracy March and Rally held during the European Summit in Edinburgh on 12 December, 1992, which attracted over 25 000 people and briefly seemed to bridge Labour-SNP antagonisms. The Coalition for Scottish Democracy (CSD) emerged in March 1993 as an umbrella organisation to help integrate the efforts of this new generation of civic groups, and to capitalise on the momentum generated by this rally. Close examination of the central cast of characters again reveals the strong continuing presence of the CSP and various people instrumental to the Constitutional Convention. The CSD was chaired by Campbell Christie, the respected and influential General Secretary of the Scottish Trades Union Congress at the time.

The CSD had two main projects. One was to design, circulate and deliver a petition to the European parliament to request its support for the right of the people of Scotland to self-determination. This was primarily a symbolic gesture. The European parliament is something of a talking shop, and its support, or lack of it, is of limited political consequence, the real power lying in the Council of Ministers. This latter body is highly unlikely to pass any judgement that would appear to set a precedent for meddling in the internal affairs or territorial sovereignty of member nations. The other project was originally known as The Scottish Senate, and came to be called the Civic Assembly. This idea, developed primarily by members of the CSP, came out of a concern about the low profile of the Constitutional Convention in the mid-1990s, and a sense that what was needed was some kind of standing body, a kind of 'shadow parliament', in which the people and institutions of Scottish civic life could come together and discuss Scottish problems and express their dissent from the UK government's handling of Scotland's affairs. This would achieve two ends. By not relying on the political parties, it would by-pass the inter-party struggles that often derailed co-operation in the movement, and it would create a permanent vehicle for publicising the cause and strengthening the connection in the popular imagination between everyday practical concerns (e.g., jobs, housing, poverty, adequate health care) and self-government. On 18 June 1994 the CSD sponsored a 'Consultative Conference on the Establishment of a Scottish Senate', symbolically held at the Old Royal High School in Edinburgh in the chamber that had been outfitted for an anticipated assembly back in 1979.[4]

The conference was attended by a wide variety of representatives from local governments, trade unions, churches, voluntary associations, political groups, and other home rule campaigning bodies. Some were dismayed however, by the poor representation of the Scottish business and finance community, arguing that these interests need to be involved in the process as well. The meeting was opened with a 'civic welcome' by one of the Edinburgh District Councillors. This was followed by 'three contributions from civic life', in which representatives from three voluntary associations, the Scottish Parent Teacher Council (education), Age Concern (for senior citizens), and Action of Churches Together in Scotland (ACTS – addressing various aspects of poverty relief), spoke about the negative effects of the 'democratic deficit' on the ability of these organisations to achieve their goals and serve their constituencies. The idea behind these interventions was to give a sense of the kinds of issues a senate might discuss and issue public statements on. The rest of the meeting involved a presentation of proposals on how to organise the senate, followed by open discussion. Participants addressed the need for broad and balanced representation of the populace, and grassroots, 'bottom-up' forms of democracy. There was also a familiar sceptical refrain from those less integrated into the circle of 'high profile' activists behind this project, that the entire affair might simply become another 'central belt talking shop', another context in which politicos and civic leaders in the Glasgow-Edinburgh circuit get together to appear to be 'doing something', while in effect doing little of consequence. This constant tension between a resurgent hope and optimism and a deep seated cynicism about politics has been a defining feature of the movement discourse and its dynamic.

It was debated whether this senate might be confused with a parliament, being seen either as a substitution or as an unelected parliament-in-waiting. The organisers tried to allay these fears, although it is true that for some of them, the senate was seen as potentially evolving into a second chamber if a parliament was established. It was in light of these concerns that the less threatening title of Civic Assembly was adopted. By the time of the referendum the Civic Assembly had held three plenary meetings on topical issues for Scottish social life. The project has now evolved into what is called the Civic Forum, and key activists are currently hoping that the new parliament will choose to provide institutional support so that the Civic Forum can continue to function as a more accessible popular forum for raising and discussing issues of popular concern, playing a consultative role to the parliament.

– THE ETHNIC NATIONALIST FRINGE –

In the Introduction I discussed the common distinction between civic versus ethnic nationalisms. The preceding I think amply demonstrates how the Scottish movement can be seen as heavily weighted toward the civic end of this spectrum. None the less, much to the chagrin of the civic nationalists, especially those in the SNP, there is a distinct fringe of intense ethnic nationalism in the movement. The story of this fringe could be given a much deeper treatment, going back to the cultural revival movements of the 1920s and '30s, which played a part in the founding of the SNP, addressing the influence of Celtic-romantic authors like Fionn McColla and Peter Berresford-Ellis, and the eccentric activities of Wendy Wood, and the 1320 Club. But I will limit myself to what was going on while I was in the field, involving people in and around the rather shadowy 'cultural and fraternal organisation' Siol Nan Gaidheal (SNG, meaning Seed of the Gael, pronounced 'sheel na gay-l').[5]

SNG has gone through two incarnations. The first ran roughly from 1979 to 1985, when the group was closely associated with the membership of the SNP, although not wholly an internal faction. Like the SNP's '79 Group, with its republican-socialist orientation, SNG was also a product of the frustration that followed the failures of 1979. Its purpose however was one of cultural and moral revival; aimed especially at young men, SNG was politically vague, yet with a distinct anti-socialist/anti-left wing bias. In its early days, through its participation in marches, rallies and ceilidhs,[6] it was quite successful in rallying morale among some nationalists, and attracted the support of some right-to-middle-of-the-road leading members in the SNP. SNG was known for showing up at SNP marches, and marching separately with a colour guard of young men in full highland gear waving black flags. Some found the image inspiring, others, ominous. In time SNG voiced an increasingly militant position, associating with other small, fringe militant groups advocating the use of violence. At the 1982 Conference the then fundamentalist leadership of the SNP killed two birds with one stone, proscribing internal factions, namely SNG and the '79 Group.

By the mid-1980s the first SNG had fizzled out, and its successor, formed in 1988, disavowed violence. This second incarnation was, however, still inclined to produce posters and literature that expressed extreme hostility and antagonism toward 'the English'. One familiar poster during my fieldwork showed a person wearing military gear and balaclava, and brandishing a rifle. The text read: 'so long as 100 of us remain alive we will never submit to English rule' a passage from the famous Declaration of Arbroath written in 1320 (which was a letter to the Pope from the Scottish nobility asking him to intercede in the ongoing conflicts with England at that time). SNG's 'constitution' claims to eschew 'the divisive codes of party politics' and 'economic expediency':

> In their place we advocate a foundation of Truth, Compassion and Common Sense. Our vision of the way ahead recognises spiritual health rather than political creeds. We would thus by-pass the impenetrable bog-lands of party political manifestos, and in their place project a simple vision of a people on the march, fired with the excitement and adventure of rebuilding this ancient country and of endowing our children with qualities that stem from sound moral principles. (Siol Nan Gaidheal 1990: 6)

The harsh anti-English tone of the group's rhetoric also comes out in a statement of 'Aims and Principles of our Movement':

> Our aim is to promote and reassert the historical sovereignty of the indigenous ethnic community which is Scotland, and in doing so rekindle the will of the

Scots to take their political destiny into their own hands . . . We do not recognise the sovereignty of the English Parliament and therefore shall neither petition nor seek election to it. Rather, we shall unstintingly campaign against English imperialism in Scotland and highlight the insidious effects of its spiritual twin – Scottish Unionism. (Siol Nan Gaidheal 1993: 36)

The exact size and membership of SNG is difficult to determine, due to its shadowy nature. I strongly suspect the core members that I met exaggerated levels of participation. My own speculation based on impressions is that the organisational work and publications are primarily produced by a fairly small and shifting core group, perhaps just over a dozen people, but that there is a much larger floating/fluctuating membership of young people, mostly male recruits, who participate in occasional projects and events. Despite the continued ban on the group, some are active in the SNP, keeping their SNG membership a secret. Still, these would be a muted minority within the SNP. My attempts to meet core members generally involved a bit of skulduggery and chains of phone calls. Near the beginning of my fieldwork, the group appeared to go underground, partly in response to heat it was taking for the actions of two new splinter groups, Scottish Watch and Settler Watch, discussed below. It was also indicated to me that the leadership of the group was in flux, that the previous leader was pulling away from the group, and it appeared that one of the founders of the original SNG was again asserting greater influence. At the time of writing however, the group has almost no public profile.

During October of 1993, shortly after I arrived in Scotland, a series of news stories began to break about the activities of two new organisations – Settler Watch and Scottish Watch. Both evolved out of the SNG milieu, the former being based in the north-east around Aberdeen, the latter in the south-west around Dumfries. Both were dedicated to exposing and opposing the impact of English incomers, often referred to as 'English settlers' or 'white settlers'. The 'English problem' has many dimensions, but the three main areas are: competition for housing in rural areas, competition for places at Scottish universities, and disproportionate English presence in managerial and administrative positions, especially in the arts. The strongest feelings are for the first issue, and this was the main focus of Settler Watch and Scottish Watch. While these groups are prone to exaggeration, there are real problems of rural gentrification, as people from the south who prospered in the 1980s were able to buy vacation/retirement homes, driving rural housing prices out of the reach of locals in some areas, where employment in the rural economy is already scarce. While the aggregate information on English immigration to Scotland does not seem to support the massive 'invasion' these groups describe, it seems likely that there are many pockets in rural areas where this gentrification effect has been quite pronounced (cf. Dickson 1994; Jedrej and Nuttall 1996).

Settler Watch was the more militant of the two groups, if they can indeed be called groups, and not just small circles of SNG-type activists. Its activities included putting up threatening posters, leaving threatening packages with Celtic designs on doorsteps, and spray-painting 'English Out' and 'Settler Watch' on houses with English occupants. I was surprised to find a flurry of news stories that revolved around a woman I had met briefly while on a preliminary research trip in the summer of 1992, who had helped me make my first contact with the leadership of SNG at that time. From Germany, she had taken on a Scottish name, was working on a doctorate in Scottish medieval history, spoke fluent Gaelic, and was vice-convenor of the SNP's South Aberdeen association. She and a friend had been caught putting up Settler Watch posters – a major embarrassment to the SNP. The SNP quickly proscribed membership in both of the 'Watch' groups for all SNP members. By the beginning of 1994 there was also another response by the SNP – the formation of a group called New Scots for Independence, made up of SNP members from outside Scotland (primarily England), meant to counter the impression that the SNP is racist or unwelcoming to non-native Scots.

The main organiser of Scottish Watch was Iain Sutherland, a mild mannered history teacher from Dumfries, who also has long-standing SNG associations. Sutherland has condemned Settler Watch's activities, but some of his co-organisers have expressed sympathy. Scottish Watch defines itself as a non-violent, anti-colonialist organisation, its approach being to inform and persuade through publications and public meetings. An early flyer defines the group's aims as:

1. To investigate the extent of the English white settler exploitation of Scotland and inform our fellow Scots of what is happening in their own areas and in Scotland as a whole.
2. To create an organisation to protest at the economic colonialism being inflicted upon the Scottish people and to defend them particularly in the areas of housing and employment.
3. To counter the English Tory generated climate of despair and fear, also to create a will to resist.

Toward this end Scottish Watch organised a series of public meetings around Scotland. The first one in March of 1994 drew around 100 people, some receptive, and some not. I was unable to attend any of these meetings, but a fellow researcher reported to me that the one he went to had a fairly hostile audience, which seemed confirmed by the audio tape he played for me. The meeting I tried to attend was cancelled due either to poor planning, or to second thoughts on the part of the person leasing the venue.

A small booklet published by the group is entitled *The New Scottish Clearances*, making a familiar reference to the Highland Clearances of c. 1790–1830, in which Highland tenants were thrown off their traditional lands by ennobled and anglified clan chiefs who sought to improve their lands by raising sheep.[7] The statement on the inside cover of this booklet indicates the stance of the group (primarily of Sutherland I suspect) on political and economic issues, mixed with a kind of communitarian yearning characteristic of the Scottish movement as a whole:

> Scottish Watch is a nationalist group which is positively anti-imperialist. We reject political ideologies which are based on economic dogma. Among these are international capitalism and socialism, the twin evils of the modern imperialist state. International capitalism is based on individual greed and results in exploitation of the weak. International socialism depends upon a divisive class-based analysis and has an inherently anti-social materialism at root. International socialism and capitalism are geared to exploit the environment and people to the maximum degree. This inhuman materialism contains the seeds of its own destruction. Scottish Watch adopts the concept of nationalism because only nationalism can unite a cultural or social group in the war against the imperialism of economic theories and dogma. We believe in people, not money. The cultural values of human society come first and financial matters must be subordinate to them. The false modern values of liberal cosmopolitanism are based on an essentially Anglo-Saxon mercantilism. The nonsense of so-called political correctness is a by-product of middle-income liberalism. (Scottish Watch 1994: 2)

While there was only limited public support for these 'Watch' groups, which appear to be defunct at the time of writing, they tapped into a widespread but poorly articulated discontent in Scotland, and many people I met, especially in the SNP, expressed a degree of sympathy for them, even if they found their methods distasteful and wrongheaded. Passages such as the one above speak to a general distrust of 'ideologies' and 'systems' that are seen as external, remote, and inhuman. Something reminiscent of Weber's anxieties about the disenchantment of the modern bureaucratised world comes through here. While activists would tend to place themselves at either end of the polarised spectrum from civic to ethnic nationalism presented in these last two sections, and the larger and more strategic share is at the civic end, it is important to acknowledge certain continuities. Across the board there is an understanding of Scotland as a real political community, oriented by common interests and values, which are in turn organically rooted in Scottish history and culture. Despite profound differences over the analysis of Scotland's situation, and strategies for improving it, these basic assumptions pervade the movement.

– NEW LABOUR, NEW REFERENDUM, NEW PARLIAMENT –

By the mid-1990s the Conservative Party was beginning to show the strains of too many years in government, its popular mandate weakening, as internal divisions around the terms and pace of incorporation into the EU, and between moderates and Thatcherite stalwarts, led to internecine struggles. In this context the business and finance community of London began to shift its allegiance to the Labour Party. As it became increasingly apparent that the 'New' Labour Party was poised to win the next general election, the desperate Scottish Tories fell into in-fighting, with well-timed rumours of indiscretions and infidelities forcing several prominent party figures to bow out of the political arena. In the language of the Scottish press, the Tories appeared to be in 'meltdown', paving the way for their subsequent 'wipe-out' at the general election.

Meanwhile, Tony Blair's Labour Party consolidated its position, taking care to quell worries about the possibility of Labour raising taxes, and to marginalise the left-wing of the party. Thus in the Scottish party conference before the general election many from the left-wing and home rule end of the party, including those associated with Scottish Labour Action, were forced off the Executive in what some called a 'purge'. One of Blair's other moves to safeguard the election, especially against the Tory charge that a Scottish parliament would impose an unwanted 'Tartan Tax' on the Scots, was to announce in June of 1996 that there would be a referendum on Scottish devolution, and that it would contain two opportunities to vote yes or no, first on the establishment of a parliament, and then on its ability to vary the UK personal income tax rate in Scotland by 3 per cent. Because earlier the Labour Party had indicated that the popular will of the Scots on this issue was clear, and that legislation for a parliament was a foregone conclusion of a Labour victory, many in the pro-parliament movement felt betrayed when this referendum was announced, seeing it as back-peddling on the entire issue, and generally being uncertain of Blair's commitment to the idea, in contrast to his predecessor in the leadership, the late John Smith. Despite the outrage and strong protests, movement activists became resigned to this strategy, shifting their concerns to the success of the referendum. With hindsight, many who had objected conceded the tactical wisdom of the referendum, in a sense clinching the issue, whether or not that was Blair's objective.

The strength of the Labour victory at the May 1997 general election, with its 179 seat majority, enabled the party to move quickly on legislation. By July it had published the white paper on Scottish devolution, *Scotland's Parliament* (Scottish Office 1997), modelled on the final report of the Scottish Constitutional Convention: *Scotland's Parliament, Scotland's Right* (1995). The white paper managed to make the best-seller lists of Scottish booksellers, while work in the Scottish Office on the drafting of the Bill had already begun. The parliament established consists of 129 members elected by an Additional Member System, which combines seventy-three first-past-the-post constituency seats with a 'top up' of fifty-six representatives from party lists, seven from each of the eight Euro-parliamentary regions, to approximate proportional representation. The parliament receives an annual block grant of around £14 billion from the UK Treasury, according to a formula already established for funding the Scottish Office. In addition to the tax-varying power, the matters on which the Scottish parliament is competent to pass legislation include: health, education, local government, social work, housing, economic development, transport, law, environmental matters, agriculture, fishing, forestry, sport, the arts, the licensing and protection of animals, and statistical record keeping. Broadly, the powers reserved by the UK parliament include: international relations and foreign policy, defence and national security, regulation of national borders, macroeconomic policy and business regulation, employment legislation, social security, and regulations in the areas of medical practices, transportation, and a miscellaneous list including such things as nuclear safety, abortion, firearms, and broadcasting. The stated desire of the Constitutional Convention to see the Scottish parliament's powers entrenched was not realised. Another early hope of some members of the Convention, to require 50/50 gender representation in the parliament, was not included in the Scotland Act 1998. However, under the guidance of the Convention, Labour adopted a policy of 'twinning' male and female candidates in comparably winnable seats. Much concern has been focused on the nature of the Standing Orders of the new parliament, which aim for strong and consultative committees that can check executive power and receive substantial input from relevant experts and concerned citizens. Working hours are designed to create a process more accessible to the public, and to participation by members with families and children, than the system at Westminster (Consultative Steering Group 1999).[8]

There were only seven weeks between the release of the white paper and the 11 September referendum. In May Scotland FORward was formed, backed by the businessman Nigel Smith, in order to create a unified campaign for a double yes vote, activists having learned from the experience of the divisive 1979 referendum when each party organised its campaign separately amid internal splits. In July, after some protest from the fundamentalists, Alex Salmond led the SNP to support the Yes/Yes campaign and Scotland FORward. In August the actor Sean Connery, long a supporter of the SNP, put his charismatic weight behind the campaign. When Princess Diana was killed in a car accident on 1 September, campaigning was suspended for a week, and many feared a backlash of British patriotism and affection for the union. But Diana was not exactly the best symbol of the solidarity of the monarchy and the British people, and the tragedy seems to have had no effect on the final vote. For the last 100 hours of the campaign, inspired by an idea from the German novelist Günter Grass, Common Cause organised a 'bus party' of artists, writers, and other public figures, touring nine towns in Scotland, holding forums on the issue in schools, churches, community centres, and such.

While the entire spectrum of the home rule movement showed exceptional unity for the Yes/Yes campaign, the opposition was almost invisible. In June the 'No' camp organised its 'Think Twice' campaign, but its natural leadership and support would have had to have come from the Tory Party, which was so demoralised and discredited at this point that the campaign was minimal. In July Arthur Bell, member of the Scottish Tory Reform Group and long-time Tory advocate of devolution, left the Party (later to join the Liberal Democrats); and Margaret Thatcher's stern warnings of a 'backlash of English nationalism' in a lecture in Glasgow two days before the vote may have done more harm than good to the No cause. While one or two members of the business community, such as the Governor of the Bank of Scotland, tried to raise fears about the effects on business of a parliament with tax-raising powers, they were lone voices, the majority quietly waiting to do business in the new order of things.

On the evening of the 1997 general election, as people realised the Tories would finally be decimated, and Labour would win comfortably, the mood in much of Scotland was one of jubilation, of long awaited vindication. By contrast, the response to the success of the referendum was more circumspect. Part of the sweetness of victory is in the defeat of one's enemies, and in the latter case the only enemy to worry about was political apathy and reservation. Furthermore, the mood around the referendum seems to have been caught between a combination of caution based on past experience, and reasonable expectations of success based on the general political climate following the general election. In the event, with a 60% voter turnout,

74.3% voted 'yes' to the Parliament, and 63.5% voted 'yes' to its tax varying powers. Both questions received a majority of 'yes' votes in all districts, with the exception of the tax varying question in Orkney (47.4%) and Dumfries and Galloway (48.8%). Overall, support was stronger in the urban and central belt areas, and weaker in rural and Highland areas, reflecting basic differences in economic interests in urban and rural areas, and concerns that urban interests are more likely to dominate in the Scottish parliament. From the perspective of rural Scotland, Edinburgh may be just as remote as London.

In the wake of the referendum, two decades of mobilisation and oppositional politics melted into a sea of preparations and readjustments. The Vigil on Calton Hill closed up shop, Scottish Labour Action is defunct, the CSP wound-up its affairs in the autumn of 1998, with many members shifting their energies to the future of the Civic Forum. Common Cause is hoping to continue its mission to create popular forums on civic politics, and is in search of the backing to transform itself into a kind of think-tank on issues of democracy.

Early opinion polls in the Summer of 1993 suggested a much greater willingness to elect the SNP to the Scottish parliament, and that Labour and the SNP might have a roughly 40/40 split of the seats in the first parliament. But as time wore on, Labour re-established its lead, frequently deploying a rhetoric of the 'defence of the union' that was strangely reminiscent of the Tories. The process of selecting candidates was clearly being overseen from London, and the marginalisation and domestication of the party's left wing in Scotland continued apace. Even so, the make-up of the Scottish party is inevitably to the left of that in London, which may create serious intra-party strains around the unity of policy north and south of the border. After an early emphasis on business-friendly policies and 'enterprise with compassion', the SNP increasingly sought to differentiate itself by claiming political space to the left of Labour. When the UK Chancellor Gordon Brown announced plans to lower UK income taxes by one per cent, the SNP seized on the opportunity with it's 'Penny for Scotland' campaign, which would use the Scottish parliament's tax varying power by one per cent, thus forgoing the tax cut in order to raise revenues to invest in health and education. Then, on 29 March, Salmond took a publicly critical stance in regard to the NATO/Serbia war over Kosovo, arguing that the project needed UN backing and was likely to cause more suffering than it would prevent. Neither of these strategies appear to have radically altered the SNP's support. Meanwhile, it was becoming abundantly clear that the Liberal Democrats would be playing the role of 'king-makers' in a coalition government with Labour, and thus that they would 'win' no matter what. The Tories approached the election as though they were starting from scratch and had nothing to lose, which was indeed the case, and attempted some of the most daring and stylish political advertising of the election.

Election day, 6 May, was another rainy day in Scotland, which when combined with general fatigue from an atmosphere of campaigning that seemed to have been going on ever since the 1997 general election, and a certain disenchantment with the usual mud-slinging between the parties, may account for an electoral turn-out somewhat lower than that of the referendum. The ballot allowed two votes for each voter, one for a constituency candidate, and one for a party list. As expected the SNP and the Tories benefited the most from proportional representation:

Table 1: The Party Breakdown of the First Scottish Parliament.

Party	Constituency Seats	Party List Seats	Total
Labour	53	3	56
SNP	7	28	35
Tories	0	18	18
Lib. Dems	12	5	17
Scottish Socialists	0	1	1
Greens	0	1	1
Independent	1	0	1
TOTAL	73	56	129

The first parliament includes 81 men and 48 women (38 per cent), most of whom are either in Labour or the SNP. As noted above, the Scottish Socialist Party and the Greens managed to gain one seat each via the party lists. The sole Independent elected was Dennis Canavan, who chose to stand that way when he was de-selected by the Labour Party, presumably for his left-wing views, despite his well known popularity with his constituents in Falkirk West. His handy victory was a clear embarrassment to the Labour Party – he is likely to be a thorn in the rose's side. The vast majority of the candidates come to the parliament from positions in local government and national politics, and from the educational and legal professions, comprising a highly educated and professionalised body over-all. Labour and the Liberal Democrats negotiated a coalition government within days of the election, as predicted, and on 1 July, a much sunnier and more festive day, Queen Elizabeth came to the official opening ceremony to confer power on the new parliament in her role as sovereign. However, there are widespread republican sentiments in this parliament, and many commentators on the day stressed that this was a symbolic confirmation of a de facto power already in place. Meanwhile, the ominous sounds occasionally made in regard to devolution by the business community have now shifted to the possibility of independence, but lobbyists are setting up shop in Edinburgh, where property values have been rising.

– NOTES –

1. For a developed version of these debates among economists of Scotland, see the exchanges in the *Quarterly Economic Commentary* (a journal of the Fraser of Allander Institute), and specifically: Hood (1995); McGregor et al. (1997); Stevens (1997); Wilson (1997) and Wood (1997).

2. The Queen and her successors would be maintained as Head of State in a constitutional monarchy, 'until such time as the people decide otherwise' (Scottish National Party 1992a: 4). The party is divided on this last question, with the younger members having a decidedly republican, and anti-monarchy bias.

3. It is worth noting that there are many people in this circle who are also associated with Charter 88, the UK wide group organised in 1988 which advocates democratic and constitutional reform and the establishment and protection of civil rights.

4. It is also telling that although the Tory administration of the Scottish Office had announced plans to sell the building, the Edinburgh District Council had exercised its option to re-purchase it, thus blocking this manoeuvre, and symbolically reasserting the fundamental opposition that existed between Scottish local government and the Tory government in Westminster on the home rule issue.

5. *Britain's Secret War: Tartan Terrorism and the Anglo-American State* (Scott and Macleay 1990) provides an interesting although sensationalistic view of the murky hodge-podge of revolutionary nationalism, letter-bombs and quasi-secret societies that have inhabited the fringes of the movement since the 1960s. But considering that at least one of the authors has been intimately involved in Siol Nan Gaidheal, and founded Scottish Watch, this should not be taken as entirely objective reporting. See Marr (1992: 187–9) for a much briefer and deflating assessment of this militant milieu.

6. Traditionally a ceilidh (pronounced 'kay-lee') is an informal social gathering involving music, dance, story-telling and lively conversation. But it has also come to refer to public dances in which traditional set dances are done to traditional (usually fiddle) tunes. Ceilidhs, like Scottish culture as a whole, are enjoying something of a revival, and are quite popular with young people.

7. This is the typical scenario, though there was a whole range of economic 'modernising' processes at work, a continuation of the process of

'improvement' begun in the Lowlands a century earlier (cf. Gray 1988; Macinnes 1988). The Highland Clearances provided case material for Marx's discussion of 'the so-called primitive accumulation' in Vol. I of Capital (1967: 728-9).

8. For introductions to the new Scottish parliament, see: Hassan (1999); Himsworth and Munro (1998); McFadden and Lazarowicz (1999); and Scottish Office (1997).

CHAPTER 4

The Public Sphere

– INTRODUCTION –

A key question in the study of nationalism, and social movements more generally, is how core ideas, ways of thinking and talking about the project, get created and disseminated. Part of this in the Scottish case has been an extensive academic discussion of the issue of nationalism, which I engage at various points in this book. My main focus here, however, is on the kinds of work that reach a more general, popular audience, rather than on the considerable growth in scholarship in this area. In and around the array of parties and campaigning groups described in the last chapter is a network of intellectuals, academics, artists, writers, journalists and media figures through whom the ideas and attitudes of the movement are constantly being articulated and re-articulated. These people and their ideas can be seen as inhabiting what Jürgen Habermas has called the public sphere, 'a domain of our social life in which such a thing as public opinion can be formed' (1989a: 231). Habermas sees the public sphere as an historically emergent phenomenon associated with the rise of the modern, liberal, democratic constitutional state in the eighteenth century, but also one at odds with and threatened by corresponding processes of capitalism and bureaucratisation. It relies on social and institutional conditions conducive to the relatively unconstrained production and intercourse of ideas.[1] There are similarities between the idea of the public sphere and that of civil society, though it is perhaps useful to regard the former as highlighting processes of communication, while civil society usually identifies networks of institutions and patterns of social organisation through which people interact. This chapter focuses on the Scottish public sphere, but with civil society clearly looming in the background.

If we are concerned with the formation of public opinion, it is worth comparing the ideas of consensus and hegemony. Consensus is usually regarded as uncoerced agreement, or at least approximate agreement, the product of an ideal public sphere, whereas hegemony is a more ambiguous term. In the writings of Gramsci hegemony is used to suggest both political domination and leadership achieved through active consent (Gramsci 1971: 12–13), which are cultivated through the institutions of civil society. Our concern in this chapter hovers between consensus and hegemony. It is partly about how certain understandings of Scotland's situation and how it should be remedied became widely held common sense, through steady processes of discursive reinforcement. But it is also about how those with strong political commitments and public social roles actively articulated and promoted this common sense, and the larger structural conditions that helped make this possible.[2]

Since the 1970s there has been a cultural revival, placing new emphasis on Scottish language, culture, and politics in books and other publications (fiction, non-fiction, poetry), television and radio shows, the plastic arts, theatre, and popular music. The amount of work being produced is too great to attempt a comprehensive treatment here, so what follows is only a suggestive sampling, shaped by the particular contacts I made while doing fieldwork. The content of movement discourse will be examined more closely in Part Three. Here, in keeping with the organisational focus of the last chapter, I am primarily interested in mapping out the social milieu, institutions, and forms of media through which popular nationalist discourse has been generated. The following description of the public sphere through which left-nationalist hegemony was produced highlights several key factors. One is the numerous ways in which 'Scotland' is reinforced as the given universe of discourse, in both explicitly political, and relatively apolitical contexts. Another is a wide variety of media through which ideas about nationalism are created and disseminated. A third is the density of multiplex social networks, so that key activists participate through various roles and contexts. And finally, there is the basic issue of the mobilisation of material resources, in the form of economic and institutional support (Zald and McCarthy 1987). The dominance of local government by a Labour Party broadly sympathetic to the cause is significant in this regard, as is the support of sections of the Church and University communities.

– NATIONALIST DISCOURSE IN THE PUBLIC SPHERE –

In recent years many Scottish novelists, such as William McIlvanney, James Kelman, Irvine Welsh, and Alasdair Gray have been particularly concerned with producing work that reflects and speaks to the Scottish experience, especially the central-belt working-class experience. A major part of this is writing in vernacular Scots. This in itself has certain cultural-nationalist implications, although not necessarily of the sort associated with groups like Siol Nan Gaidheal. It is worth noting, moreover, that some of these authors also write explicitly on the issue of Scottish nationalism. Thus Gray has offered the booklet essay *Why Scots Should Rule Scotland* (1992), somewhat whimsically framed as an imaginary dialogue with his sceptical publisher, and McIlvanney has published numerous newspaper and journal essays under the title *Surviving the Shipwreck* (1991), his metaphor for the Tory assault on Scottish socialism. As we have seen, McIlvanney is one of several writers/artists who frequently make public speeches at movement events. Another author who participates in this way is Billy Kay, whose highly popular book on the structure and history of Scots, *Scots: The Mither Tongue* (1993), was made into a popular television series in Scotland. That book concludes with the Hugh MacDiarmid quote, embedded in the Democracy Cairn, that opened this book, and I suspect that Kay's book is one reason why the members of Democracy for Scotland remembered it, and selected it for this purpose.

Central Scotland abounds with journals that have helped sustain the movement discourse. *Cencrastus* (a mythical snake that consumes its tail, again a reference to MacDiarmid's poetry), is a glossy 'magazine of Scottish and international arts, literature and affairs' that has been published since 1979. It contains a mixture of vernacular fiction and poetry, book and performance reviews, letters, and essays of political and social analysis. Nationalist issues and debates are a recurring theme throughout. *Chapman*, also published since the 1970s, is a literary magazine of fiction, poetry and essays. While less explicitly political, the central theme of the self-definition and autonomy of the Scottish writer creates clear linkages to the broader discourse. Editor Joy Hendry is one of several founding members of Artists for Independence, another group formed in the wave of activism around the 1992 general election. The *Edinburgh Review*, a book-like journal published by Edinburgh University Press, is a more eclectic mix of writings, interviews and reviews organised under headings like 'works' and 'ideas'.[3] Murdo MacDonald, one of the associate editors during my research, ran the Centre for Continuing Education at the University of Edinburgh, and has social connections with the Adult Learning Project discussed below. All three of these journals have received significant support from the Scottish Arts Council, and *Chapman* also received support from the Edinburgh District Council, the point being that such journals are notoriously hard to sustain economically, and their continued existence as vehicles for public discourse is due both to the demand for such intellectual outlets/forums, and to a system of substantial institutional provisioning. Also worth noting is

Polygon, a division of Edinburgh University Press which, although specialising in literature, is an important publisher of non-fiction texts relevant to the nationalist movement (and thus is prominent in the bibliography of this book). Polygon grew out of the student publications division of Edinburgh University Press two decades ago, has also been supported by the Scottish Arts Council, and is another important component in the arts-publishing milieu that has evolved in Edinburgh since the 1970s.

Scottish Affairs, founded in 1993, grew out of the now defunct *Scottish Government Yearbook*, a major academic digest of materials relevant to Scottish politics that had been administered through various divisions of the University since 1978. While addressing a somewhat more professional/academic community than the journals just mentioned, the *Yearbook* also served as a major forum for the nationalist debate. Broadening this forum is one of the main aims of the newer journal, which in the words of the editors 'takes up a position between informed journalism and academic analysis, and provides a forum for dialogue between the two. The readers and contributors include journalists, politicians, civil servants, business people, academics, and people in general who take an informed interest in current affairs'. *Scottish Affairs* is published by the Unit for the Study of Government at Edinburgh University, and thus, as with Polygon and the *Edinburgh Review*, the institutional support of the University helps make the journal possible. Several of the journal's editors are major researchers and writers in the study of Scottish nationalism (e.g., Brown et al. 1998a, 1998b; McCrone 1992; Paterson 1994).

There is broad agreement around the movement that the now defunct *Radical Scotland* was the most important journal for Scottish politics, nationalist or otherwise, throughout the 1980s. In fact, part of the motivation behind broadening the scope of *Scottish Affairs* when it succeeded the *Yearbook* was to help compensate for the loss of *Radical Scotland*. The magazine published fifty-one issues between 1983 and 1991, and a list of its contributors over the years is both a 'Who's Who' of the movement and a sound guide to the spectrum of ideological and strategic positions found there. For the latter half of its life, it was primarily organised and run by Alan Lawson, a key figure in the Campaign for a Scottish Assembly and one of the initial instigators of the Constitutional Convention. Although highly respected, the journal was not well subsidised, just barely meeting production costs, and relying on the volunteered labour of its small staff. The editors' explanation in the final issue of their decision to close down is instructive; even if many on the scene would have disagreed:

> After considering all relevant factors, the RS editorial board have reluctantly decided that this issue will be the last. The main reason for this is a positive one –

namely, that the Scottish political situation has developed so much in the years of the magazine's existence that the uniqueness of RS and its line has been overtaken by events. Today, the case for self-government – and for a separate Scottish political and cultural identity – has been accepted in all but the darkest corners of Scotland. Developments on the self-government front (and allied topics) are now taking place so rapidly that a bi-monthly magazine simply can't properly keep up with events. The much improved Scottish daily and weekly press and radio and television programmes are now producing new angles, new debates, and new analysis almost every day. Because of these developments, RS was enjoying less influence than it had done, and the future therefore held the prospect of declining relevance and (probably) declining sales. So we agreed that it would be better to quit whilst our reputation remained strong, believing that the magazine has played an important part in bringing Scotland to the stage where it now is. (Lawson 1991: 3)

The cover of this issue was a cartoon portraying Ian Lang, then Tory Secretary of State for Scotland, standing ankle deep in water on the beach and staring uncomprehendingly off into space as a huge wave labelled 'Home Rule' looms up behind him. The coming year was one of high hopes for a Tory downfall in the 1992 general election which, as we have seen, did not materialise. Had the *Radical Scotland* editors anticipated this they might have chosen to hang on a bit longer. Still, there is substance to the general argument that the intelligentsia-media milieu had grown tremendously.

One place this was reflected was in the editorial columnists for major newspapers. *The Scotsman*, the major Edinburgh daily (tabloids aside), now carried a regular Monday column by Tom Nairn, long a key observer, thinker and writer in the movement. Also new was the upscale weekly sister paper to the *Scotsman*, *Scotland on Sunday*. Here the regular editorial page column by Joyce MacMillan, theatre critic, social commentator, and supporter of the parliamentary cause, provides a quintessential example of the social democratic moral discourse that pervades the movement.[4] The ravages of capitalism, the cynicism of the political parties (especially the Tories), the starvation of the democratic process, and the alienation from and erosion of community are her central themes. Her tone is frequently both moralistic and caustic. While she has particularly strong and developed views, the fact that she has a regular audience through a weekly paper with a broad middle-class readership shows that her basic outlook is widely shared. Some examples:

sooner or later, British public opinion will have to get real again about the nature of capitalism, which is not some jolly nice show run by decent chaps from public schools, but a system which, in its nature, will exploit labour and discard burnt-out human lives unless people band together to regulate it and protect themselves. (MacMillan 1993a)

For the paradox with which the right in Britain and America has not even begun to grapple is that economic internationalisation, if it is to proceed without provoking the most frightening kind of backlash, actually requires not less government, as the dominant market ideology suggests, but more government; enough government, in fact, at enough levels, to reassure people that whatever changes may sweep through the international market-place, their basic needs in terms of health, education, environment, income support, and the protection of cultural identity, will always, without fail, be met. (MacMillan 1993b)

Like many Scots, in the days of anger and despair after the last general election, I felt that there must be a way for the broad mass of Scottish opinion that is social-democratic by inclination, and would like to see a measure of home rule for Scotland, to form a common front against a reactionary brand of Conservatism that we all oppose. But in the two intervening years, I have learned, if nothing else, to recognise the deep and real gulf that separates those who do not dispute the Tory theory of national sovereignty, but would simply like to replace British sovereignty with the Scottish variety; and those who reject that nationalist perspective in favour of a culture of federalism, decentralisation, and multiple identities, expressed through subtle and, if necessary, complex political structures. (MacMillan 1994)

MacMillan's commentaries can be taken as a rough gauge of Scottish public opinion on these issues. Many might find her too idealistic and strident, but there would tend to be sympathy, if not always agreement, with her point of view.

A network of pro-parliamentary opinion-formers exists in the non-print media as well. There has been a remarkable growth of theatre dealing with relevant themes and politics, much of it in the various Scots dialects. A major example is John McGrath's *The Cheviot, The Stag, and the Black Black Oil*, a darkly humorous and immensely popular synopsis of Scottish history done in a quasi-vaudevillian style. The play focuses on three phases of exploitation of Scotland and the Scottish people: the expulsion of highland tenants to raise sheep (the cheviot) at greater profit; the transformation of highland estates into vacation game preserves (the stag) for the wealthy; and the derangement of local economies and ways of life due the impact of North Sea (black, black) oil. One of the best known radical theatre companies in Scotland today, 7:84, takes its name from the statistic that under Thatcher 84 per cent of the wealth had come to be controlled by 7 per cent of the population. One of my informants, a founding member of the journal *Cencrastus*, now works with a Canadian playwright translating plays about the Québec experience from French into vernacular Scots.

Murial Gray is another well known figure who has run a production company, Gallus Besom, that promoted Scottish oriented television and film projects. She used to write an opinion column that appeared opposite to Joyce Macmillan's in *Scotland on Sunday* where her nationalist sentiments were often in evidence. During my fieldwork she was producing and emceeing a short-lived, half-serious, half satirical game show on Scottish Television called *The Golden Cagoule* (cagoule = raincoat). On the show celebrity guests would compete to answer questions pertaining to Scotland's culture, history, and natural environment – the winner mounting a platform at the back of the set to don the golden cagoule and be lightly drizzled upon from a shower nozzle.

One of the show's frequent guests, Donnie Munro, was the lead singer of the popular Scottish rock band Runrig. The band hails from the island of Skye, their original songs in both Gaelic and English revolving around the themes of lost tradition, cultural alienation and political exploitation. Like many highlanders, Munro, a pro-parliament Labour supporter, has somewhat more reserved and cautious attitudes regarding nationalism than many central belt activists. Coming from a marginalised cultural and geographic background that represents what one highland informant described to me as 'a minority within a minority', highland Gaelic speakers have often shown a more patient and pragmatic attitude toward the goals of greater political autonomy. Munro made an unsuccessful bid as a Labour candidate for the Scottish parliamentary constituency seat of Ross, Skye and Inverness West in the first Scottish parliamentary election.

Pat Kane is a member of the Glasgow based, soul-inflected pop band Hue and Cry, and also a public figure on television and radio shows. He writes regularly for *The Herald*, the major daily newspaper in Glasgow, and has published a book of essays on politics, culture and the arts. Kane sees himself as both an artist and a social critic, and supports the SNP, fitting into its republican-socialist wing. Both Kane and Munro's bands are known for being supportive of the movement and playing at fund-raising events.

All three – Gray, Munro and Kane – share something in common: they have all been Rectors of Scottish universities (at Edinburgh and Glasgow). An old custom in Scotland, the Rector is elected annually by the student bodies to represent student interests to the administration. It is common for the elected to be popular and outspoken public figures, and the election of these three is a mark of the receptiveness of younger Scots to nationalist ideas. (Support for nationalism in the universities has a long history, however, ante-dating the post 1960s upswing in nationalist politics.) Iain Hamilton, SNP member and motorcycle riding lawyer, was elected rector of Aberdeen University during my fieldwork. His major claim to fame comes from being a key player in the plucky bunch of young Scottish nationalists who briefly 'liberated' the Stone of Destiny from Westminster Abbey back in 1951, smuggling it around Scotland for a brief period until it was returned (see note 4, Chapter 1).

The people mentioned in this section live in social circles that intersect and overlap – some know each other well, some are merely acquainted, but all would know of each other. And as I have tried to indicate in regard to some of them, their social networks link up with those of the politicians and activists described above. I would maintain, and I know other observers of the scene would agree, that there are particularly dense and interconnected social networks around the movement. This extends to the realm of professional politicians as well, where key figures from opposing parties may have been close friends since their university days. Although I cannot offer any operationalised measures, part of my objective in this chapter is to give a sense of this interconnectedness. As one SNP official observed to me, the style of Scottish politics is shaped by the fact that the players, even when on opposite sides of an issue, frequently know each other on a personal level, and have some mutual history.

– THE ADULT LEARNING PROJECT –

This next section deals with one specific organisation in which I did intensive participant-observation. Unlike the preceding, it is less an over-view and more an attempt to capture a 'slice' of Scottish life. Unlike campaigning organisations in the movement, the Adult Learning Project (ALP) was a context in which I could regularly discuss issues of culture and politics with everyday working-to-middle-class Scots, only some of whom were or had been active in the movement.

ALP is an adult community education project located in the working-class neighbourhood of Gorgie/Dalry on the south-west side of central Edinburgh. It is a particularly successful case in the broader system of community education in Scotland, explicitly founded on the philosophy of Paulo Freire, the Brazilian theorist of critical socialist pedagogy (Freire 1970; Kirkwood and Kirkwood 1989). ALP grew out of the efforts of a small group of neighbourhood women working with a community educa-tion worker in 1977. They created a successful local program offering such things as preparation for English 'O' Grade exams and yoga.[5] In 1979, the program was redefined as an Urban Aid project receiving combined central and regional government funds. After five more years it became wholly funded by Regional Government, in combination with its own fund-raising efforts. By the time I became involved, ALP was running courses on:

1. Scottish history, including women's history.
2. The environment and land ownership/laws/reforms.
3. Scottish politics, focusing on constitutional and democratic reform.
4. Photography.
5. Multi-culturalism in Scotland.
6. Gaelic language instruction.
7. Women's studies.
8. Writers workshops, including a women's writing group.
9. Traditional music and instrument instruction.
10. Traditional dance instruction.

ALP is run by an organising group of students and staff, which sets policy and plans curriculum, fees, and special projects and events. Individual study groups around the topics above collect minimal fees and rely on the collective efforts of the group. There is a core co-ordinating staff supported by regional funds who play a leading role, and most groups work with at least one of these instructors, but the direction of the project as a whole, and each study group, is highly co-operative. Some of the largest and most popular groups are those working on music, dance and writing.

In February 1994 I began participating regularly in two groups, the History Group and the Democracy Group. The History Group was an ongoing project which had worked its way up to the latter half of the nineteenth century when I joined. Discussions revolved around the Dickensian conditions of the working poor, and the successes and failures of working-class political organisation during the period. An explicit concern of the group was to relate Scotland's past problems to its present ones. The orientation of the group as a whole was left, socialist, and nationalist. With the exception of one older man who quietly admitted to me that he voted Conservative, the political sympathies fell along the Labour-SNP spectrum. Of the two staff co-ordinators, one was a specialist in local history who led Edinburgh history tours and was once active in Scottish Labour Action (see Chapter 3), the other was a member of the young republican-socialist wing of the SNP and involved in that group's magazine *Liberation*. By the end of the term the group had produced, through the written contributions of members, the first volume of the ALP History Journal entitled *Reform and Revolution*. The volume addressed topics such as housing and prostitution in nineteenth-century Edinburgh, and the eighteenth-century radical Thomas Muir.

The piece on Thomas Muir grew out of a small theatrical presentation put on in a nearby pub as part of a fund-raiser for the group. The 'play', comprised of dramatic readings and minimal props, told the story of Muir, a radical lawyer agitating for the expansion of the suffrage, who was convicted on trumped-up charges and transported to Botany Bay in 1794. Toward the end of the story one of the narrators reads:[6]

> Yet today, 200 years after Thomas Muir's transportation, Scotland's political system is still dominated by patronage, and corruption. Just as in Muir's time, the opinion of the vast majority of Scots is not listened to by Government. Just as in Muir's time the taxation system is unfair to the poor and generous to the rich, just as in Muir's time, the system of government is full of unelected appointees who are chosen for their loyalty to the Tory Party.

The play ends with Muir speaking:

> I was transported because I was found guilty of sedition, which was defined by the lawyers of the time as 'a commotion of the people without authority'. Therefore I urge you all to involve yourself in sedition. Make a huge commotion of the people, demand your natural rights. You do not have to face transportation so there is no need to be timid. We are a nation – we should start behaving like one.

It is significant that the historical analogy to the present being drawn here is precisely from the period of eighteenth-century radicalism, the time in which early modern nationalism was associated with developing conceptions of citizenship and democracy, as discussed in the Introduction. This is the conception of nationalism that primarily informs the Scottish movement. In spite of the rousing and defiant tone here, the mood in the pub was actually quite light-hearted. It was a crowd of ALP friends and members, out for an evening of drink and humour, and positively predisposed toward the spirit of the play. None the less, this very point suggests the normality of the moral-political critique of the political right pervasive in Scotland at the time. This radical tone was part of everyday life.

The other group I worked with was the Democracy Group, whose central project was to study the range and types of constitutions around the world and then design its own for Scotland. Each meeting began with a brief discussion of news items of the week, especially those that seemed to mark outrageous infringements upon democratic principles. Of the two staff co-ordinators of this group, one was a fairly typical Labour supporter, the other an active member of the fledgling Communist Party of Scotland, having been a member of the CPB before its fragmentation. People took turns doing presentations; I did one on the American federal system of government. By the end of the term, some constitutional principles had been agreed upon, rough constitutional designs suggested and discussed, but nothing finalised. Ambiguity concerning whether what was being discussed was a parliament within the UK, or an independent state, sometimes led to confusion. Also, as part of the 'civic life of Scotland' invitations were sent to ALP by the Coalition for Scottish Democracy to attend the Consultative Conference on the Scottish Senate discussed in the last chapter, and two members of the Democracy Group went as representatives. One of the co-ordinators of the Democracy Group, and core ALP staff member, has continued to be a key representative of the continuing education community to the Civic Forum as it is now called. In a revisit to the Democracy Group in May of 1993, I found the discussions continuing in the same spirit, but now oriented to the impending reality of the parliament, concerned with questions about popular participation in the first general election, and voter education in regard to the somewhat complex PR voting system. As politicians sought to bolster the legitimacy of the impending parliament, and various civic activists sought to scrutinise its formation, groups like ALP were being inundated with opportunities to go to meetings and be 'consulted' as representatives of a more grassroots political culture.

While many of the students and staff of ALP have or have had memberships in some of the parties and campaigning bodies already discussed, it should be understood that ALP is not an instrument of any of these. The focus of the groups I worked with was a response to a genuine popular interest and demand. These issues were in the air, and while many people did not pay too much attention, cynically uninterested in politics, many were concerned enough to take a more active step by participating in the kinds of classes ALP offers. In short, I believe the ALP curriculum and activities provide a good gauge of matters of interest and concern in the popular imagination.

ALP provides a context for extensive social interaction beyond its various classes. The weekly evening classes were usually followed by a visit to a popular local pub, for a couple of pints and continued conversation on the themes of politics, history and society, as well as lighter fare. I participated in several study trips to historical sites in Scotland and a two-week long summer trip to Brittany, to stay at a Breton language and culture centre and learn about and compare the situations between Scotland and Brittany, both regions within larger states with Celtic cultural roots. In all these ways ALP supports a broader culture of interest in all things Scottish.[7]

– THE PUBLIC SPHERE REVIEWED –

This broad milieu of active discussions around politics, culture and the constitutional question was sustained by a highly varied network of organisations – publications, radio shows, community education projects and so on – which in turn received substantial support through the institutional channels of regional and local government. And this social milieu was of course intertwined with the system of more explicitly political organisations discussed in the last chapter. Moreover, these processes developed around a long-standing framework of explicitly national institutions, which to varying degrees have been supportive of the movement. The churches, the universities, various organs of local government, especially the Convention of Scottish Local Authorities, have regularly provided support for public debate on the issues, if not always for the cause itself. The competing political parties all have a distinctly Scottish level of organisation, thus encouraging the idea of Scotland as frame of reference for political issues. And beyond the core campaigning groups is a host of civic voluntary organisations oriented toward various needs and issues at the Scottish level. The more dis-course-oriented groups and organisations described in this chapter in-habit the same generalised social space as this complex nexus of institutions. This is how the public sphere in Scotland has been con-stituted in recent years, and it is through this public sphere that a social democratic nationalist hegemony has been created.

To help clarify this context, it is worth considering differences in the basic infrastructures of civil society in Gramsci's Italy and modern Scot-land, differences which bear upon the conception of a public sphere in Scotland. Ultimately, hegemony needs broad and deep roots to flourish, and this requires an extensive organic system of social 'cells' in which it is generated and reproduced. That is why Gramsci was so concerned with the role of Factory Councils in his conception of proletarian revolution (Gramsci 1994: 163–7). There is nothing that exactly corresponds to this in contemporary Scotland. There are political parties, but party-branch membership has fallen drastically across the board in the last two decades, and the old system of Labour clubs and trade unions has been radically undermined. Church membership is also down, and membership in the various pro-parliament campaigning bodies was always limited. Although under the right circumstances, rallies and marches could turn out large supportive crowds, and the success of the last referendum is clear evidence of this potential for mobilisation at crucial moments, this does not translate easily into steady activity and participation through the social structures of daily life.

None the less left nationalism has had some success in achieving hegemony in Scotland. Asking why points us toward a fundamental, familiar and widespread shift in how hegemony is produced in modern states, from community based social institutions, print media, and face-to-face communication, to newer forms of mass consumption and mass media. Scotland has retained many organs of the earlier forms of hegemony production, in terms of print media, a lively pub-culture where politics is discussed, and a range of civic and voluntary organisations like ALP. But while these organisations occupy a relatively supportive environment generated by Labour dominated local government, and share a social democratic philosophy, they are differentiated and thus fragmented in their primary aims and interests (e.g., community education, helping the poor, senior citizen concerns, etc.). In other words, they lack the more or less uniform cell-like structure that Gramsci was attracted to in the Factory Councils (his version of the soviet), and that characterised the institutions of mid-century Labour-culture.

Regarding newer organs of mass media and mass consumption in Scotland, it is significant that these exhibit a Scottish orientation (despite incessant cultural Americanisation). Scotland has its own radio and television stations, which beyond giving time to nationalist issues, treat Scotland and Scottish culture as an important reality, a defining feature of social life, and this approach is actively promoted in the Scottish broadcasting industry (cf. Linklater 1992; MacInnes 1994). Of course, these modes of disseminating information and ideas have their familiar isolating and fragmenting social effects, yet they do this within an explicitly and self-consciously Scottish national framework.

As I indicated above, there are several pop bands (e.g., Hue and Cry, Runrig, Capercaillie, The Proclaimers) who emphasise Scottish themes and sometimes nationalist politics. These also generate products for consumption in the form of tapes, compact disks, and concerts. More generally, there is a specifically Scottish framework of mass consumption, however un- or only subliminally-political. Thus there is the national soft drink Irn Bru, as well as Scottish ales and lagers such as Tenants and McEwans, not to mention many foods. I would argue that football, which is a major pastime (for some a preoccupation) in Scotland, should also be viewed in the context of modern mass consumption. But the story here is also more complex, in that football in Scotland is deeply connected with national (especially masculine) identity, as well as Protestant-Catholic rivalry. During the mid-1970s surge of the SNP, nationalist sentiments became heavily invested in Scottish football teams and their performance abroad, including against England. It is widely suggested in Scotland that the blow delivered to the national psyche by Scotland's failure in Argentina in the 1978 World Cup is causally related to the failure of nerve in passing the 1979 referendum on a parliament (cf. Forsythe 1992: 352–3).

What I am generally suggesting here is that although strong community based channels of hegemony have undoubtedly weakened, newer channels have taken hold at a distinctively Scottish national level, thus reinforcing the construction of political conflict along a Scottish versus English/British axis. I would also argue, and here I am anticipating the issues at the end of Chapter 7, that developments in the organs of hegemony in Scotland have been shaped by the creation of a corporate middle class out of the former working class, via the institutions and standards of the Keynesian welfare state. Theorists of the welfare state sometimes refer to 'decommodification', that is, the management and regulation of consumption and demand by the state rather than the free market (cf. Keane 1984: 14–18). Scotland is, in a sense, simultaneously constituted as a framework for both commodified and decommodified consumption. These are not entirely separate social processes, because national identity and community are shaped through patterns of consumption in their entirety, from nationalised health care and rail services, to pop music, soft drinks, tourism and television shows. Although relatively de-politicised, this national context of consumption seems to provide a frame of reference which at least latently supports the more politicised conceptions of Scotland generated by the nationalist movement (cf. Billig 1995). In other words, due to the peculiarities of history, these newer media of hegemony have braced rather than defused this particular movement.

– INTELLECTUALS, CIVIL SOCIETY, AND 'THE NEW CLASS' –

It is well established that intellectuals and middle classes often play a key role in the development of nationalism, and Scotland is no exception.[8] Many of the specific people discussed above can, in some broad sense, be understood as intellectuals of the Scottish middle classes. In keeping with a distinctive Scottish a pattern, many would probably identify themselves as working class, despite having been upwardly mobile, achieving levels of consumption, education, and professional status unknown to their parents. This provides an important clue to the historical specificity of this process.

Tom Nairn (1981) and many other observers of the Scottish movement have argued that the general co-optation of intellectuals and the middle classes through the Union of 1707, and their orientation toward questions of political liberty and economic improvement within a British framework, was an important factor militating against the development a vibrant nationalism in the eighteenth and nineteenth centuries. Graeme Morton's (1998) counter-thesis of unionist nationalism, that Scottish elites and middle classes of the nineteenth century simply exhibited nationalist sentiments and goals that were compatible with the union, is instructive, but does not alter the basic point that there was no strong or unified intellectual leadership for a separatist nationalism during this period.[9] By contrast, the post-1960s rise of nationalism has seen a corresponding flourishing of a new national intelligentsia actively engaged in Scottish political and cultural issues linked to the home rule cause.

The current generation of activists came of age during the US-driven post-World War II economic expansion that fuelled a remarkable growth in accessibility and levels of education for new middle classes, only to see their new-found opportunities threatened by protracted withdrawal of the state's commitment to the national economy under the influence of neoliberalism. It is a period in which the career options for activists of a left/liberal/progressive political persuasion shifted from being centred on the labour movement, unions, and political parties, to a more diffuse network of movement and community organisations and NGOs, as well as a defensive entrenchment in the academy. Finally, as has so often been noted (e.g., Wood 1986), it is a period in which the very idea of left politics has experienced both an opening up and a fragmentation, as 'identity-politics' around a diverse array of issues of injustice and social exclusion have displaced notions of a unifying theme of class politics. Instead, struggles for more complex understandings of liberal citizenship and entitlement have taken precedence. As I have tried to suggest, Scotland's liberal/civic nationalism is a peculiar local permutation of this tendency, in which national and class identities have tended to converge (cf. Foster 1989).

About twenty years ago Alvin Gouldner (1979) coined the term 'The New Class' to describe the social tier of technocrats, experts and managers generated by the interacting demands of capitalism and the modern state over the last century. Narrowly defined this referred to a new species of intellectuals commanding specialised knowledge and cultural capital; applied more broadly it included the new educated middle classes associated with the expanding service and public sectors. At the turn of the century members of this New Class often provided leadership and key sectors of support to both nationalist (cf. Mann 1993: 546–96) and socialist (cf. Levy 1987) movements. During the middle years of this century, these New Classes became strongly associated with the technocratic projects of Keynesian and socialist states in the west and east respectively. But with the retrenchments of the state since the 1970s, the latest generation of the New Class has had to reconfigure, and rethink, its social role. The Scottish movement, and I strongly suspect neo-nationalisms more generally, reflect in part this process of New Class intellectuals redefining and reconstructing their class positions, including conceptions of social obligation and responsibility, in a changing political economic environment. In a sense they are reclaiming the institutions of state and civil society, and reaffirming their interdependent relationship, because that is where this sector of society is bound to find its way in life. The fact that 'civil society' has become a label of self-ascription for middle-class intellectuals and activists in recent years in Scotland indicates, I would argue, a need to re-establish and revalorise the legitimacy of the New Class in a world where its estrangement from the state, and in some cases redefinition as a threat to society, has created a crisis of identity and social standing.

– NOTES –

1. This social-analytic concept should not be confused with Habermas's normative arguments about 'discourse ethics' (1990, 1993), which attempt to offer philosophical justifications for trying to realise something like the public sphere, based on the belief that reaching agreements and discerning disagreements through communicative action is fundamental to being human.
2. In this instance we are interested in what conditions and processes have helped produce the peculiar local consensus around a fusion of nationalist and social democratic values in Scotland. However, we must remember that the generation of this consensus was conditioned by a situation of opposition between the Conservative Party and the opposition parties in Scotland. With the parliament a reality, the political discourse is bound to shift, and the oppositional consensus liable to deteriorate.
3. This journal is a revived version of the original *Edinburgh Review*, an influential middle-class, Whig periodical founded in 1802 which helped to shape the political reform movements in the nineteenth century.
4. MacMillan was also highly active as a member of the Steering Committee of the Constitutional Convention, and as part of a commission set up by the Convention to investigate the problems and alternatives involved in insuring balanced gender representation in the prospective parliament.
5. The 'O' or Ordinary Grade, is a general course of study leading to qualifying exams indicating the student's level of accomplishment at the secondary education level, and preparedness for higher education.
6. In fact, I read this part myself.
7. All these situations provided extended leisure time to get to know fellow ALPers and establish real friendships. My work with ALP was by far the most engaging and personally rewarding part of fieldwork, where I felt I was most able to participate, and not simply observe.
8. On the role of intellectuals see: Hobsbawm (1984), Hroch (1985), Kedourie (1993) and Llobera (1994: 149–76). On the roles of middling classes, see:

Anderson (1991: 47–65), Frykman and Löfgren (1987), Mann (1993: 546–96), and Seton-Watson (1977: 417–42).

9. Some of the leading figures of the Radical movement of the late eighteenth and early nineteenth centuries might be considered an exception, but these represented only a fragment of the middle classes allied with artisan/working classes, not a relatively unified national intelligentsia.

PART TWO

History

In the search for understanding, we must always begin with what is most immediate and demanding of our attention. Having surveyed the contemporary nationalist movement, we now turn to a deeper history of the Scottish nation, in order to put that movement in a larger frame. In this way we can get a fuller sense of the various historical processes that have fed into the movement, and at the same time introduce and locate many of the iconic persons and events that populate nationalist discourse in their historical context. This will be helpful when these come up again in Part Three. In three short, synoptic chapters, the aim is to underscore the development of major social institutions that have given form to Scottish politics and identities, and provided the framework through which key social groups and classes have contended over Scotland's future. In Part Three I will try to show that the language and imagery of contemporary nationalism owes debts to earlier modes of contention, and that that is why this historical perspective is needed. Chapter 5 takes us from the formative years of the Scottish kingdom (c. 500 AD) on up through the Reformation and the politico-religious conflicts of the seventeenth century. Chapter 6 examines the effects of capitalism, the British Empire, and Victorian Liberalism on Scotland, from the Treaty of Union in 1707 to the rise of modern socialist politics at the end of the nineteenth century. Chapter 7 considers the rise and retrenchment of the welfare state in the twentieth century, arguing that this process is the most basic and immediate one shaping Scottish nationalism in this century.

As we saw in the Introduction, one of the major debates in nationalism studies revolves around whether it is better understood as a product of modernity (Gellner 1983), or whether we need to give more weight to the role of ethnicity, which often has deep pre-modern roots (Smith 1986).[1] In part this debate hinges on preferences for different modes of explanation. Modernists such as Gellner are primarily concerned with the functional demand for nations that modernity generates – the need for a mobile and literate mass culture. History is in some sense irrelevant to functionalist explanations which focus on the interdependence of the parts in a system. Those who, like Smith, stress prior ethnicities, are interested in origins and sequencing – what happens 'after' depends upon what came 'before'. Both ways of accounting for nationalism can be construed as causal, but the former approach is more synchronic, involving a closed and mutually reinforcing circle of causes, while the latter is more diachronic, causation as a linear, temporal process. We need to be careful not to be misled by the terms of this debate, which tend to suggest that ethnicity is, in its nature, old and pre-modern, because of the way in which it gets logically opposed to modernity. But culture (i.e., ethnicity) is a part of our general human make-up, always with us, and as much a part of the modern world as the pre-modern one (though perhaps tending toward some homogenisation). Moreover, as I have already argued, specific cultures are unstable, mutable processes, with fuzzy boundaries, and should not be thought of as essentialised historical subjects.

This points us toward an issue on which 'modernists' and 'ethnicists' generally agree, that whatever the duration and significance of the raw materials of culture involved, nationalist movements actively incorporate these into contemporary visions of the nation, constructing supposedly coherent national histories and identities out of a much messier heritage. However, in my opinion, it is insufficient to try to explain this process of historiographic self-construction in terms of some primordial need for group identity, for this simply begs the question, why do people need their identities confirmed in this way? And why is this need so strong in some instances, and so weak in others? The answer, I think, lies in the fact that we are claim-making creatures, forever trying to lay hold of material and symbolic goods, and we do this in a social context. Thus we highlight and intensify our social and cultural bonds with those with whom we make similar claims, and nations and states have become dominant social forms through which this is done. While I would agree that nationalism arises out of the complex interactions of ethnicity, modernity, and the state, in contrast to those who would seek to prove that one of these is a prime mover of the process, I am inclined instead to focus on asking what claims are being made, what rights asserted? For it is actual people, with passions, motives, desires, and goals, that set social life in motion, not the huge sociological categories with which we try to make sense of them. Nations and nationalisms are social idioms through which real people pursue social goods, however obscurely and unequally.

Metaphors of birth and awakening pervade nationalist discourses, and play into debates about the historical depth of nations. As Walker Connor put it: 'When is a nation?' (1990). I am not convinced that this is a terribly useful question. Unlike the founding of modern constitutional states, which can be dated and located in historical acts, the origins of nations are murky, and depend on what criteria one uses to define a nation. And this is further confused by the efforts of nationalists to lay claim rhetorically to a past that becomes them. For the Scottish case at least, I am more inclined to think in terms of accretion, the gradual building up of important factors, that converge, slowly in some periods, more rapidly in others, into something we would recognise as a nation. To fix on a point of origin is inevitably a rhetorical gesture, whether made by nationalists or social theorists. The next three chapters attempt to show how Scottish nationhood is layered on over time, with certain corporate institutions and processes – particularly the Reformed Kirk[2] and the welfare state – being central to its formation. There is nothing inevitable about this. Any number of counterfactual histories can be imagined in which nationalist potential would have been diffused and Scottishness fragmented and assimilated to other identities. But that is not what has happened, and so instead we must try to reconstruct how the circumstances for the current nationalist project came together.

– NOTES –

1. On this debate, see the exchange between Ernest Gellner (1996) and Anthony Smith (1996a, and 1996b) in the Warwick Debates, published in *Nations and Nationalism* 2(3), pp. 357–70.
2. Both Liah Greenfeld (1992) and Adrian Hastings (1997) have argued for the key importance of the language of the Bible and the Reformation in England's precocious development of national consciousness, a line of argument which has important ramifications for the Scottish case.

CHAPTER 5

Kingdom to Nation

– HISTORICAL SYNOPSIS[1] –

– KINGDOM FORMATION –

At the end of the eighth century the territory of modern Scotland included five cultural-political groups. The Scots, 'men of Ireland who raided Britain for its wealth in silver in the days of declining Roman rule' (Duncan 1991: 1), had established a kingdom in Argyll ('the shore of the Gael') on the west coast. Below the Forth-Clyde line and to the west lived the Britons, Celtic-Welsh peoples who had been pushed back by the Anglo-Saxons invading from the south and east. The latter by this time occupied the eastern coast up to the Clyde, and parts of Lothian (the area of Edinburgh and east-central Scotland). In the east to the north of the Clyde, was the stronghold of the Picts, who probably spoke a Celtic language, were descendants of long-time inhabitants of northern Scotland, and had been increasingly pushed back from the west by the expanding Scottish kingdom. Finally, these groups were becoming partially encircled by Scandinavian settlements established by Vikings in the Northern and Western Isles, and intermittently down the western coast of Scotland.

Combined with the mountainous terrain of the Anglo-Scottish border lands, this Scandinavian encirclement resulted in the relative isolation of this northern part of the British Isles from the south and Ireland. It was in this context, along with the missionising expansion of Celtic Christianity, that the Scots were able to achieve a degree of political unification. By 843 the Scots had incorporated the Picts into the new unified Kingdom of Alba, and by 1034 the Britons and the Angles to the south had also been brought into this system. However, as Smout observes, in that these different cultural groups followed different forms of law, 'Scotland, in fact, was much less an identifiable state than a confederacy of peoples with distinct characteristics and traditions, each prone to rebellion and internecine war, held together only by allegiance to the person of the king' (Smout 1972: 20).

– KINGDOM INTEGRATION –

By the end of the thirteenth century, after two centuries of importing features of Norman feudalism, this ethnic patchwork was significantly altered. Now the political heartland of the kingdom lay in the diocese[2] of St Andrews, which encompassed the major burghs along the east coast and its estuaries, from Aberdeen in the north, to Stirling on its western edge, and to Berwick in the south. To the west, running the length of the Scottish mainland from Caithness in the north to Galloway in the south, was a wide belt of earldoms, more Celtic in custom, and less firmly under kingly control. Still further, the western coast and islands, though nominally subject to church and king, were relatively autonomous in culture, economy and politics (Smout 1972: 31). Although the distinction was not being made at this point, the stage was set for the formation of the now familiar Highland-Lowland divide.

Several processes had brought about these changes. First, Scotland enjoyed an unusually stable series of competent kings, who were impressed by the Norman system of government in England after 1066, and eagerly incorporated the new ways. It is worth noting however, that this was not so much Normanisation 'by conquest', as in England, as 'by invitation' (Grant 1991b: 17–19). Thus while the kings actively inserted Anglo-Normans and their ideas into the Church and nobility, this did not result in any wholesale displacement of the indigenous aristocracy. Instead, the more powerful Celtic earls (called 'mormaers'), were drawn into the more feudal forms that were developing, resulting in a hybrid and regionally varied system that fused aspects of chiefdoms and feudalism, with a strong emphasis on obligations based on kinship, both real and fictive, throughout.[3]

Of crucial importance in this period were profound changes in the size and organisation of the Church. Religious practices were standardised and brought into greater conformity with Rome; a system of eleven dioceses each made up of many parishes was created; and over twenty new abbeys were established, primarily in the east and south. These monastic houses were major corporate institutions and economic agents in the areas of sheep and arable farming and early coal and lead mining. They also created a new literate class, whose corporate identity was strengthened by Rome's recognition of the Scottish Church as a distinct entity (the Pope's 'special daughter'), separate from the English Church.

The other major force during this period was the foundation of burghs – towns in which merchants and craftsmen were granted special trading rights. These included the major burghs of the east coast involved in foreign trade, and many smaller burghs, often associated with new royal castles, established by the king, barons, or the Church. This network of burghs faded out as one moved north and west to the Highlands and Islands. They were frequently settled with immigrant populations of Flemings, Normans, English and Scandinavians, and fostered the beginnings of a new, hybrid, urban Lowland culture in which the older distinctions between Scots, Picts, Britons and Angles were eroded, and Scots became the lingua franca, as Gaelic receded into the Highlands.

– KINGDOM FRAGMENTATION –

From the late thirteenth century until the time of the Reformation (1560–7) the political system became unstable and fragmented. When the Scottish royal line died out without a clear heir in 1290, the rulership of Scotland was contested from all sides. The years from 1286 to 1371 have been styled the 'Wars of Independence', a period of protracted warfare and negotiation when the kings of England and rival Scottish noble houses all competed for overlordship. This process was complicated by the fact that competing noble families often held lands on both sides of the border, creating ambivalent and shifting allegiances. Many of the key icons of Scottish nationhood come from this period, such as William Wallace, the rebel military leader from a knightly family, and temporary 'guardian of the realm' while factions of greater nobles could not agree on leadership; the 'defender king' Robert the Bruce and his victory against the English at Bannockburn in 1314; and the Declaration of Arbroath of 1320, a letter to the Pope asking for his intervention in the Anglo-Scottish conflict, which asserted Scotland's historical political autonomy from England, and the right of the 'people' (as represented by the nobility) to choose, and replace, their own king.

While the following 175 years saw longer periods of peace, English pretensions and internal strife were still recurrent. A major factor here is that for much of this entire period the Scottish monarchs were either absent, imprisoned in England, or in their minority. Thus leadership often fell to competing nobles who vied for regency. As one might expect, this situation fostered the rise of new power centres throughout Scotland, the most striking of which was the Lordship of the Isles, centred in Argyll, where the Clan Donald 'approached the status of a second royal house in Scotland' (Smout 1972: 40), after the collapse of Norse power there in 1263. As Wormald (1980) has argued however, it is a mistake to view this process as simply decline and anarchy. While their were new factions, there were also new forms of alliance and negotiation. Of particular interest here is the custom of bonding (or banding), which flourished from the middle of the fifteenth century to the beginning of the seventeenth century. Bonds were signed agreements or contracts, written in the vernacular (Scots), sometimes regarding debts or commercial transactions, but more often establishing rights and duties between parties, either clientelistically between lords and lesser men, or horizontally between peers, such as nobles, lairds (a rank of substantial landowners below the nobility) and burgesses. In the absence of a strong political centre, bonds were part of the fabric of an indigenous politico-jural system in which power was constantly being locally managed and renegotiated (Wormald 1980, 1985).

Meanwhile, the respective fates of the Church and burghs were setting the stage for the Reformation. From the fourteenth to the sixteenth centuries the Church went from a dynamic economic and cultural force, to a decaying institutional redoubt of monarchs and nobles, who filled higher church offices with their offspring, and extracted the material resources of monasteries, cathedrals, and church lands, allowing many local parishes to go derelict. On the other hand, the years after 1450 saw steady growth of wealth and trade in the larger royal burghs of the east coast, and the establishment of many new, smaller baronial burghs, thus strengthening networks for the influx of European goods and ideas.

Beyond urban growth and church decline, two other factors were key. First, through a combination of dynastic contingencies and machinations, Scotland was heading toward monarchical union with France, a situation which grew out of a history of political and military alliances made during many years of war and conflict with England since the late thirteenth century. Many Scots resented this. Second, at the same time that the burghs were becoming stronger, noble power was being overtaken by the rising class of lairds. Many of these substantial landholders enjoyed tenancy agreements whereby they paid fixed rents to their lords in money, while extracting rents in kind from their tenants. Over the troubled times of the fourteenth to sixteenth centuries, this process of subinfeudation had become a common means for the nobility to generate much needed cash. In the context of rampant inflation due to the arrival of New World gold and silver, this meant the lairds now found themselves in an advantageous position, paying out relatively cheap fixed rents, while generating revenues from the productivity of their tenants (Makey 1979: 3).

– THE REFORMATION –

Scotland actually had two Reformations. The first, in 1560, was led by a large faction of the nobility and was a relatively moderate expression of resistance to the possibility of political absorption by France. The second, in

1567, was much more radical and Calvinist, bringing together the forces of a new class alliance between parts of the nobility, the upwardly mobile lairds, the burgesses, and the growing elite of clergy and lawyers. The new kirk that came out of this was expansionist and proselytising in outlook, quickly taking hold of the lowland burghs and steadily expanding into the towns and countryside (the Highlands tended to remain Catholic until much later). The kirk leaders saw their role as one of overseeing and instructing the civil authorities, and through the system of parishes, took responsibility for poor relief, a widespread system of education so that all parishioners could be literate and read the Bible, and often harsh social and moral discipline. The result, especially for the first hundred years or so, was a theocratic society intensely concerned with piety and godly discipline (Smout 1972: 65–93).

– THE UNION OF CROWNS –

After a period of struggle between this new church/class and the Catholic Mary 'Queen of Scots' (1561–7) there existed an uneasy balance of forces as the alliance developed, and the minority of Mary's son James VI was managed by a series of regencies. After coming of age and ruling Scotland from 1587, James VI took advantage of dynastic dilemmas in England and made good his own claim to that throne, becoming also James I of England, with the Union of the Crowns in 1603. Inevitably, James moved his court to London, and ruled the realm from there with his dramatically expanded powers. This began a trend toward anglicising the Reformed Kirk's organisational structure and liturgical practices on the one hand, and toward absolutist government on the other, that reached a breaking point under the rule of his son Charles I (1625–49). A key point of tension was the Crown's efforts to extend and integrate its administrative powers by grafting the Episcopal (i.e., Church of England) form of church organisation, based on a hierarchy of appointed bishops, on top of the new presbyterian system. The latter was, in principle, more democratic, composed of embedded levels of elected representation from the parish kirk sessions, through the presbyteries, and up to the national level of the General Assembly.

Charles's reign was toppled by a complex mixture of English parliamentary struggles between its nobility and developing bourgeoisie, and the rebellion of the alliance of new Scottish classes under the banner of the Presbyterian Church. The Scots elites who banded together to pressure Charles to change his policies, and the armies they eventually led in their part of the 'English Civil War', were known as Covenanters, because of their practice of using covenants to formulate and present their religious and political demands. Crucial during this period were the National

Covenant of 1638, which bound the signatories, the members of Scotland's new class alliance, to mutually defend Presbyterianism and oppose Catholicism,[4] and the Solemn League and Covenant of 1643, which pledged mutual support between the Covenanters and the English parliament in the same cause. The former was intended as a device to compel Charles (through his signature) to recognise the Covenanters' demands; the latter was in fact an expedient device for the English parliament to enlist the Scottish armies in their cause. Although the Covenanters vainly hoped that the outcome of this alliance would be a humbled King Charles, administering his kingdoms through a unified Presbyterian Church, they got instead a beheaded king and the harsh military government of Cromwell's occupying army of puritan independents during the interregnum of 1650 to 1660. Despite these reversals, smaller and somewhat millenarian sects of Covenanters endured, particularly in the south-west, and were the objects of harsh royal persecution late into the century.

Politics in Britain as a whole became more stable in the second half of the seventeenth century, especially when the new royal line of William and Mary was established in 1689, thus making the various forms of Protestantism in England and Scotland, and the powers of parliaments, more secure. In the Lowlands this greater stability led to some intensification of agricultural production. Whereas there had long been a gradient of mixed agro-pastoralism from the Lowlands to the Highlands, by this time there had developed a pronounced split between the agricultural lowlands and the pastoral highlands, where cattle were raised, driven to the lowlands to be sold and fattened, and then driven further south for final sale. But there were also problems. After the Reformation, trade with Catholic France declined, and Scotland was largely shut out of the New World circuits. Its wealthy class lost huge investments in a failed scheme to establish a colony at Darien (Panama) in 1698, which was actively obstructed by both the English merchants and the Crown for economic and political reasons. Combined with a series of disastrous crop failures and famines, Scotland's position by the end of the century looked precarious. After a century of monarchical union, parliamentary union was soon to follow.

– DISCUSSION –

Anthony Smith offers a list of 'six main attributes of ethnic community', what he often calls an 'ethnie'. These include: '1. a collective proper name; 2. a myth of common ancestry; 3. shared historical memories; 4. one or more differentiating elements of common culture; 5. an association with a specific "homeland"; 6. a sense of solidarity for significant sectors of the population' (1991: 21). It would be difficult to mark a starting point for a Scottish ethnie in these terms. The picture that emerges here is one of an ethnic and political patchwork, gradually coalescing around a somewhat unstable hierarchy of kingly power, feudal fealty, and clan organisation, and perhaps somewhat integrated by recurring military mobilisation in response to English pretensions to overlordship. Out of this political system with a relatively weak centre, especially in the fourteenth and fifteenth centuries, emerges a new alliance of classes, made of lesser nobility, lairds, burgesses, clergy, and lawyers, that gather together under the banner of the Reformed Kirk. A new kind of national identity, more grounded in the lowlands and urban ways of life, is attached to the development of this dominant social institution. With the removal of the royal court to London in 1603, the kirk increasingly becomes the focus of a national, corporate identity, and Scotland again finds itself at odds with power to the south.

Along with the familiar story of the decline of feudalism and the shift in the locus of power to the growing system of burghs, there is in the Scottish case a distinct shift from 'court' to 'kirk' as the main embodiment of national will and identity. If we take one of the defining features of the modern nation-state to be the displacement of networks of kinship-based fealty and ownership by more bureaucratic structures through which people of the middling ranks can advance, then the combination of the Scottish Reformation and the Union of Crowns appear to have given Scotland a precocious experience of this new political form, only to be subsequently obscured and preserved in the Union of Parliaments. Moreover, the core idea of modern nationalism, that political legitimacy lies in the consent of the governed, with 'the people', has important roots in Reformation theology with its emphasis on the direct relationship between the believer and God. Later conceptions of the relationship between the citizen and the nation-state were in many ways incubated within the reformers' critiques of the Catholic Church (cf. Llobera 1994: 134–47; Skinner 1978: 349–58, passim).

– Notes –

1. The main sources for this section include: Barrow (1989); Duncan (1991); Grant (1991a, 1991b); Lynch (1992); Marshall (1992); Mitchison (1990); Smout (1972); Smyth (1989); Wormald (1991).
2. A diocese is a district under the jurisdiction of a bishop.
3. The entire hierarchy of lord-vassal relations was overseen and administered by a system of sheriffdoms, and itinerant royal officers who collected revenues and monitored local legal practices.

4. More specifically, the Covenanters opposed 'papacy' and 'prelacy' (administration by bishops); in other words, their objections were directed at the 'Catholic' practices of the Anglican Church that were being grafted on from above to the more decentralised Presbyterian system.

CHAPTER 6

Liberalism and Empire

– HISTORICAL SYNOPSIS[1] –

– THE UNION OF PARLIAMENTS –

In the lore of modern Scottish nationalism, the Act of Union of 1707 is portrayed as a dark and sordid episode – a deal struck by a venal Scottish nobility under the influence of personal bribes and military and economic coercion (cf. Scott 1979). There is some truth to this picture, but as Paterson has argued, it may well have been the best deal possible under the circumstances (1994: 27–31). It was a deal between unequals, with the Scottish ruling class seeking economic security and opportunities, and the English elites seeking political and military security of the northern border against their rivals in France and Spain. In order to survive amid these European superpowers of the time, Scotland had to make alliances, and here the common Protestantism of Scotland and England was decisive. Indeed, Scottish Presbyterians since the Reformation had often argued for stronger ties between the two countries in order to consolidate and defend the reformed faith, and since the agreements reached under the Revolution Settlement of 1689–90 protected the Presbyterian Church from royal interference, many Scots felt able to pursue this path without threatening this most basic of Scottish institutions (Paterson 1994: 30). Thus, although Scotland lost its parliament in the Treaty of Union of 1707, it retained its own legal system, its church, including the extensive educational system it administered, and its system of local government. It was this nexus of institutions that shaped daily politics in Scotland, and its preservation meant that a significant degree of political autonomy was retained, despite the Union.

– THE EIGHTEENTH CENTURY: MERCANTILISM –

The initial economic effects of the Union were rough, as protectionist tariffs, recently built up, were removed, causing Scottish manufacturers, and the economy as a whole, to suffer. Widespread rioting in lowland Scotland at the time of Union, especially in burghs like Edinburgh, seem to indicate that the populace anticipated these hardships. But by the middle of the century, as Scotland's role in British and then global markets grew, as old exports of raw materials (cattle, wool, leather) were augmented by manufactured exports, and as opportunities for indigenous capital accumulation and reinvestment opened up, the lowland economy began to flourish. Crucial to this process was the growth of the tobacco trade, which was dominated from the 1740s to the American Revolution by a network of Glasgow merchants that came to be known as the 'Tobacco Lords' (Devine 1990). From this point on Scotland's economic centre shifted from Edinburgh in the east, to Glasgow in the west. Participating merchants reinvested their profits in Lowland agricultural improvements and industries, such as linen weaving, which grew dramatically during the century from a domestic system of production that had been well established in the seventeenth century to more mechanised factory production. Significantly, the Highland economy remained anchored in the export of cattle, accentuating its role as a kind of internal colony, which fed into the profound disruptions that came at the turn of the century (Macinnes 1988: 85).

The political system that emerged in the eighteenth century was one in which a Scottish elite managed Scottish affairs, negotiating with London in Scotland's interest, or at least their conception of it. Thus a series of political managers such as the Earl of Seafield, the Duke of Argyll and, most importantly in the latter half of the century, Viscount Henry Dundas (the 'uncrowned king of Scotland'), were powerful figures, co-ordinating the votes of Scottish MPs and governing by patronage. The fact that the right to vote was limited to an extremely small portion of society (as compared to England) made it all the easier for this system of narrow elite control to work. At the local level the key agents of government were the Sherrifs who administered and enforced the law and regularly convened the Commissioners of Supply – the local land-owning electors of the countryside and towns who managed the collection and expenditure of taxes. The Royal Burghs, the larger towns, were relatively autonomous from this system, being governed by councils that, while elected, were in effect self-selecting (Paterson 1994: 35).

The most important component of this system was the Church and its parishes, which played a direct role in people's daily lives, and provided the major forum for ideas on what we would today call social policy. The parishes handled poor relief and education, as well as matters of morality and social discipline. Each parish was administered by a kirk session, a body of church elders in principle democratically elected by the male members of the congregation, though in practice tending to become a self-reproducing oligarchy of the locally powerful.[2] The parishes were united into regional presbyteries, which in turn came together as the General Assembly, which as Paterson observes,

> was Scotland's parliament for domestic matters in the eighteenth century. It was much more democratic than the parliament at Westminster, or than the episcopalian Church in England. The general assembly consisted of ministers, elders, and representatives of the burghs, the universities and other bodies. In theory, the ministers and elders were elected by all the male members of local congregations, and at the very least they were more closely in touch with local opinion than the members of parliament or than any of the other personnel of the state. In theory also, the representatives had equal voices in the assembly, although in practice the Edinburgh-based academics and others were able to exercise undue influence. (Paterson 1994: 38)

Indicative of the role of the Kirk as a mediating body between the elites and the broader populace was its internal division into Moderates (the men of 'undue influence' Paterson refers to) and those that came to be known as Evangelicals by the beginning of the nineteenth century. A central issue here was the objection of many congregations to the principle of patronage, the right of local landowners, often Episcopalian in rural areas, to appoint kirk ministers in their parishes. This privilege, granted by Westminster in the Patronage Act of 1712, had overturned the right of the local kirk sessions to appoint their own ministers – the established practice at the time of the Treaty of Union in 1707. Moderates, more closely tied to the networks of political patronage, tended to actively support, or at least tolerate this situation, while Evangelicals opposed it. The power of patronage not only ran afoul of strong Calvinist views about the separation of secular and divine authority and the right of the Kirk to govern its own affairs, it also suggested the point where the system of government by patronage which characterised the century began to reach its limits of legitimacy at the grassroots level. This specific conflict led to the formation of two secession churches, the Associate Presbytery in 1733, and the Relief Church in 1761, the former especially attracting strong support in central and southern Scotland, and drawing heavily on the language of covenanting from the previous century (Reid 1960: 118–23).

As we saw in Chapter 2, resistance to the new regime also appeared on two other, and very different fronts: from the Jacobites during the first half of the century, and the Radicals toward the end of the century. The Jacobites,[3] led mainly by factions of the highland nobility that held to Episcopalianism or Catholicism and the legitimacy of the succession of the

House of Stuart, was undoubtedly partly a response to the weakening political and economic position of rural, and especially Highland Scotland. The first Jacobite rebellion in 1715, led by James VIII, was unfortunate, poorly planned, and abortive, as was the second in 1719. The third in 1745, led by James's son 'Bonnie Prince Charlie', had French support; its adherents managed to occupy the Lowlands and invade England. They did not elicit decisive support, however, and were driven back by government forces, ending in the disastrous battle of Culloden (1746). The majority of Scottish lowlanders were hostile to the Jacobite cause, and the aftermath of 'the Forty-Five' was the decimation of what remained of the traditional highland socio-political system. Rebel leaders were executed or escaped to the continent, estates were seized and forfeited, legal powers of clan chiefs were abolished, and draconian laws banning the bearing of arms and wearing of traditional highland dress were imposed. This was in effect the last and hardest blow in a long history of efforts by Britain's political centre, ever since James VI/I moved his court to London in 1603, to break the political autonomy of the Highlands.

The Radical movement, supported by artisan and middle classes, began in the 1790s and grew to be central to nineteenth-century politics. Inspired by the French Revolution and secular and rationalist ideas of the Enlightenment, Radical figures such as the lawyer Thomas Muir (1765–99) (mentioned in Chapter 4), and the societies they helped to found such as the Scottish Friends of the People, advocated political reforms, in particular universal male suffrage and annual parliaments. In the context of war with France this was seen as especially subversive, and Muir and many fellow Radicals, now remembered as the 'Scottish Martyrs', were transported to Botany Bay.

Finally, this was the century of the Scottish Enlightenment. The various responses of rebellion and reformism that economic growth and political patronage generated were outweighed by an increasingly hegemonic view of the world in which freedom of religion, freedom of thought, and freedom of trade, were bound together and elevated in the overarching ideal of liberty – and the Union was seen as the main guarantor of that liberty. The Union came to be seen as the context and agent of progress, even while conceptions of that progress were already beginning to diverge within that ideological framework (Paterson 1994: 40–1). The urban elites and middle classes were primary agents in the promotion of these ideas, but they filtered out to pervade Scottish society, partly through their associations with Protestant identity. The key intellectual figures of the Enlightenment were involved in various attempts to restructure their mental maps of the world and the social order. One of their main goals was to explain in more naturalistic as opposed to theological terms how a social and moral order was even possible in a world where traditional anchors of life had become unmoored, and communication in every sense of the word was expanding geometrically. They sought to define, through notions of historical development, economic improvement, and civil society, new principles of social order that would safeguard this new-found freedom from despotic government. It was in this process of conceptual re-mapping that the idea of civil society that we encounter throughout this study, as a locus for the creation of values and morality outside of the state proper, first developed.

– THE NINETEENTH CENTURY: CAPITALISM –

Despite the growth of the tobacco trade and linen weaving, in 1760 Scotland was still primarily a peasant society, the characteristic class of landless urban industrial wage labourers still only nascent. But the years spanning the later eighteenth and early nineteenth centuries were ones of rapid and traumatic economic transformation, especially when compared to England where the shift to industrialisation had been more gradual (Devine 1988: 3–4). Demographic changes were profound. In 1700 the Scottish population was around 1 million, in 1800 just over 1.5 million, and in 1900 just under 4.5 million (Donnachie and Hewitt 1989: 152–3). Meanwhile the new industrial centre of Glasgow which contained about 5 per cent of the Scottish population in 1801 held 20 per cent by 1891.

Weaving was central to the industrial transformation that helped drive this demographic explosion. The expansion of cotton textile production that began in the latter eighteenth century (surpassing linen), continued until the 1860s. Then as the cotton industry declined, due to the American Civil War, the next twenty years saw a trebling of employment in the woollen industries. Meanwhile, in the 1830s, the newer 'heavy industries' that revolved around coal and iron mining, railways, and especially shipbuilding, developed, becoming the heart of the Scottish economy by the end of the century. These industries were mutually reinforcing, driven by technological innovations in ship designs (for example shifts from wood, to iron, to steel hulls), and creating satellite industries in locomotives, girders, bridges, rails, textile machinery and machine tools. The second half of the 1800s saw the rise of the great industrial manufacturing companies of the central belt which nearly all owned coal mines and furnaces. At the same time, lowland agriculture became much more rationalised and productive, replacing human labour with steam power, so that agricultural employment dropped from around 500,000 to around 200,000 over the course of the century.

This rapid expansion in productivity was made possible by the existence of British Empire. In addition to underwriting vast markets, the Empire created new overseas career opportunities, and functioned as a kind of release valve, feeding upper- and middle-class Scots into the colonial, administrative and diplomatic services, and working-class Scots into the army and navy. Scotland provided a large portion of professionals, bureaucrats, and adventurers to the cause of Empire – for the most part with great patriotism and enthusiasm.

In the Highlands the effects of the new economy were the most rapid and traumatic of all. The highland peasant economy, based on potatoes, turnips, and the cattle trade, was aggressively dismantled in the years of 1790–1830, during the Highland Clearances. Arguing along Malthusian lines that their lands were over populated and under productive, the absentee land-owning nobility, descendants of clan chiefs, through the factors and middlemen who managed their estates, removed huge numbers of tenants from their lands, often by force. The highland tenants emigrated either to the burgeoning central belt, or to Canada, Australia, New Zealand, and to a lesser extent South Africa and the United States. The initial strategy was to raise sheep (the new Cheviot breed) on the depopulated lands. This turned out not to be as economically profitable as hoped, because the sheep often over-grazed and degraded the land and, ironically, the Australian sheep industry became more competitive. Another part of this program of 'improvement' was the establishing of coastal villages, with attendant industries, to which some of the tenants were relocated. The short-lived kelp industry on the west coast collapsed after the Napoleonic wars, but herring fishing (men) and processing (women) became a key industry in the Highlands, eventually to be controlled by large companies by the end of the century. After the 1880s, amid the Victorian era, many highland estates were turned into hunting and fishing retreats, catering to the upper classes from the Lowlands and England.

In keeping with all these changes, control over the system of political management and patronage shifted from the old land-owning aristocracy to the new urban industrial bourgeoisie. The periods of political mobilisation and party formation in Scotland (and Britain as a whole) are clearly linked to the three Reform Acts that expanded the franchise in 1832, 1868 and 1884. The first half of the century saw diverse forms of radicalism and early socialist experimentation, such as Robert Owen's innovative though rather authoritarian industrial weaving town at New Lanark (1813–21). Most notable during this period was the 'Radical War' of 1820 which involved marches on industrial sites and a well co-ordinated week-long general strike of some 60,000 workers in the west of Scotland. Extending the right to vote was central to their demands.

This action was brought on especially by the recession that followed the Napoleonic wars and by the rapidly worsening position of handloom weavers as factory production forced them out of the market; small tradespeople such as shoe makers and tailors were also key participants. The insurrection was put down by government troops and three leaders were executed, but political agitation continued and in 1832 the franchise was increased from 5,000 to 60,000, incorporating a significant portion of the artisan middle class. Further pressure for extension of the franchise, of a more moderate and reformist variety, came from this same sector of society in the form of Chartism in the 1840s.

The first half of the nineteenth century also saw the rise of the Whigs and their transformation into the Liberal Party, which managed to absorb radical energies during the middle years of the century. The nomenclature has a long and shifting history, but in short, the Tories represented the older, conservative landed elite, more committed to the system of royal patronage, while the Whigs were more connected to an urban commercial elite that preferred to place parliament above the monarchy in the business of politics. Fusing progressive political ideas inspired by the French Revolution with a strong commitment to the developing system of capitalism, the Liberals became the hegemonic party in Scotland, rising to dominance (first as Whigs) with the first Reform Act of 1832. During its heyday the party consisted of three major factions: 'the paternalist land-owning Whigs; the new middle-class Liberals of the towns and cities; and the working-class Radicals' (Donnachie and Hewitt 1989: 118).

Politics was relatively quiescent in Scotland during this mid-century period of 'Victorian Liberalism', with a further increase of the middle-class franchise with the 1868 Reform Act. The Liberal Party managed to contain both the reformist tendencies of the commercial/middle classes and the radical tendencies of the working class up to the 1880s. But the latter's advocacy of unions, factory acts, and further extensions of the franchise tended to push the limits of the party's moderate centre, and after the Reform Act of 1884 its grip on Scotland began to slip, as a series of new parties were formed, in particular the Crofters' Party (1885), the Scottish Labour Party (1888), and the Independent Labour Party (1893), the last two merging in 1895. Thus the stage was set for a modern class-based politics featuring a Labour movement. The Liberals were further weakened when they split over Gladstone's introduction of the Irish Home Rule Bill in 1886, the seceders forming the Liberal Unionists under Chamberlain and taking nearly a third of the Scottish Liberal seats in a forced general election that year. The remaining Liberal Party, now with a more coherent social reformist (but anti-class struggle) program, briefly swept to power again in 1906, only to head into a long decline after World War I that did not begin to reverse until the 1960s.

The Conservative Party was established in the 1830s in response to the growing success of the Whig/Liberal Party. It was an attempt by the older Tory land-owning class to counter the new political hegemony of the Whig commercial class. The party had limited success in nineteenth-century Scotland, except in a few rural counties where land owners still had considerable control over tenants and voters. But in 1912 the Conservatives and the break-away Liberal Unionists in Scotland merged to form the Scottish Unionist Association, which created new strength for the party in Scotland in the mid-twentieth century.[4]

The major radical event of this period was the Crofters' War, a series of riots and land raids on the islands of Skye, Lewis and Tiree that led to the formation of the Highland Land League of 1882, apparently modelled on the Irish Land League. These crofters, small holding tenant farmers and fishers in the Highlands and Islands, were responding to extremely precarious conditions, and were suppressed by a contingent of police sent from Glasgow. Public outcry led to the formation of the Crofter's Commission, which in turn produced the Crofter's Holding Act in 1886, which guaranteed fixity of tenure, fair rents, and freedom to inherit holdings. A significant victory on one level, the Act nevertheless fixed croft sizes in such a way that they normally could not support tenants year round, thus producing a class of small holders who were compelled to sell their labour periodically in order to maintain their way of life (cf. Hunter 1976).

Not surprisingly, many of the political factions and tensions described above were paralleled within the Kirk, which became more intensely divided between the Moderates, social conservatives, often lawyers and landlords, who subscribed to the sober and cautious values of the Edinburgh Enlightenment milieu, and the Evangelicals, who held 'a much more strenuous view of religion and the social responsibilities it imposed on the more fortunate' (Checkland and Checkland 1989: 68). These latter, more from the lower middle class, while still subscribing to notions of the sanctity of property and the need for industriousness, felt compelled to respond to the social upheaval and profound urban poverty being created by industrialisation. In 1834, the Evangelicals won control over the General Assembly, leading to ten years of struggle between the two factions. Matters came to a head in 1842 when the General Assembly issued a Claim of Right to parliament protesting against the right of lay patrons to appoint ministers in their parishes. When parliament refused to acknowledge the Claim of Right, it precipitated the 'Great Disruption' of 1843 in which more than a third of the entire membership of the Church of Scotland, ministers, elders and laity withdrew in protest, establishing the Free Church of Scotland.

Within a decade, Scotland had two parallel Presbyterian Churches, along with the smaller secessionist churches from the previous century. On the one hand this released a flurry of religious energy and activity as new churches and schools were established across the country. But on the other it marked the fragmentation and decline of the Kirk as an integrated and hegemonic social institution, and opened the way for a greater role for the secular state. For instance, whereas poor laws had always been administered at the parish level by the kirk sessions, the divided Kirk was ill-equipped to keep pace with growing poverty, and thus the Poor Law Act of 1845 established a new secular system of Parochial Boards under a national Board of Supervision. Still, despite the schisms, the later nineteenth century saw a florescence of middle-class philanthropic activity that was informed by the Calvinist/Presbyterian ethos and the social gospel, a world view which also greatly influenced the early socialists around the turn of the century (cf. Knox 1988).

As the institutional structure of the Church fragmented and lost some of its more direct influence on daily life, secular state structures correspondingly began to grow. As Paterson points out:

> Scottish social policy was governed by the system of supervisory boards that grew from the 1840s onwards – local and national committees of lawyers, other professionals, and aristocrats who were put in charge of administering all the subsequent social legislation that parliament produced in the nineteenth century. They ran the poor law, the rudimentary system of public health, and the lunatic asylums. They managed the prisons and industrial schools for young offenders. They were in charge of registering births, marriages and deaths; and they oversaw the provision of burial grounds. Later they took charge of elementary schools, agriculture and the development of the highlands. (Paterson 1994: 51)

This burgeoning system of middle-class and elite management, which relied for the most part on locally raised tax revenues, dovetailed with other developments. In the rural counties the powers of Sheriffs expanded as they played a key role in implementing the policies of the local boards. In the meantime burgh government became more independent, and the stronghold of the Evangelicals and the Liberal Party. Thus the Convention of Royal Burghs, dating from the middle ages, became newly influential, paralleling the powers of the Church and the boards. At the national level the latter half of the century saw a dramatic increase in the creation of Royal Commissions (for example the Crofter's Commission mentioned above) to address specific social problems. With this rapid expansion of bureaucratic bodies responding to the incredible growth and social displacement of capitalist industrialisation, it is not surprising that the post of Secretary for Scotland was established in 1885, with a Scottish Office in Whitehall soon to follow in 1887, in order to co-ordinate the new governmental system that Liberal hegemony had wrought.

The creation of the Scottish Office and Secretary is a prime example of UK level responses to what has been called 'unionist nationalism' (Morton 1998), the nationalist sentiments of the dominant middle class which were commonly seen as compatible with, and even complementary and necessary to the larger project of Britain and the Empire. Such sentiments have been symbolically preserved in structures such as the monuments to William Wallace in Stirling and Walter Scott in Edinburgh, built largely through subscriptions from pro-union elites and middle classes. This dual Scottish/British nationalism was possible because the UK was still a very devolved, locally managed, laissez-faire based political system, and many Scots saw Scotland as a distinct and important partner in the project of Empire. While middle-class Scots freely appropriated English forms of speech and manners, and even ideas on matters such as education (Paterson 1994: 66–70), these were seen as the rational choices of an active modernising nation, not as the erasure of Scottishness.

– DISCUSSION –

Let us review the main themes of this period, bearing in mind earlier discussions of civil society. I have tried to show that current Scottish devolution, far from being a sudden, anomalous and historically retrograde phenomenon, is a coherent, comprehensible outgrowth of Scotland's modern history. Despite the Unions of Crowns and Parliaments, Scotland has endured as a sphere of governance and moral and political discourse, negotiating its position within the larger British political system through its own political elites. This was possible because of a strong indigenous network of institutions (often highly clientelistic) that gave form and focus to Scottish civil society.

The British state of the eighteenth and nineteenth centuries was unusually decentralised, the first and ultimate example of the laissez-faire system. This was no doubt partly made possible by the outward focus of an expanding Empire which absorbed internal political pressures and brought in substantial wealth to defray the costs. In this context Scotland's institutional nexus of church, schools, universities, law, and local government, operated with a remarkable degree of autonomy as the domestic side of the state, managing social relations in daily life. The Kirk was the key institution in this mix, bridging divisions of class, profession, and regional and local affiliations, and exhibiting precisely that pervasive presence and cell-like structure that Gramsci considered crucial to the production of hegemony. But civil society is also the site of competition and ruptures, even within its core institutions. The Kirk contained ideological contradictions, simultaneously generating support for a Calvinist ethic that honoured work and private property and scorned indigence, complementing the developing capitalist system, while also allowing room for ideas of liberal reform and a social critique of the effects of industrialisation. There is something characteristically Scottish in this peculiar tension between Moderate caution and conformism, and Evangelical indignation and reformism, and the attempt to accommodate both these tendencies under the rubric of nineteenth-century liberalism. The Kirk seemed to strain to face in two directions at once, to both accommodate and criticise the social changes going on around it, until it finally split in 1843.

In the eighteenth century, the Kirk clearly stood as a mediating body between the state and civil society, controlling such things as poor laws and social discipline, and guiding information back and forth along the social hierarchy. With the nineteenth-century expansion of the franchise, modern political parties increasingly filled this mediating role, with the Kirk, especially after the Disruption, becoming more of an adjunct in this process – more of a moral voice and conscience, and less of an opinion forming and decision taking administrative body. This is a posture that continues to this day, some sections of the Kirk having taken a leading role in criticising Thatcher and the Conservative government, and supporting the call for parliamentary self-government. Today, thanks to this shift, and to secularisation in general, the Kirk is more purely 'of' civil society and not 'of' the state. Thus kirk minister and theologian the Rev. Will Storrar, a driving force behind the campaigning body Common Cause discussed in Chapter 3, saw that group's project as one of reviving Scottish civil society, and monitoring the behaviour of the political parties from that position.

The creation of the Scottish Office in 1887 amid the precipitous growth of secular governmental bodies in the latter nineteenth century, can be seen as the culmination of this process of transferring the role of political mediator from church to state (and the party system). And correspondingly this period also saw the growth of non-governmental voluntary associations such as trade unions and co-operatives, that further 'filled in' this more secular version of civil society. It is also important to remember the massive growth of economic firms and corporations, in manufacturing, trading and finance. Tobacco Lords, linen firms, banks and ship building enterprises, and their control of capital and social power, were a central aspect of this evolving civil society. Thus, in keeping with an argument made earlier, what might appear as simply the political-economic backdrop to the development of civic institutions in the preceding account, should rather be seen as the private/commercial dimension of Scottish civil society, in dynamic interaction with the development of other institutions of civil society, such as the Kirk, governing boards political parties, etc.

It is also important to note the continuities as well as the differences in this overall shift, how new forms carried on older functions (cf. Steward 1972: 91). The party system in Scotland was in many ways incubated and hatched within the Kirk – the major lines of ideological division already articulated within that institution's polarisation of Moderates and Evangelicals. Further, the genealogies of Evangelicalism, Liberalism, and Socialism in Scotland are tightly interwoven and cannot be neatly separated. Together they feed into a larger tradition of political and moral protest (Brotherstone 1989a; Walker and Gallagher 1990), which often positioned itself in opposition to the external power at Westminster.

I would sum up this chapter by stressing that while Scotland became part of the larger British project, it remained just that – a part within the whole – with its own internal foci of conflict and community, of struggles over the distribution of wealth and power. Moreover, its external relations to Britain as a whole evolved and changed. Manichean debates that seem to oppose absolute absorption to absolute autonomy obscure the actual historical process: an evolving web of social institutions that negotiated political, economic and moral relations, and shaped the linkages between civil society and the state.

– NOTES –

1. The main sources for this section include Checkland and Checkland (1989); Devine and Mitchison (1988); Fry (1987); Lenman (1981); Lynch (1993); Smout (1972, 1987); Withers (1988). My thinking here is particularly indebted to Lindsay Paterson (1994), who argues convincingly for a greater recognition of the relative political autonomy of Scotland during this period.
2. In the urban context kirk sessions sometimes came into direct conflict with burgh councils, as competing centres of power and opinion formation.
3. 'Jacobite' comes from 'Jacobus', Latin for James, namely James VIII, son of James VII, exiled in the 'Glorious Revolution' of 1688-90.
4. They campaigned under that name in Scotland until 1966, when they became the Scottish Conservative Party, although the local or 'voluntary' level of party organisation still goes by the name The Scottish Conservative and Unionist Association (SCUA).

CHAPTER 7

Welfare State

– HISTORICAL SYNOPSIS[1] –

Increasingly in the 1930s, in response to the failures of the free market, the politicians and managerial-professional elites across the UK political spectrum began to converge on a 'middle opinion' (Paterson 1994: 104–5) which advocated a mixed economy with greater state intervention in public welfare. This shift had been foreshadowed by the moderate reforms of the last major Liberal governments of 1906–14, such as old age pensions and the National Insurance Act. But after the collective hardships of World War II, which also furthered the intervention of government in the economy, this middle opinion came into its own with the Labour governments of 1945–51, and the modern British welfare state was truly established. Guided by the influential Beveridge Report of 1942, the new Labour government's program led to the contributory National Insurance Act of 1946, to provide pensions and sickness and unemployment benefits, the National Assistance Act of 1948 providing relief to 'non-contributors', and the creation of the National Health Service, a cornerstone of the welfare system, in 1948 (Bryson 1992: 83). At the same time the government nationalised key industries such as coal and steel in order to help stabilise the economy.

This agenda grew out of an attitude which sought to 'solve social and economic problems by removing them from politics and placing them in the hands of experts' (Paterson 1994: 130), resulting in a form of government that has frequently been called 'technocracy'. Also basic to this middle opinion was the pervasive influence of Keynesian economic theories, which questioned the self-regulating properties of the market, and instead sought to maintain full employment through government regulation of consumption and investment by manipulating such things as interest rates, taxation, monetary policy, and public works (Pierson 1991: 27). Despite shifts between Labour and Conservative governments, this basic technocratic/

Keynesian consensus around the functions of the state remained stable down to the 1970s.[2]

From the 1930s on, the new UK political order was paralleled at the Scottish level by the establishment of new problem-solving political bodies such as the Scottish National Development Council (1930), the Scottish Economic Committee (1936), and the Scottish Council Development and Industry (1946); all became basic to how Scottish economic problems were addressed. This new political and ideological environment fostered substantial growth in the powers of the Scottish Office (which moved from London to Edinburgh in 1930) and the Scottish Secretary of State. The leadership of Scottish Secretary Tom Johnston in the wartime coalition government, who promoted major infrastructural investments such as the North of Scotland Hydro-Electric Board (established 1943), exemplifies this trend. Meanwhile, the Barlow Commission of the late 1930s led to the formation of the Council on Industry by 1942, its purpose being to co-ordinate industrial investment throughout the UK. Policies of regional planning evolved that treated Scotland, like other parts of Britain, as a distinct unit of economic management. With the institutions of the Scottish Office, local government, and Scottish civil society already well entrenched, this conception of Scotland found fertile ground (McCrone 1993). One key outgrowth of this regional planning perspective was the establishment of five New Towns (a UK-wide program) between 1949 and 1966. Designed to relieve urban population/housing pressure and provide sites for new industries, especially branch plants from outside Scotland, these were relatively successful, although perhaps also hastening the urban decay of places like Glasgow. Interestingly, students of Scottish nationalism have often noted greater levels of support for the SNP in the New Towns, attributing this to the relative social detachment from well established local traditions of politics and voting (usually for Labour) (McCrone 1992: 164–9).

The system of government that developed in Scotland has been described by Moore and Booth as a form of 'meso-corporatism' with a 'negotiated order' (1989). By this they mean a system in which the Scottish Office and its various departments brought together representatives from both public and private interest groups (business firms, unions, financial institutions, etc.), creating policy networks for negotiating political exchanges, thereby guiding and shaping the realisation of central government policy. Within the larger context of UK regional planning, this gave Scotland an exceptional degree of autonomy, fostering a sense of distinctively national interest, and sustaining a broad based, policy-making elite with a sense of its own right to participate in political decisions (Paterson 1994: 118–22).

This relative autonomy is revealed in various policy areas. Scotland has historically suffered from very poor housing stock, and through Scottish Office policies has shown a stronger support for state subsidies and house-building by public authorities than in the rest of the UK. Similarly, the Scottish Education Department (SED) played a key role in implementing the UK-wide shift from specialised to comprehensive secondary education in the 1960s in such a way that major partisan struggles experienced in England over this Labour initiative were avoided. Later in the 1980s when a new Tory push for more vocational training seemed to threaten compre-hensive education, the SED policy networks found ways to redirect central government mandates, thus protecting the Scottish preference for more generalised education.[3]

So the degree of Scottish political autonomy within the UK was excep-tional. None the less, bureaucratic growth and the centralisation of power and domestic policy-making in the UK led to efforts to rationalise local government to keep pace with these changes. In 1973, under the Con-servatives, Scottish local government was reorganised, abolishing the patchwork of district, county, and small and large burgh councils that had been in place since an earlier reorganisation in 1929. The new two-tiered system was made up of nine Regions administering planning, transport, social work and education, and fifty-three Districts dealing primarily with housing.[4] This attempt to make local government more efficient cut the number of local councillors by around two-thirds. In 1995–6 local government was again reorganised in search of greater efficiency, when these Regions and Districts were merged into a system of thirty-two Councils.

Although Labour has clearly dominated Scottish politics in this century, local government had tended to reflect the spirit of cross-party consensus. Somewhat paradoxically however, this post-1973 system of local govern-ment became a power base for the Labour Party, which increasingly came to control the Regional and District Councils after it was forced into opposi-tion in 1979. The Convention of Scottish Local Authorities (COSLA), the new co-ordinating body of local government since 1973, and in a sense the descendent of the medieval Convention of Royal Burghs, became a Labour stronghold, often articulating opposition to Tory policies coming from the Scottish Office and supporting pro-parliamentary political projects such as the Constitutional Convention (cf. Jones 1992b: 180–203). After 1979 Scottish politics was increasingly shaped by this structured opposition between the Scottish Secretary of State, appointed by a Conservative Prime Minister and controlling the Scottish Office, and Labour dominated Regions and Districts organised by COSLA. Here the north-south divide in

UK voting preferences for Labour and the Tories (respectively) took on a very concrete form. Meanwhile the meso-corporatist policy networks, somewhat beleaguered, continued to buffer and negotiate this institutionalised conflict.

Still, the ideological divergence and break-down of 'consensus' since the 1970s has been profound. Conservative policies, based on the monetarist economic theories articulated by F. A. Hayek, Milton Friedman, and the Adam Smith Institute, have emphasised shrinking government, primarily through a shift from public to private provisioning in the areas of education, health, housing, social work and public transport. The Scottish public has been generally unreceptive and/or resistant to these initiatives. This tension was exacerbated by the patronising political rhetoric of Thatcher and her cohort, which characterised the Scots as suffering from a debilitating 'dependency culture', relying on a 'nanny state', and ignorant of their own intellectual heritage in Adam Smith (Mitchell 1990: 119–31). Thatcher's introduction of the regressive 'Poll Tax' to fund local government a year earlier in Scotland (1987) than in the rest of the UK was deeply resented, and resistance to this policy in the south was instrumental in her ultimate political downfall. Her successor John Major's Conservative government tried at least to appear more consultative, through such efforts as the slyly titled White Paper report *Scotland in the Union: a partnership for good* (HMSO: 1993), which considered ways of making the unionist system of government more 'responsive' to Scottish concerns. Although Major professed some minimal commitment to social welfare, there was now a deep pattern of distrust and resistance to Tory policies. During my fieldwork this was exemplified by popular campaigns to oppose the imposition of the Value Added Tax on domestic fuel, and plans to reorganise the administration of the Scottish water supply industry, shifting administration from local government to a non-elected body appointed by the (Tory) Secretary of State. Many saw this as the first step toward the privatisation of water services, following the English model. Movement participants commonly pointed to these government initiatives as further reasons why a parliament was needed.

So far the New Right can only claim qualified success in achieving its goals of rolling back the state: while government budgets have achieved surpluses, this is due to income from privatisation and tax increases – government expenditure has continued to grow (Midwinter et al. 1991: 167). Furthermore, the paradoxical result of the policies of the Conservative Party was that they undercut its pro-union stance. In the first place, the Thatcher generation abandoned earlier strains of Tory philosophy that emphasised a more decentralised, paternalistic politics, stemming from its landed heritage, sometimes referred to as 'one nation' toryism. But perhaps more fundamentally, during the middle of this century public welfare provisioning and regional planning came to be major integrating forces in the UK state, especially as the ideological 'glue' of Protestantism, the monarchy, and World War II solidarity and anti-fascism slowly weakened (cf. Colley 1992). As the Tories took apart the co-ordinating role of central government, they simultaneously dismantled the very integrity they claimed to uphold (cf. McCrone 1993). Under New Labour, which in many ways is following rather than countering the neoliberal trends of the last few decades, the new Scottish parliament could serve a new integrative function, much as the Scottish Office has in the past. It may absorb and defray political tensions between north and south, and could possibly lead the rest of the British system toward a more symmetrical federalism, as many in the movement advocate. But Britain's constitutional history has been organic and piecemeal, not the product of a single revolutionary-constitutional event, and each new change, such as the Scottish parliament, creates new anomalies for the political system, and this could eventually lead to unresolvable constitutional conflicts and full separation.

Finally, another factor must be considered – the European Union (EU). The EU also grew out of the post-World War II initiatives to rebuild, and to co-ordinate the industrial policies of the more highly industrialised European countries to help prevent the occurrence of outright war. It has grown to become one of the three major competing world zones of capital mobility and accumulation. It has also grown to become a competing centre for sovereignty in a Europe that appears to be edging toward a kind of quasi-federalism. Within it the leading economic powers, namely Germany and to a lesser degree France, tend to set the tone of economic and social policy. Although the overall thrust of EU policies is toward open markets and greater freedom for capital, none the less,

> the harmonisation of social policy throughout the European Community [now the EU], the adjudications of the European Court and the enactment of the European Social Charter will force certain member states to *increase* their welfare provision. (Pierson 1991: 188, emphasis in original)

This is exactly the position that recent Conservative British governments found themselves in, partially accounting for their demands for opt-outs from, and slower schedules of conformity to, EU policies. Correspondingly, the SNP, and Labour and Scottish nationalists in general, have tended to be increasingly pro-Europe since the 1970s, seeing the EU, perhaps over-optimistically, as a context for rebuilding a social democratic consensus (cf. Paterson 1994: 179).

At the end of a century of vast governmental expansion, and eighteen years of Conservative rule, Scotland is a considerably changed place. Overall, Scottish economic trends follow these of the UK as a whole – the decline of heavy industries, capital flight, and growth of foreign owned branch plants. The goal of full employment slipped away in the 1960s and 1970s, with unemployment as a percentage of the workforce in Scotland climbing to just over 13% in 1986 (it has since fallen back to the 7–8% range). In the south of England, around the London core, this same trajectory peaked at around 8% unemployment in 1986, falling back to around 4–5% (Aitken 1992: 244). Who is employed, and where and how, has also dramatically changed. The heavy industries, including coal, steel, and especially shipbuilding, once a defining symbol of the Scottish economy as a whole, have drastically declined in importance and share of employment. Economic decline has been offset, though not reversed, by other industries. North Sea oil and gas has caused substantial growth in the Aberdeen area and the Shetland economy since the 1970s, reaching peak production in the mid-1980s. It is, however, a volatile industry, susceptible to global market fluctuations, with relatively weak labour organisation and its support industries sub-contracted out and likewise heavily exposed to market uncertainties. New 'light industries' such as electronics and computer wafer manufactures, largely owned by US and Japanese corporations, have grown substantially since the 1940s, but do not create new employment on the same scale as the older heavy industries once did.[5] Meanwhile the whisky industry underwent deep restructuring in the 1980s, and is fighting hard to maintain its export market share. Agriculture and especially fishing are more important in Scotland than in England, but are highly technologised, employing relatively few people.

But perhaps more important has been the massive shift away from industrial and toward service sector employment, accompanied by a dramatic increase in the number of women in the paid workforce. This includes tourism, which is a major and growing part of the Scottish economy, and Scotland's highly developed financial sector (banking and insurance) which generates around 15 per cent of Scottish GDP. But the largest number of service sector employees are in the public sector, as teachers, nurses, civil servants, and such, which is not surprising considering the growth of the state we have been discussing (cf. McCrone 1992: 62–87). It is often noted, I think rightly, that Scotland's high level of public sector employment, combined with higher levels of public sector housing, no doubt help account for the tendency to vote Labour and stand by the basic principles of the welfare state.[6] But these factors should also be seen in combination with the enduring pattern of meso-corporatism discussed above – as another dimension of the remarkable interpenetration, by current British standards, of public and private life and institutions. A relatively integrated, bureaucratic-corporateness permeates this small country, setting it off from its neighbour to the south.

– DISCUSSION –

It is in this broad context of the growth and current retrenchment of the welfare state that shifting attitudes toward twentieth-century Scottish nationalism should be viewed. During the 1920s and 1930s nationalism expressed a diverse array of anxieties about Scotland's weakening economy, and the encroaching centralisation of power that seemed to undermine the considerable managerial autonomy that Scotland had enjoyed in the previous century. By the middle of the century Labour had arrived as a strong advocate of Scottish interests in the process of centralisation, in a sense continuing the Liberal tradition of seeing Scottish and British level nationalisms as distinct yet compatible, at the same time damping more separatist sentiments. Meanwhile the sense of a common set of British concerns and a common fate was consolidated by the entire welfare state project and the experiences of the Second World War. Ironically, Scottish members of the Conservative Party, distrusting big government, sometimes flirted with devolutionist ideas during the years of Labour's ascendancy (1940s–70s). Since the 1960s, a revived nationalism has coalesced around a continuing distrust of powerful centralised government, newly informed by the radical politics of the 1960s, while at the same time holding to a belief in a collective responsibility for social welfare, in ways that hearken back simultaneously to presbyterian, liberal, and socialist traditions. Since 1979 this new brand of nationalism has intensified, becoming a key element in the political and ideological polarisation between Scotland and the UK core of London and south-east England.

– THE WELFARE STATE –

The synopsis of welfare state development in Scotland presented in this chapter fits well within most standard accounts of this transnational process. Such accounts generally chart initial experiments with welfare provisions from the later nineteenth century up to World War I, consolidation of support for the idea between the wars, dramatic expansion after World War II up to the mid 1970s, and crisis and retrenchment after that time.[7] Explanations for the rise of the welfare state have varied. Some have

seen it as primarily a natural result of functional requirements of industrialised society and its demographic and bureaucratic effects (Wilensky
1975). For others it was a necessary response by the state, compensating for
the corrosive effects of capitalist markets on social reproduction (Therborn
1987). Still others have placed greater emphasis on the political process,
seeing the welfare state as primarily the result of gains won by strong labour
movements and class-based left political parties (Esping-Anderson and
Korpi 1987). A similar but divergent explanation treats these 'gains' as
also a means of defusing left political mobilisation and subsidising capital
accumulation (Thane 1984). As Gough observes however, there is truth in
both of the last two positions: the welfare state is inherently a product of
contradictory tendencies (1979: 153).

During the heyday of the welfare state from the mid 1940s to the mid
1970s, there was often a tendency to talk in terms of the gradual extension
of citizens' rights. The quintessential example can be found in T. H.
Marshall's model (focusing primarily on England) of an unfolding sequence: of 'civil rights' in the eighteenth century, including freedom of
thought, speech, and the right to form contracts; of 'political rights' in the
nineteenth century, to participation in the political process; and finally of
'social rights' in the twentieth century, to the basic conditions for health,
economic welfare, and full participation in society (Marshall 1983). From
our present vantage point this may seem like a naively optimistic projec-
tion, but at the time it appeared to many to be a commonsense extra-
polation from the history of the modern state. The important point is that
the modern idea of the nation was bound up early on with the idea of the
citizenry claiming its rights, and this process in this century has been
channelled into the making of the welfare state. Even if those rights were
won through processes of class struggle, they are constituted as citizens
rights, not working-class rights (cf. Hasenfeld, Rafferty and Zald 1987:
395–7; Pierson 1991: 22–4). This is not to deny the very real inequalities
and exclusions involved in the provisions offered by welfare states. There
are of course substantial variations between such states, but the largest
share of social entitlements tend to go to white, middle-class men, with
systems of provisioning being biased against women and ethnic minorities
(Bryson 1992; Goodin and Le Grand 1987). None the less, there is an
underlying logic of the extension of rights under welfare states, even if the
contradictions of capitalism and the modern state have always managed to
realise this process in uneven and divisive ways.

Attempts to provide an overview of the literature on the 'crisis' of the
welfare state often end up, almost as an afterthought, by noting the impact
of the changing global political economy (e.g., Bryson 1992: 230; Esping-

Anderson and van Kersbergen 1992: 203). When asking comparative questions about the relative fates of welfare states it is perhaps natural to focus on endogenous factors that can then be compared, but this tends to draw our attention away from the larger, encompassing picture. As Pierson has observed,

> [i]t is above all changes in the international political economy that have undermined the circumstances for the promotion of national Keynesian institutions. The powers of national governments, national labour movements and nationally based capital – between whom agreements about economic and social policy were typically constructed – have been undermined by the greater internationalisation and deregulation of the modern world economy. Even the domestic difficulties of Keynesian social democracy must often be understood as the local expression of international processes. At the risk of some over-simplification, one could say that Keynesianism and its characteristic welfare state form are increasingly incompatible with the new international political economy. (1995: 49)

Pierson goes on to note that the international system of post-World War II Keynesian welfare states was underwritten by the global strength of the United States economy, and the stable exchange rates based on the reserve currency status of the US dollar, which have declined and collapsed, respectively, since the early 1970s. This has made it much more difficult to use the traditional Keynesian monetary policies to control inflation and interest rates within domestic economies. Combined with the growth of multinational corporations, the heightened mobility of capital, and the deregulation of financial institutions, national economies, especially of small nations, have become much more open and vulnerable.[8] Lash and Urry (1987) attribute this process to a new stage of 'disorganised capitalism' in contrast to the 'organised capitalism' of mid-century, based on fordist production techniques, Keynesian regulations, and the welfare state compromise between capital and labour. Developing this thesis, Offe sees various effects: fragmentation of the work force and working-class organisation; middle-class defection from the ideal of the welfare state; an individualistic self-survival ethos; and general declining faith in the state (1987: 529–34). David Harvey has succinctly posed the central paradox:

> The state is now in a much more problematic position. It is called upon to regulate the activities of corporate capital in the national interest at the same time as it is forced, also in the national interest, to create a 'good business climate' to act as an inducement to trans-national and global finance capital, and to deter (by means other than exchange controls) capital flight to greener and more profitable pastures. (Harvey 1989: 170)

Harvey also directs our attention to the effects of capitalism, with its hyper-mobility, on the social construction of space and time as sources of social power. He argues that capital, with its tendencies toward ever greater expansion and acceleration, dominates global 'space' in general, and that working-class and other social movements that resist capital correspondingly tend to take opposing stands in specific 'places' (1939: 236–9). This argument again seems to confirm what I have suggested above about the Scottish case. As the social contract between capital and labour under the welfare state regime, which is at the same time a contract between a state and its citizens, has become weakened and threatened, that contract/conflict has tended to become reconfigured in terms of places: Scotland and England or, more precisely, Scotland and the London-centred core of the UK economy. It is intriguing to note that Harvey offers as an example of the bourgeoisie's need to dominate empowered spaces Thatcher's abolition of the Greater London Council, controlled by the marxist left during 1981–5 (1989: 237). In this light the Greater London Council and the Scottish movement appear as parallel processes of resistance, the one located at the politico-spatial heart of the current conflicts with capital interests, the other on the northern third of the isalnd. The conflict between Thatcher and the GLC encapsulated the tensions of the 'north-south divide' within the boundaries of London.

– THE SCOTTISH INSTITUTIONAL NEXUS –

In Scottish discussions of nationalism the critical role of the institutions of Scottish civil society has often been noted. Nairn stressed early on the importance of the preservation of the indigenous lowland bourgeoisie and the institutions through which they governed – church, law, education, royal burghs and other forms of local government (1981: 132–48). Jack Brand (1978) pointed out how this older nexus of institutions has been augmented by twentieth-century structural developments in Scotland, including a more national press and television stations, and increasing articulation of specifically Scottish economic problems with the rise of regional economic management, exemplified by such projects as the New Towns discussed above. He saw these changes as providing the basis for rising confidence and expectations that have not always been adequately fulfilled by the programs of UK-wide political parties – and thus stimulating a regionally based form of politics. One of the best general statements of the relevance of this institutional framework for Scottish nationalism is Lindsay Paterson's essay *Ane End of Ane Auld Sang: Sovereignty and the Re-Negotiation of the Union* (1991; elaborated in 1994). He criticises commentators on the Scottish situation for exaggerating Scotland's traumatic loss of sovereignty in 1707, arguing that in fact Scotland's elites and middle-classes long retained a high degree of autonomy within the decentralised system of the eighteenth and nineteenth centuries, and effective UK representation through the Labour movement in this century. Since World War I there has developed a kind of middle class managerial autonomy, based on a network of institutions including the old triumvirate of law, church, and schools, and crucially involving such bodies as the Scottish Office itself, the Scottish Trades Union Congress (STUC), and the Convention of Scottish Local Authorities (COSLA). The political and economic changes discussed above have meant that '[f]aced with near exclusion from even a peripheral access to sovereignty, the Scottish institutions have found that their legitimacy can no longer derive from above: they must trust the people, or die' (1991: 113); in other words, the ability of these institutions to manage Scottish affairs during the Tory reign depended on their ability to rally popular support. It remains to be seen how a Scottish parliament and a Labour controlled Westminster will affect this situation.

Scotland's political situation has been rendered problematic not only by the concentration of political power in Westminster, but also by the siphoning off of economic power by external capital. It is this parallelism in the loss of sovereignty and control, to both the state and capital, that has helped fuse understandings of interests based on membership in a corporate working middle class with those based on membership in a nation. The recent processes of capital and state development have meant that the conflicts between 'workers' and 'capital', and between 'Scotland' and 'Britain', have tended to become mapped on to one another in the popular imagination in Scotland (cf. Foster 1989; Dickson 1989), a point I explore further in relation to the concept of the social contract in Chapter 10.

– THE 'NEW OBSCURITY' –

I would like to conclude by considering some ideas put forth by Jürgen Habermas on this general subject. He attempts to place the welfare state crisis within an analysis of the contemporary Zeitgeist, which he describes as 'the new obscurity' (1989b: 288). By this he means a fading of the utopian vision based on the idea of humanity's mastery of its own productive powers and nature, which has inspired and guided liberal and left-socialist politics over the last 200 years, as well as the building of the welfare state in this century. This stems from the failings and contradictions of the Keynesian compromise as we have discussed, but perhaps more profoundly, from the realisation of the vastly destructive potential, for both humanity and nature, that our productive powers have attained (ibid.: 286). The result is an 'exhaustion of utopian energies', a period of ideological uncertainty and unclarity, which Habermas suggests elicits three main types of re-sponses. The first tries to defend the legitimacy of the welfare state and industrial society. As he puts it: '[t]oday the legitimists are the true conservatives, who want to stabilise what has been achieved' (ibid.: 293). The second response is that of the neoconservatives, who pursue a roll back of the state and greater freedom for capital, bolstered by a return to 'traditional culture and the stabilising forces of conventional morality, patriotism, bourgeois religion, and folk culture' (ibid.: 294). The third response he labels 'the *dissidence of the critics of growth,* who have an ambivalent attitude toward the welfare state' (ibid.: emphasis in original). Here he includes what are generally called new social movements, based on identities and interests not directly tied to relations of production and class. He argues that although the first two responses represent continuing commitments to the productivist paradigm, the first seeking to stabilise the situation through the political power of the state, the second through the economic power of the market, the last response seeks to reassert the autonomy of the 'lifeworld', his term for the culturally constructed world of negotiated and shared meanings. Thus the 'critics of growth', mostly partially and inarticulately, reject the 'colonisation' of daily life by both the state and the market driven economy (Habermas 1989: 295).

While clearly schematic, and influenced by the German political context (particularly in the characterisation of new social movements as generally 'antiproductivist'), I think Habermas's portrayal of the situation helps us to further characterise the Scottish movement, which I would cast as a unique mixture of his first and third responses – as merging both a conservative defence of the welfare state, and a reassertion of the 'lifeworld' in a Scottish mode. This merging has been facilitated by the fact that the 'utopian vision' in this case has been focused not only on competing futures for the UK state/society, but also on a hypothetical 'state-society-to-be', an imagined alternative, or new beginning. Likewise, the blurring of state and society that I have just implied, and that is characteristic of movement discourse, has also been made possible by this idealised conception. in which the normal tensions, ruptures, and condition of alienation that characterise the society-state relationship, are elided in imagination. As I have tried to suggest, the quasi-state-like nature of Scottish civil society further facilitates this peculiar intimacy and interpenetration of the very ideas of state and society in Scotland.

To re-trace the argument thus far: our present moment is one in which the mid-century compromise between capital and labour, which was necessarily also a kind of social contract between modern industrialised states and their citizens, has become severely stressed, and those arrangements are undergoing crisis and retrenchment. In Scotland, a unique conjunction of a strong, quasi-state-like civil society (although, as we have seen, by no means univocal), and strong, intertwined public traditions of socialism, liberal reformism, and politico-religious resistance to the state, have provided a context for grounding a vision of an alternative and less alienated future, in the form of greater Scottish political autonomy. But there is a real tension here, between a hopeful vision of the future and a pragmatic defence of a present connected to an idealised past. This discourse is defensive and conservative, but it is also an attempt to convey chosen aspects of the past and present into the future – to argue for a certain kind of future by arguing from a certain kind of past.

– NOTES –

1. Key sources for this section include Devine and Finlay (1996), Dickson and Treble (1992), Harvie (1981), Lynch (1993), Paterson (1994), and Smout (1987). As in the last chapter, Paterson (1994) is a major influence here.
2. Britain's mediating role between the US, USSR, and Europe during the Cold War undoubtedly played an important part in this special balance of internal political forces.
3. There is a common argument in Scotland which asserts that Scots, due to cultural temperament, prefer a generalised and philosophical approach to education. This ideal is more true of the university system in the eighteenth and nineteenth centuries than of twentieth-century secondary education. Still, the recent defence of 'Scottish generalism' has often been seen as a defence of a deeply rooted Scottish tradition, that contrasts with the narrow particularism of the 'English' world view (cf. Davie 1981; Macdonald 1993).
4. In the less populous and more remote islands of Shetland, Orkney, and the Western coast all functions were combined in a single tier.
5. A good portion of this industry is driven by the larger global defence industry (cf. Henderson 1989: 118–38).
6. For examples of this line of argument, see Kendrick and McCrone (1989); Midwinter et al. (1991: 18–19); McCrone and Bechhofer (1993).
7. For standard accounts of this process, see Bryson (1992: 69–120); Heclo (1981); Pierson (1991: 102–40).
8. On this point, Esping-Anderson and Van Kersbergen cite the work of D. R. Cameron who has argued that 'the vulnerability that small, open economies face favours the expansion of the public economy so as to reduce uncertainty via social guarantees, full employment, and more active government management of the economy . . . Since small open economies tend to be industrially concentrated, they also tend to develop strong and unified interest organisations. The capacity to forge broad consensus and to mobilise power is further

helped by the homogeneity and concentration of the labour force' (Esping-Anderson and Van Kersbergen 1992: 192). Perhaps the broad support for the welfare state in Scotland fits particularly well within this model, a fit that is obscured by its being embedded within the UK state and economy. These same authors also note Tilton's (1990) argument that Swedish social democracy, often seen as the type-case of the welfare state, may have more to do with 'a radical-liberal commitment to freedom of choice rather than to socialism' (Esping-Anderson and Van Kersbergen 1992: 191), an argument which is suggestive for the Scottish case when we recall the roots of Scotland's twentieth-century socialism in its nineteenth-century liberalism.

PART THREE

Culture

In the last part of this book we are concerned with the relationship between history and culture. Not only with the idea that culture is a social process, with a history that can be described, but also with the idea that culture, as a somewhat contradictory cluster of beliefs and assumptions, convictions and prejudices, opinions and inklings, is frequently integrated in the popular imagination through notions of history. Despite their fragmentary composition and permeable borders, we think of cultures as having their own histories. This is true of culture in general, and especially so when it is caught up in social movements which seek to justify and advance an agenda. Chapter 8 examines the widespread idea in Scotland that Scottish culture has a characteristic egalitarian ethos, exploring the different ways people in the movement draw on Scotland's past to confirm or questions this belief. Chapter 9 argues that there is a distinctive tradition of political practice in Scotland encoded in the idea of the Covenant, that has been rearticulated and redeployed throughout the last 500 years of political history, informing twentieth-century nationalism in crucial ways. Going deeper into the implications of this argument, Chapter 10 relates the idea of the Covenant to those of the social contract and social convention, highlighting the importance of metaphorical thought in these connections.

The themes of these chapters are recognisable as ones central to the standard story of the rise of liberalism and modernity in Europe, and indeed the account given should be viewed as one of a local variation within that wider process. Once again, a key aim of this last section is to convey how the histories and core concepts of liberalism and nationalism are complexly intertwined. Another goal is to show how present political projects are legitimated by being referenced to a past that is represented as leading up to them, often with a certain inexorable logic. Such constructions are commonly referred to as 'whig interpretations' of history (Butterfield 1978), after the Whig Party of eighteenth- and nineteenth-century Britain, whose ideologues sought to justify its rise to power, and the increasing power of the parliament over the monarchy, in terms of a deep history of Anglo-Saxon commitments to individual liberty, achieving their natural ascendancy. But the epithet 'whiggish history' is commonly used to refer to any political history that proceeds in this manner, and there are several competing whiggisms at issue in the following chapters. First, as Colin Kidd has argued (1993), both Scotland and England had traditions of constitutional theory, and their own respective versions of whig historiography prior to the Union of 1707 (see also Mason 1998). The Scottish version however, tended to offer historical justifications for the godly authority of the Kirk, the Reformation, and the Covenanters, unlike the English whiggism, centred on the power of parliament and the development of 'liberty'.

Kidd observes that after the Union, rather than fusing into a combined whiggism that was truly British, the English tradition came to dominate – and thus British conceptions of constitutionalism have come to be seen as rooted in England's history. This Anglo-British whiggism has been a powerful ideological force in the glorification of the Union and delegitimation of the idea of devolution. There is a well established practice of representing Scotland's history as one of inevitable incorporation into that of England, and of its political history as effectively ending in 1707 (Fry 1992). The historical ideas and narratives that shape Scottish nationalism today can be seen as a new, counter-whiggism. But it is one that both draws on Scotland's deeper past of politico-religious struggles between kirk and court, and incorporates the standard contemporary themes of liberalism: egalitarianism, democracy, freedom. It is a new synthesis, at times taking on the familiar form of the Whig historical narrative. The point here is not to discredit the movement, but rather to try to understand how it gets legitimated, because this is an example of a very general process, of which most major political mobilisations must partake.

CHAPTER 8

Egalitarian Myths

We have seen throughout this study the recurring claim in Scottish nationalism to both be and become a fairer kind of society. As William McIlvanney put it, the most appropriate motto for a Scottish flag would be 'Hey – that's no' fair!' This sentiment is so broadly recognised in Scotland that it tends to go by the common appellation 'the myth of Scottish egalitarianism'.[1] I explore this myth in this chapter, first through a consideration of academic discussions of it, and then by surveying statements by various informants in order to create a layered ethnographic assessment of the current state of this idea, and to disaggregate it into some of the key motifs out of which it is composed.

– THE SCOTTISH MYTH OF EGALITARIANISM –

– ACADEMIC DISCUSSIONS –

The idea of an egalitarian ethos in Scotland is so widespread that many recent major texts on Scottish culture and politics address it at the outset.[2] Peter Jones summarises the myth concisely in his introduction to *The Anatomy of Scotland: How Scotland Works* (Linklater and Denniston 1992):

> the so-called 'democratic intellect' [is] a national perception that all Scots share skills and opportunities to an extent not widely echoed elsewhere. It is perhaps part of a wider myth, that of egalitarian Scotland which has its clearest expression in the Presbyterian church and the Scottish education system. The democracy of the Kirk, governed not by bishops but by locally chosen kirk sessions, presbyteries, synods and the General Assembly, contributes strongly to the idea of an egalitarian state, while the tradition that Scottish education offers every pupil, irrespective of class or wealth, the potential to attain the highest academic standards, informs policy-making right across the political spectrum and is widely accepted south as well as north of the border. The egalitarian myth permeates political debate and underpins much of Scotland's institutional structures. The Scottish Nationalist leader, Alex Salmond, put it thus in

September 1990: 'I think that people are looking for a political party which is collectivist in terms of its view of social provision. In terms of how society looks after the disadvantaged, people want to see a collective ethos. That has a very keen response in Scottish society. [There is] great resonance and support for the health services, and a state led comprehensive education system'. (Jones 1992c: 4, second insertion in original)

The myth is not without its Scottish critics (e.g., Maxwell 1976; McCrone, et al. 1982; McCreadie 1991). To further flesh it out and identify its fallacies, I focus on David McCrone's recent critical assessment (1992: 88–120). McCrone, a Scottish sociologist, tackles the myth in a chapter on social mobility in Scotland, quickly pointing out its simultaneously radical and conservative import. At times the claim appears to be that Scots have a stronger yearning for equality, to set right social inequity; but in other contexts the assertion seems to be that there is a real underlying equality of social status in Scotland, that egalitarianism is a condition that actually exists (ibid.: 90, 115). This latter version of the myth rests especially on the notion of equality of opportunity – that Scotland is an effectively merito-cratic society. It is this version of the myth that McCrone targets.

Equality of opportunity depends upon levels of literacy and education. There is a long-standing belief among Scots that their society has benefited historically from higher than usual levels of literacy, particularly in the Lowlands, resulting from the Reformed Kirk's policy of establishing a school in every parish, so that the faithful could read the Bible. Taking the ability to sign one's name on a marriage register as evidence scholars have offered support for this belief, arguing that, already in the seventeenth century, the Scottish peasantry was comparatively advanced in terms of literacy in Europe. With the dislocations of increasing industrialisation in the eight-eenth and nineteenth centuries, Scotland's exceptional literacy increasingly became a conceit of the Scottish middle class, most strenuously argued from the latter nineteenth century as Scottish educational institutions, tradi-tionally controlled by this class, were under pressure to assimilate to English models. Still, data as late as 1855 show higher levels of literacy for both men and women in Scotland than in England and Wales (in each country male literacy is higher than female) (McCrone 1992: 94).

The latter nineteenth century also saw the development of what is known as the Kailyard literature (c. 1880–1914), named after the cabbage gardens characteristic of Scotland's rural villages. The Kailyard school defined Scotland

as wholly consisting of small towns full of small-town 'characters' given to bucolic intrigue and wise sayings. At first the central figures were usually Ministers of the

Kirk (as were most of the authors) but later on schoolteachers and doctors got into the act. Their housekeepers always have a shrewd insight into human nature. Offspring who leave for the big city frequently come to grief, and are glad to get home again (peching and hosting to hide their feelings). (Nairn, quoted in McCrone 1992: 96)

A stock character in these stories was the 'lad o' pairts', a boy of exceptional skill and talent. Conventionally, this boy from a peasant family of modest means is spotted by the local kirk minister or school teacher (often the same person), who then takes a hand in promoting the boy's career by winning support for him from the local well-to-do so he can go to university and pursue a professional career as a doctor, lawyer or minister. Celebrating an indigenous system of meritocracy is the central idea here. However, rooted as it is in a rural, pre-industrial, paternalist vision of Scotland, it is a prime example of McCrone's 'conservative' version of the Scottish myth, which ultimately validates social hierarchy by asserting the possibility to transcend it when appropriate.

The partial reality behind this myth appears to have been a genuine structure of opportunity for the rural middle class and some of the urban skilled artisan class, to go to university and enter the educated professions. But this system of meritocracy had little relevance to the vast majority of peasants and labourers. McCrone notes that studies of post-World War II Scotland suggest greater educational opportunity there than in the US, and that educational opportunities for the skilled working class are similar to those found in mainland Europe, significantly exceeding their counterparts in England. The offspring of the Scottish petit bourgeoisie also fares unusually well in the educational system when compared with England (McCrone 1992: 103–4). Considering the large proportion of my informants who were in the first generation of their family to go to university, and who tended to attribute this to the opportunities created by the post-1945 welfare state, I would suggest that the lad o' pairts myth survives in part because the welfare state in some measure echoes the opportunity structures created by the Kirk and its school system in earlier centuries. Idealised egalitarianism, and the cultural validation of education, appear to endure in a way that over-arches the specific historical institutional mechanisms at work.

Analysing large-scale survey research done on social mobility in Scotland, England and Wales in the 1970s and 1980s, McCrone argues that apart from an unusually high continuity (from father to son) within the petit bourgeoisie in Scotland, patterns of mobility are substantially similar throughout the UK. He concludes that the basic facts of social mobility in Scotland as compared with England do not account for the presence of the Scottish myth, nor the absence of any corollary myth in England. The origins and function of the myth appear to be more ideological than social structural.

McCrone suggests that the explanation for the myth lies primarily in two areas. First, to echo the anthropologist Clifford Geertz (1973: 448), it is a story Scots tell themselves about themselves, which has been sustained and given shape by two literary movements. One romanticised the Gaidhealtachd – the culture of the Gaelic speaking Highlands. Here the 'sturdy communalism' of the clan system was taken as a metonym for Scotland as a whole (McCrone 1992: 117). The other, the Kailyard school described above, where the Calvinist communalism and paternalism of rural Lowland Scotland is taken as the representation of the whole, seems to have appealed and been marketed especially to expatriate Scots living abroad. Both these literary movements have contributed to the Scottish myth, although they tell us more about how it was created and sustained, than why.

Secondly, McCrone avers that 'institutional and social arrangements within Scotland cannot be ignored' (ibid.: 120). While patterns of social mobility are not all that different from the rest of the UK, it does appear that the Kirk and educational system, as pervasive social institutions, have played a central role in the history of social mobility in Scotland. Although opportunity and egalitarianism in Scotland lack the mythic proportions often attributed to them, to the extent that they do exist, their long association with these extensive and dominant social institutions is quite real. Moreover, the Presbyterian emphasis on civic duties, communal values and social responsibility lives on in a secular form, influencing other areas of Scottish life, such as the trade union movement (cf. Walker and Gallagher 1990). Thus, despite the manifest patterns of social mobility and stratification, a social ethos of egalitarianism has been nurtured by these core institutions.

– INTERVIEW DATA –

The major thrust of McCrone's analysis is to show that the Scottish myth has no simple, direct basis in Scottish social structure. I now look more closely at how my informants tried to explain Scotland's 'egalitarian ethos'. The people I interviewed often cited the standard explanations mentioned above, some enthusiastically, and some in a rather perfunctory manner, as though rehearsing a familiar, well-worn argument. The influence of the Kirk, the working class solidarity of the Labour movement, and to a lesser extent the clan system, were the main recurring themes. But these were often offered with an air of perplexity. Informants sometimes puzzled over whether Scottish social institutions generated egalitarian values, or vice versa. Many seemed to feel that Scottish egalitarianism was a self-evident fact, difficult to explain simply in terms of historical causes. But overall the standard arguments were reproduced, although with critical elaborations that one does not normally find in the encapsulated versions of the myth presented in more academic treatments. On the presumption that such 'myths' are constantly evolving and being adapted to new contexts and purposes, and that the version I encountered reflects especially the attitudes of nationalist minded Scots, I suggest that an overview of these critical elaborations of the standard myth can provide clues as to how it is currently being reinterpreted and redirected to meet the needs of the Scottish movement.

– THE KIRK –

The role of the Kirk was diversely interpreted. The two main themes were the idea of the Kirk as an institution with proto-democratic structures, and the psychological impact of Calvinist theology. Allan, a free lance journalist and television producer specialising in Scottish issues argued

> Presbyterianism is usually blamed for all this . . . it's said that it produced this authoritarian, therefore deferential view of things etc., etc., etc . . . but, what Knox was talking about in the First Book of Discipline, was a school in every parish, and a college in every toon [town]. Yeah? That was an essential sort of aim of the First Book of Discipline. But not only that, but that every congregation, or at least the male members of the congregation, had the right to elect their own minister – elect – now your talking about rough democracy here in the sixteenth century. This was not reactionary, this was revolutionary. The reason that the English took a nasty turn against the Scots in the end of the sixteenth century was that they were seen as such a . . . ach . . . a threat from the left, this was a kind of radicalism that they didn't want to cope with . . .

Allan is very much arguing against one conventional trend among the intelligentsia, which has been to emphasise the oppressive and stultifying effects of Calvinism. And he is clearly drawing a deep parallel between the reformed Kirk's impetus toward democratic organisation, and the recent Scottish complaint about a democratic deficit within the UK. Hamish, a graphic designer in Glasgow from a 'respectable working class' (his words) background, and Labour oriented in his own politics, offered a similar, but more double-edged assessment of the impact of the Kirk:

> You've got to look at the Reformation here. I mean, lets face it, Scotland was the Iran of its day. There are democratic things about the Ayatollah's revolu-tion, I mean there were democratic things, some of them are still there . . . If you think of the Reformation in those kinds of terms, there was tremendous democratic things about it. Even with the 'school in every parish', they never

really managed to come out with it. I read in this book [. . .] about the seventeen years after the Reformation, and it was about the Knoxian . . . the Kirk Session, which again, think about it, the Kirk Session is like the Revolutionary Committee, or Street Committee in China, or something like that, except they had, well, they're very puritanical in the Street Committee in China [. . .] but these puritanical bodies were democratic. They were also tremendously powerful on a local level, they set up [word unclear] they banned drinking, dancing, and all the rest of it. All the socially, sexually, and psychologically repressive things were allowed to go on, but they also at the same time said 'wealth is a sin, we must do everything we can over the next few decades to take wealth away from rich people'. They never got that one through, because it was a compromise between them on the ground, and the kind of landed, which they were at the time, ruling class . . . now them on the ground filled a kind of democratic, [word unclear] workshop, early capitalism, didn't they? Not very successful, Scotland was a dreadfully poor country. And they spent the next century having doctrinal arguments and fighting to defend what . . . So I think if you go back it does come out of, in the Lowlands it comes out of that Presbyterian kind of, the good aspects of the Calvinist revolution . . . which we did, like, you know, lots of terrible things . . . grim, you know, your heart was filled when you were part of the elect and all of that, but it must have been pretty turgid, eh? But I mean it comes out of the poverty of Scotland and the climate and all the rest of it. No wonder people thought they were sinners.

Here the tensions between the democratic and authoritarian aspects of early Calvinism are compared to Islamic fundamentalism and Communism, suggesting a basic underlying problematic of political revolution. As with Allan there is an explicit parallel to twentieth-century politics, but with the further suggestion that there is not an 'either/or' choice in positive versus negative evaluations of the historical impact of the Kirk.

Christopher, a Church of Scotland minister active in Charter 88 and several pro-parliament campaigning groups, comes from a more rural working-class background, and described his political orientation as socialist and globalist, with emphasis on the decentralisation of political power. I asked him about the Kirk's role in the egalitarian ethos. Once again the approach to the Kirk is mixed and cautious:

Well, I think that is an element [. . .] but I think that is overdone. It's often said that the Church of Scotland is democratic, it's not, it's oligarchic. So yes there is a significant difference between the monarchism of the Church of England, and the oligarchism of the Church of Scotland. And of course that is an extension, there certainly is, within the Church of Scotland, a strong emphasis on . . . parity. But if you look more closely it is first of all the parity among ministers, and secondly, at least in [class] position, a parity, near parity, between ministers and elders. But there is quite a marked distance between ministers and elders on the one hand, and ordinary members, the people, on the other. [. . .] OK., so, within the limits . . . of that broad group of people, and its quite a broad band of people . . . there is that strong [word unclear] of parity. The other thing again, if we can take the contrast with the Church of England, which is quite helpful, is, there are not grades of ministers – rector, dean, bishop, archbishop – there's just the Church ministers. Now there may be all sorts of informal hierarchies, but they're not structured. And there's not that sense, which I have detected in the Church of England, of promotion. And, if you look at the eldership, the elders are drawn widely, from the community. I mean in the early days of course, the elders were the people who were leaders in the community, with a strong bias to the well to do, the professionals [. . .] people who were figures of some standing in the community.

Christopher is drawing here on experiences gained from working with the British Council of Churches, which enhanced his comparative view of the differences between the Scottish and English Churches. The major tendency among my informants on this point was for those more closely involved in what I have called the intelligentsia, and the milieu of the CSP and the Constitutional Convention, to put the influence of the Kirk in a positive light. This is partly due to a high level of participation by ministers of the Kirk and other churches in these circles. But it also reflects the strong orientation of this segment of the movement toward the fundamental reform of the constitution and political institutions. I would suggest that this legal-institutional orientation in recent debates about sovereignty logically inclines activists in these circles to anchor their critiques in the major quasi-state institution of Scotland's modern history. Portrayals of the Kirk as a grassroots, democratic institution, often presented in tandem with the historical weakness of the Scottish royalty in relation to the nobility and the Kirk, create an historical precedent for current complaints about the overweening power of the Prime Minister and Westminster as a whole, and the illegitimacy of the recent Tory government in Scotland.

Another argument I encountered, especially in Labour Party circles, sought to synthesise the roles of both the Presbyterian Kirk and the Catholic Church. John, a Labour Party activist for home rule, offered this response to my general query about the differences between Scotland and England in terms of support for the welfare state:

One of the current theories is, eh, is that there's a synthesis between a Presbyterian form of Protestantism, which has got a very egalitarian ethos, right? And at the same time the Catholic tradition – which is much larger in Scotland than it is in England 'cause of the Irish immigration – and the communal nature, of that culture. And a lot of sociologists would say, Scottish sociologists would say it was a marrying of those two cultures, which produced the eh, that kind of, attitude . . .

I asked John about the relative importance of the Churches on this point when compared to the general history of the socialist movement in Scotland:

> I think the socialist movement in Scotland benefited from the kind of value background that was created by religion in Scotland, because, Scotland is one of the very, very few countries in the world where the Party of the left is associated with the Roman Catholic Church. Equally, having said that, if you go back in the movement, to the 1920s and early 30s, and look at the role of the ILP [Independent Labour Party] as the pioneer of the Labour movement, the number of either Church of Scotland ministers or Free Church of Scotland ministers that were actually ILP MPs or leading figures in the ILP, is really quite phenomenal, in a way in which I think the clergy and religion have never had that association with the socialist movement in England.

This argument reflects the strong historical relationship between the Scottish Catholic community and the Scottish Labour Party, which has been a major force in integrating Catholics into Scottish society, despite persistent sectarianism in some areas. It also reflects an awareness of the need to counter an underlying tendency in movement rhetoric to assimilate Scottishness, Presbyterianism, and nationalism in ways that would seem to exclude the Catholic community. It is a kind of inclusive, 'broad church' interpretation.

– CLANS, KINSHIP, AND CLASS –

The modern significance of the clan system was generally approached more cautiously, with most informants conceding the difficulty of tracing connections between contemporary social relations and the old clan structures, seriously weakened in the Highlands after 1745, and eroded in the Lowlands long before that. However, this issue tends to blend into a more general question about the role of kinship and social networks in a relatively small country. Informants frequently cited the likelihood of cross-class encounters within the same extended family, as well as the likelihood of having long-term personal acquaintances with one's political opponents. Gavin joined the SNP in the late 1970s, eventually becoming active in its left-wing. He was raised in London by working-class Scottish parents, and came back to Scotland to study law. Talking about the tendency of middle class voters in Scotland to view as unfair and oppose such things as the Poll

Tax and water privatisation, even though these might be to their economic advantage, he argued:

> It is because of a sense of community, it's not just, you know, a sort of abstract concern with the poor at large. It's because, you know, there has been a fair bit of social mobility, a lot of geographic mobility in Scotland, and you know virtually everyone in Scotland, even if they're a middle-class lawyer living in Glasgow, they'll have a granny living in a croft in the Western Isles, or they'll have a grandfather who's a miner a Ayrshire . . . You know, they'll be concerned about them. It's not that it's completely unselfish and . . . altruistic, for its own sake, its that, you know, Scottish society is such that, we're a small nation, there are lots of cross-overs, the divide, the class divide is not nearly so great, and that, you know, people actually come in contact with . . . You know, if you're living in the stockbroker belt around London . . . it's quite unusual to meet, poor people . . . and you know, you talk about people living in council houses, lot of them have probably never seen a council house apart from on television, or on the train into central London.

Gavin's argument is that a rather dense interlacing of social networks fosters a corporatist attitude in Scotland, such that people see their fortunes as interdependent. Another aspect of this which came up frequently is a strong tendency toward social levelling in interpersonal discourse – a strong contempt for any one who pretends to disassociate themselves from their social origins. The satirical poetry of Robert Burns was frequently offered as a prime example of this attitude. Informants noted that this tendency is summed up in the common, cutting expression 'I kent his faither' ('I knew his father' – he doesn't fool me, I know where he comes from). Catherine, a key figure in a cross-party pro-parliament organisation, touched on many of the central themes of the myth of Scottish egalitarianism. After pointing up the stronger tradition of rural radicalism and anti-landlordism in Scotland as compared with England, she recalled:

> And certainly the Scots on the whole have always had, and this is something I can remember very strongly from childhood, they have had a very strong dislike of pretension, of people putting on airs and graces, no matter how important their position, it was always something that was viewed very critically . . . And part of it was the idea of people getting above themselves, it was a mechanism for maintaining social equality, or at least for limiting social distance, and I think that's always been very powerful in Scotland, both through satire, [and] through ordinary language . . .

I mentioned that many people had pointed out the phrase 'I kent his faither' to me:

Oh yes, and that was very much a way of saying that 'this person, in order to, whatever his pretentiousness now may be, was really one of us, so there's no need for a change in accent'. [laughter] But that's something people always used to listen very carefully for . . . When people had been away from Scotland, migrated and come home, people would listen carefully to their accents, and talk about it later, and they approved people who had kept their accent exactly as it was, and there was a definite disapproval of people who had altered their accents . . . You would hear, I can still hear my aunt, or other people saying 'you'd never know she'd been away for thirty years'.

Obviously this levelling discourse would not be an issue if there were not real anxieties surrounding the possibility of abandoning one's social origins. And it seems certain that the opportunities for careers in the Empire and emigration to England and abroad have provided a real basis for these anxieties. In any case, this appears as the other side of collectivist inter-dependence, a distrust of anyone who attempts to leave. My informants were generally attuned to the two-edged quality of this practice, as both evidence for an egalitarian ethos, and as representing a somewhat stifling and defensive world view. The parallels to tendencies toward symbolic levelling in corporate peasant communities described by ethnographers are striking (e.g., Foster 1965), prompting me to suggest that this social form supports the argument made in Chapter 1 for a correspondence in moral economic discourse between peasant communities and welfare states.

I would also note that the theme of a tradition of levelling, together with the smallness of Scotland and density of its social networks argument, was brought up more often by activists in the SNP than by others. I am not sure how to account for this, but part of the appeal of the SNP to active participants is its smaller scale and more informal style when compared to the much larger and more bureaucratised Labour Party, which of course exists at both the Scottish and British levels, unlike the SNP. Participation in the SNP, beyond being an expression of political convictions about Scotland's fate as a nation, is probably also an expression of a preference for a more small-scale, grassroots, local style of politics. In this light it is perhaps not surprising that questions of social scale might loom larger in the minds of SNP participants.

My informants frequently linked Scottish egalitarianism to the Labour and trade union movements, though often in combination with the themes discussed above. As one might expect, I found these connections were stressed especially by those active in the Labour/trade union wing of the home rule movement, but many in the SNP, especially of the younger, post-1979, left-leaning generation, also highlighted this theme. Campbell was a Labour Party member involved in Scotland United, the cross party (but

Labour dominated) campaign for a new national referendum on the home rule issue in the mid-1990s. His response to the question:

> one of the factors must be size . . . but I think there has been a relatively strong Labour and trade union movement and tradition in Scotland . . . which has probably survived maybe a bit better than our friends in England . . . from the attacks of the Thatcher movement . . . [word unclear]. I think people are more used to being involved, it's not such a surprise, I think, we'd be involved in the trade union, the Miner's Gala, and May Day, or the [anti-] Poll Tax campaign . . . and that's fostered by the fact that we've got a lot of representatives in local government and regional government, and a lot of MPs. But I think generally there is a feeling that we should look after each other . . . I don't know if you were sitting in the south-east of England, that people would necessarily say differently . . . 'cause though the Tories get in, they probably only get in with, what's their vote? maybe forty-two or forty-three per-cent. You're still talking about an electoral system where sixty percent don't want to vote for them . . . I don't know if you can say they [the Tories] accurately reflect people's egalitarianism in England. I tend not to get into debates that argue, well, we're more egalitarian, or we're more into collectivism, or more socialist, or more left, or more radical . . . I don't think that's a productive road to go down. I think we have to say, well, is this what we are? Is this what we're about? . . . I don't know if a comparison . . . would be accurate.

At this point I prompted him, asking if he would see whatever egalitarian values there are in Scotland as coming out of the Labour/socialist tradition:

> Yeah . . . yeah . . . the nationalist tradition as well has grown up a lot in the last few years in my opinion, I think you've got . . a kind of Labour hegemony I suppose in Scotland . . . and the nationalists have kind of swung from earlier on being a relatively right-wing nationalism to a kind of central belt, kind of urban nationalism, which is . . . I mean . . . you probably couldn't even fit a razor blade between a lot of my friends that are in the SNF's policies and my policies, and my ideas about a Labour Party in Scotland . . . not an awful lot of difference, apart from they're bigger on the national question than Labour is and Labour's bigger on the whole economics question, but I mean the two are kind of developing . . .

A characteristic reluctance of those with a Labour pro-parliament perspective to draw strong invidious comparisons between the Scots and the English comes across here. It should also be noted that as an organiser in Scotland United, which sought to foster Labour-SNP co-operation, Campbell would be more inclined than some Labour members to stress the common ground between SNP and Labour. Still, many people in the movement would agree with his comparison on this point. Lynn was a member of the SNP and the Young Scottish Nationalists, an example of the young, more left generation in the party. She had been involved in Scotland United at the start, but dropped out feeling that the moment for that initiative had been lost. She is the first in her family to go to university, where she was studying economics and politics during my fieldwork. Her response to the egalitarianism question indicates both uncertainty about how to account for it, and a strong inclination to place it within a kind of socialist history and iconography:

> It's very difficult to explain actually . . . we'd done this in the first year of university, we couldn't come up with an answer, we all believed Scotland's more egalitarian, but we couldn't really decide why . . . I think it is, we seem to have a more left-of-centre tendency, and a more egalitarian attitude than England, and I think our views against the Poll Tax, and our views against Thatcher kind of demonstrated that. As to why that is, it may be partly due to our kind of defeated . . . our kind of 'Scotland we all feel sorry for ourselves' stage. That might have partly to do with why we stick together more, we see ourselves as kind of in an embattled corner. But again, nobody does anything about it.

I prompt: the lack of political power in Scotland creates a sense of commonality?

> I think it does in a way really. I think we have a kind of common identity, which I think . . . English people seem to have a confused identity, they don't know whether they're talking about England, or they're talking about the UK, or what they're talking about . . . I think Scottish people have an identity which they all relate to, even although they might not support independence, and I think that helps them to kind of, have a common feeling, a common attitude, towards certain problems. I think you can also look at historical things as well . . . [JH: such as?] like the rise of John MacLean in 1915, the rent strikes, anti-conscription for World War One . . . Maybe, we've also been very strong in heavy industries, which does have a tendency to be more trade unionised. It was before, in anyway the case, I was born, that you were in your union, and you were loyal to your union, and you had an identity with the people in that, and you would then campaign, to help the community, and to help the union . . .

This passage brings out two points. First, perhaps a greater willingness than one might find among most Labour activists to draw a strong distinction between the Scots and the English on the question of egalitarianism (e.g., as compared to Campbell). And secondly, a pronounced tendency to root this egalitarianism in the history of trade unionism and socialism, and not in the mythic literary themes focused on by McCrone. The repertoire of historical referents for the Scottish myth are not neatly parcelled out, so that Labour devolutionists draw on Labour movement history, and SNP nationalists draw on some other stock of national imagery. This can work both ways. An interesting tendency is the tradition within the Scottish Communist Party, with its long history of support for home rule, to construct a very long history of class struggle in Scotland. Robert, a senior trade union leader from Dundee who had been in the CP for many years, provides an example. When I put the question of egalitarianism to him, he began not with John MacLean, but with the Reformation and the Kirk explored above, this time viewed from a marxist, class analysis perspective:

> Well, there's the Reformation in Scotland. The Church of Scotland is a very democratic church . . . it's part of . . . it reflects . . . The Church of England is often described as 'the Tory Party at Prayer' – it's created from above, by Henry the Eighth it was convenient, and all that carry on, it created divorces, it created a landed aristocracy . . . they took all the church lands and created a new church, called it the Church of England. But Scotland was entirely different . . . more community based after the Reformation. There certainly was a deal done with the aristocracy. The deal was that they would get the land if they supported the Reformation . . . the Lords of the Congregation.[3] As Burns said 'what a parcel o' rogues in a nation'. And you can see it in the structures of the Church of Scotland. The congregation actually decides whether the minister shall be the minister or not. You know? The Kirk Session, the elders of the Church, who are drawn from the congregation, they have a lot of say. The General Assembly of the Church of Scotland is a very democratic body/forum which is open to resolutions from churches . . . and I think that that reflects part of the difference. Plus, the Scots have had to stick together. There's been a requirement for a certain national unity, in Scotland, that didn't exist, certainly in England. And that was all about defending . . . the fight for a Scottish King, the fight for a Scottish Church, . . . all parts of the fight for a Scottish nation.

J. H. : 'Which is distinct from the English who didn't have the same . . .?'

> They didn't have the same need. I mean, they were the big nation. They were the big imperialist power . . . you know? The Scots were a small nation, and they had to have this degree of unity to defend themselves. And the only people who ever broke ranks were the aristocracy . . . that's why, in a sense, they're excluded from any rights within the debate. I mean the Lord Caithness wouldn't dare suggest, he wouldn't be taken seriously . . . or any of these people, the old aristocracy, they wouldn't be . . . Lord Elgin, the thought . . . I mean these guys were responsible for the Highland Clearances. I mean I doubt if there's ever been an aristocracy that's committed such heinous crimes, against its own people. And the question of the Highland Clearances is still a burning issue in Scotland, you know? It was only a couple of years ago when the Duke of Sutherland's wife, attempted to front the Gaelic festival the Mod. There was an absolute uproar all

over Scotland, that this relic of the dim and distant murky past, where they
actually drove their own people beneath the bloody, well, sea line, on the beaches
. . . you know?[4]

Robert's account is intriguing, in that it offers many of the older and
more romantic images from Scotland's history – the Kirk, the clearances –
while implying a clear historical lineage of class conflict and imperialist
domination running from these events on up to the recent struggle over a
parliament, which he sees in class terms as well.

Many would argue that there is a distinct and separate myth of a socialist
and radical Scotland, often summed up in the specific myth of the 'Red
Clyde', the period of labour unrest (c. 1914–22) on the Clyde which was
mistakenly viewed as a potential Bolshevik uprising by the government of
the time, and helped lead to a strong Scottish Labour showing in the
general election of 1922. Judging from my interviews, it appears to me that
the traditional myth of egalitarianism and this other tradition of Labour/
socialist lore are presently beginning to fuse into one larger myth. This is
not surprising in a political environment in which opposition parties, trade
unions, and the churches have been drawn together in a stance of
opposition to recent governments and political economic trends. And,
as I've already observed, Scottish socialism has strong roots in Scottish
Calvinism. Furthermore, the role of the movement has been one of political
opposition to, and struggle against, the effects of both global capitalism and
Westminster government. In fact the movement's greatest liability is a
tendency to collapse these into one another. Just as the struggles with
Westminster and capital become combined, the Scottish myth is tending to
integrate the histories of the Kirk's struggles with Westminster and kings,
and the Labour movement's struggles with capital, into a larger history of
egalitarian traditions in Scotland.

Although comparisons of class in Scotland and England were often quite
subtle, I was surprised more than once in interviews by jarring references to
'the English class system', as though class were a peculiar English invention
or cultural trait. There seem to be two factors at work here. First, Britain is a
land that maintains a system of peerage, of inherited class statuses. Despite
generations of marxist class analysis disseminated via the labour movement,
this still provides a powerful image of what class is all about. Secondly, there
is the pronounced tendency of working- and middle-class Scots to perceive
the Scottish aristocracy as in fact English or at least thoroughly anglified. In
terms of speech, education, and general socialisation, the Scottish nobility
does strongly resemble the English nobility, to which it has assimilated for
centuries. Thus to the extent that class is conceived in terms of inherited

social rank, rather than relations of production (leaving aside the fact that these often coincide), the egalitarian myth is further bolstered, because a portion of Scotland's elite is, almost by definition, non-Scottish. Moreover, the perception of the peerage-based class system as external and alien (i.e., English), and the reality of increasing control of the Scottish economy by external capital, sets up a reinforcing parallel, in which the superior parties in relations of inequality are located outside of Scotland. The need to examine internal causes of inequality is obviated by the strong perception that the major sources of inequality are external. When pressed, I am sure many of my informants would offer this same critique, but the notion of Scotland as a bulwark of egalitarian values under attack from outside is none the less persistently present as an over-arching background assumption that shapes movement discourse.

Still, it must be conceded that in comparison to England as a whole, Scotland does show stronger support for Labour, and a tendency to support higher levels of taxation in order to maintain the redistributive functions and key institutions of the welfare state. Middle-class voting districts such as Bearsden in Glasgow, which would have produced Tory majorities in the south throughout the 1980s and 1990s, were safe Labour seats. To some extent these can be considered indices of egalitarianism. But they also reflect a corporatist conception of Scotland's welfare, stemming from the strong integrative role of dominant bureaucratic institutions throughout modern history, and the tendency of these institutions to define and address social problems within a Scottish context.

Finally, I must note that the notion of Scottish egalitarianism was frequently confirmed to me by informants involved in the movement who were English or otherwise not Scottish by origin. In some cases this seemed to me to indicate a process of 'going native', acquiring the perspective of one's adoptive community. But this 'outside confirmation' happened frequently enough that I am inclined to give it some weight. It would seem that, even if the actual distributions of wealth and opportunity are as unequal in Scotland as they are in England, the hegemony of the Scottish ideal of the redistributive welfare state is palpable, and appealing to those from England and elsewhere who share that ideal. This, indeed, is basic to my own interest in this movement.

– NOTES –

1. I share Lindsay Paterson's (1994: 25) discomfort with the connotations of 'false consciousness' that the word myth evokes in this context. I have preserved it, however, precisely because it is often used by Scottish commentators, and by

many of my informants, indicating a complex attitude of self-questioning that I think it is important to highlight.

2. For instance, see Linklater and Denniston (1992: 4–5); McCrone, et al. (1989: 3–4); Midwinter, et al. (1991: 7–9); and Paterson (1994: 25).

3. The Lords of the Congregation were an alliance of nobles who supported the cause of the Reformation in Scotland and the developing Presbyterian Church.

4. The Sutherlands are historically associated with one of the most violent and brutal episodes in the Clearances.

CHAPTER 9

A Covenanted People

The Rally to Recall Scotland's Parliament out of Adjournment, described in Chapter 1, culminated in a ritual enactment that was deeply rooted in Scottish political traditions. After the speeches were over, the representatives of political parties and campaigning groups present on the platform all signed the Recall Declaration, which pledged the signatories to continue to work for a Scottish parliament and was explicitly cast as a reaffirmation of the Democracy Declaration of the 12 December Demonstration almost a year before. After the signing, all those present on Calton Hill were led in a collective recitation of the declaration. In one respect, this political ritual would seem to have little significance beyond reaffirming a sense of solidarity among those variously bound together in a common cause. The act itself constituted no concrete political leverage; it did not alter the political landscape. But it takes on richer meanings when we regard it as one small moment in a much deeper political tradition, a tradition which is alive, and which bears upon and frames nationalist politics in Scotland.

The crux of this tradition is a key social institution, the covenant. Here institution is meant in the sense of an established form of practice, a formalised way of doing things, as with ceremony and ritual. The covenant in this context should be understood as having a powerful metaphorical dimension, and as the underlying structure of a tradition of political thought and action. These are aspects I will discuss in more detail in the next chapter. A fuller sense of what I mean by 'covenant', and 'covenant tradition', can only be conveyed by the review of historical examples that follows, but it is useful to begin with a basic definition. Minimally, covenants create or reaffirm social bonds of common membership in a community, and mutual expectations for community members. In the history of Scottish politics, covenants are not entered into constantly, but usually at certain junctures that are defined by uncertainty, anxiety, risk and conflict. Covenants are made when solidarity and common purpose are threatened, and are often concerned with articulating those threats, with voicing concern for an untenable state of affairs. Sometimes already existing covenants are broken. So to consider this tradition thoroughly we have to look both at explicit acts of testifying to bonds of membership in a common cause, and at acts of protest and petition framed within contexts that are understood by the social actors as, in some sense, already covenanted. In other words, some of the covenant events we will consider emphasise creating and consolidating new ties, but others, perhaps less immediately recognisable as part of the same tradition, emphasise the betrayal of agreements, and the assertion of neglected rights. These are two sides of the same social form; the fundamental form of the covenant is that of a community asserting its terms of membership within a larger community. One of my goals in what follows is to elaborate this twofold conception of the covenant tradition, in which agreement and disagreement, consent and dissent, continually implicate each other.

It will quickly become apparent that my use of the term covenant is synecdochic, using the paradigmatic case to name a larger and more diverse tendency. Thus the discussion that follows will feature several variations on this contractual metaphor, but especially three types of covenant events: Covenants, Claims of Right, and Declarations. These three are important because each of them designates a kind of political act or practice that has been prominent in twentieth-century Scottish nationalism, involving more or less conscious historical allusions to earlier events in Scottish history. I would stress however that I see these three types as particular variations on a common theme: the broader, 'double' sense of covenant outlined above. Most of these covenant events have already been mentioned or discussed in their historical context in earlier chapters, so I will keep a fairly narrow focus here on the basic aims and structuring of the covenants in question.

– HISTORICAL BACKGROUND –

– THE DECLARATION OF ARBROATH –

Any discussion of this kind must begin with the famous Declaration of Arbroath of 1320. As discussed in Chapter 5, the years from 1286 to 1371 involved extensive rivalries around political leadership in Scotland and protracted 'Wars of Independence' with England. The Declaration was actually a letter to Pope John XXII from the 'barons and freeholders' of Scotland, petitioning him to intercede on their behalf in the ongoing war with England. The Papacy desired peace within Christendom so that military energies could be directed against Islam, and tended to side with the greater power, England, in prosecuting a resolution of the conflict. A masterful work of diplomatic rhetoric, the Declaration does several things. First it asserts Scotland's antiquity and long-standing sovereignty as a Christian nation 'called to faith' by the apostle Saint Andrew. Then it recounts Scotland's depredations and unfair treatment at the hands of the English kings Edward I and his son Edward II. This is followed by the most frequently quoted section, in which the noblemen praise their Lord and protector King Robert the Bruce, and assert their allegiance to him, while at the same time declaring that if he were to betray their cause and surrender to the English, they would depose him and replace him with another:

> for, as long as but a hundred of us remain alive, never will we on any conditions be brought under English rule. It is in truth not for glory, nor riches, nor honours that we are fighting, but for freedom – for that alone, which no honest man gives up but with life itself. (Fergusson 1970: 9)

The letter concludes by beseeching the Pope to intercede and urge the covetous and bullying English to desist, so that all parties may be more able to devote themselves to the Crusades. They do not hesitate to remind the Pontiff that posterity will remember him according to his success in securing the frontiers of Christendom. The Declaration in fact had little effect on the Pope's position on the conflict with England but has been remembered and kept alive by later generations as an early testament to Scottish political consciousness.

The document, with its assertion of the right of 'the community of the realm' to choose its own king, is sometimes cited as a precocious example of notions of popular sovereignty and the nation-state in Europe, emerging, as it did, well before the modern period. There is an identifiable strain of political and theological thought in mediæval and early modern Scotland that emphasises the idea that kingship rests on popular support. This interpretation is problematic, however, both because similarly early declarations of this sort can be found elsewhere in Europe, and because the document was produced by a feudal elite which claimed to represent the 'realm', but not through any process resembling modern mass democracy. Properly speaking it was simply a diplomatic letter, the term 'declaration' becoming attached to it at a later date. And yet, it fits into our covenant paradigm. It is reasonable to assume that those who participated in or sanctioned its drafting, many of whom signed it, considered themselves thereby bound to the other members of the group who helped produce the letter, and obligated to live up to its claims as far as possible. The signatories of the letter are bound one to another in protest, while simultaneously assuming the legitimacy of the larger world of the Church within which their complaint is being expressed. Though it would be anachronistic literally to consider this a covenant like those of the seventeenth century, nonetheless, the twofold nature of the covenant outlined in the working definition above is evident in this case.

– THE CUSTOM OF BONDING –

The classic covenants of the seventeenth century had roots in the much older custom of bonding mentioned in Chapter 5. This practice of formalising rights and obligations between parties through a written and signed contract was widespread from the fifteenth century to the beginning of the seventeenth century. Some bonds, usually between lords and heads of leading families within the lord's domain, were called 'bonds of manrent' in which the lesser man pledged 'manrent' – good counsel, military service, and any other services or tributes particular to the relationship – in exchange for 'maintenance' from the lord, including legal and political protection and other forms of support in times of need. Although the point was not explicitly stated in the bonds until the sixteenth century, the lesser man apparently had the power to commit his subordinate kin and his descendants to the bond (Wormald 1985: 52–5). This type of bond is clearly similar to the standard feudal relationship of fealty, but distinctive in its written form and its relatively late development (1442 is the year of the earliest surviving document).

There were other types of bonds which formed ties horizontally between peers, such as nobles, lairds and burgesses, which helped create and maintain a diverse array of social arrangements, and that clearly diverge from the standard model of feudalism. These might involve alliances in response to some political or economic threat or opportunity – such as a political faction of nobles backing a particular contender to the throne, or a coalition of burgesses responding to a threat of economic competition. Furthermore, bonds could either be between two individuals, or among a collectivity of signatories. Thus there were 'bonds of friendship' which 'were made between two people, or sometimes a small group, and were concerned with local affairs' (Wormald 1985: 374), and this form shaded into another that involved larger numbers of people, and was usually concerned with addressing or staving off some political or religious crisis (ibid.: 402–12). For instance between 1556 and 1562 there was a rash of religious bonds among various nobles, gentry, and congregations, in support of the new reformed religion. One of these, the Negative Confession (or King's Confession) that would later make up the first portion of the National Covenant of 1638, is commonly viewed as a bond of this type (Burrell 1964: 11).

Jenny Wormald argues that in Scottish historiography an exaggerated dichotomy has been set up between private/kin based and public/state-based modes of law. She rejects the conventional notion of lawless highland clans engaged in endless bloodfeuds on the one hand, and state-making lowland Calvinists and kings, bringing godly discipline and absolutist government on the other. She suggests that what these later state-making forces in fact encountered was a complex mixing of feudal and kin-based relations throughout the Highlands and Lowlands, and that bloodfeuds and bonds were a part of a working system for the local regulation and constant re-negotiation social relations (cf. Stevenson 1980: 9–10, 20). Drawing on Max Gluckman's notion of the 'peace in the feud' (1973: 1–26), that standing relations of conflict tend to create stabilising arrangements of alliances, Wormald argues that bonding was a major part of the indigenous politico-jural system, which grew up in the chronic absence of a strong centralised monarchy in Scotland from the late thirteenth century onwards. This system presented a serious obstacle to new attempts at centralisation, once the requisite forces were at work in the century following the Reformation, and particularly after the Union of Crowns under James VI/I in 1603 (Wormald 1980: 55–6; 1991: 35–6; 1985: 115–36).

In the latter half of the sixteenth century, both the Kirk and crown were evidently attuned to the importance of this idiom. James seems to have seen the practice as both a threat and a useful tool of statecraft. Thus in 1585 he promoted an act of parliament that forbade the making of private bands, recognising these as possible instruments of sedition (Stevenson 1973: 86). Conversely, James also used banding to further his political program. The most striking example of this is the 'Band and Statute of Incolmkill (Iona)' of 1609, a part of the broader effort to pacify and subdue the Gaelic political and cultural networks that spanned the Irish Sea, the same political agenda that led to the plantation of Ulster. This band was targeted at the highland clans in the western regions of Scotland in and around Argyllshire. Mackie provides a nice vignette:

> A powerful army appeared in Mull under Andrew Stewart, Lord Ochiltree, who enjoyed the co-operation of Andrew Knox, Bishop of the Isles. The chiefs were invited to a conference in the Castle of Aros, lured aboard ship to hear a sermon, kidnapped, and confined to various prisons. Under this compulsion they accepted next year from the Bishop 'the band and Statutes of Incolmkill (Iona)' which, though largely concerned with the establishment of the church and the improvement of morality, made each chief responsible for the conduct of his own clan. (Mackie 1978: 190)

More specifically, the band prohibited the support of bards, a hereditary office among the clans which carried with it the responsibility for maintaining historical and genealogical records (Mitchison 1990: 15–16), and also 'tried to insist that highland chiefs should come to the lowlands at regular intervals, and (in the re-issue of 1616) learn English as a qualification for inheritance' (Wormald 1991: 164). Thus we find James imposing a band from above, as part of a program of coercive social engineering, in which bonds are disengaged from their more embedded social function, and reintroduced in an altered form, in the project of state-making and consolidation.

– THE COVENANT TRADITION –

– THE CLASSIC COVENANTS –

As related in Chapter 5, the famous covenants of 1638 and (to a lesser degree) 1643 were responses to the absolutist and anglicising tendencies of King Charles I's government in London, and more particularly to the power of Anglican bishops grafted onto the Presbyterian church structure from above, and to the threat of royal reappropriation of church lands acquired by the nobility in the Reformation. However, it was Charles' 1637 attempt to impose a new common prayer book, which basically prescribed Anglican liturgical forms, that triggered the making of the National Covenant in 1638. Stevenson describes the event:

> The national covenant was first signed in Greyfriars Kirk on 28 February. The lairds assembled there were addressed by Loudoun [a noble] and Alexander Henderson [a minister], after which Johnston of Warriston [a lawyer] read out the covenant. A few doubts raised by some of the lairds having been answered, the nobles arrived and signed, followed by the lairds. The next day three hundred ministers and commissioners for the burghs signed, followed on the two succeeding days by the people of Edinburgh. It was decided that copies of the covenant should be provided for 'ilk shire, balzierie, stewartry, or distinct judicatorie' to be signed by the principal persons of the area, while copies for each parish should be signed by all who were admitted to the sacrament there. John Livingston rode to London with letters and copies of the covenant which were delivered to friends of the covenanters at court by Eleazer Borthwick. After the signing of the covenant most of the covenanters who had gathered in Edinburgh returned home, many of them taking copies of the covenant with them for signature locally. Before they dispersed it was arranged that six nobles and a few commissioners from each shire should remain to await the king's reaction to the covenant, and that elections should be held to chose commissioners for future meetings. Each parish or burgh was ordered to keep lists of those who signed the covenant and those who refused to do so. (Stevenson 1973: 83–4, my insertions)

Although initiated by the nobility and the developing Kirk-based elite, who no doubt used coercive measures in some cases to gain support, the National Covenant had a strong base of popular support (Stevenson 1988: 2). This Covenant was an amplification of an earlier document (referred to above) instigated by the young King James VI in 1581 known as the Negative Confession, 'the signatories of which bound themselves to uphold the true religion of the church of Scotland and oppose popery and superstition' (Stevenson 1973: 82). That document, which members of James's royal household had been required to sign, responded to fears of plots by noble factions to align with France and Spain for the restoration of Roman Catholicism. The National Covenant, quoting this earlier document in full, and citing numerous acts of parliament, called upon Charles to follow his father's established precedent, while also insisting that the signatories were still loyal to the Crown, and asserting that any changes in worship must be approved by free assemblies and parliaments. Thus Charles was presented with an earnest and urgent request to enter into this covenant with the ruling class and the people of Scotland for the common defence of the 'true Reformed religion', but the document to be signed clearly sought to demarcate his powers, especially in regard to the Presbyterian Church.

The ensuing battle of wills and power was complex – at first Charles outlawed the signatories, then he recanted and agreed to call the first General Assembly of the Church of Scotland in almost twenty years, which then struck back by abolishing bishops. From there the situation quickly slid into civil war. The Solemn League and Covenant of 1643 was basically a tactical move in this war. Its stated purpose was a pledge of mutual support between the Scottish Covenanters and the English parliament (largely Presbyterian but not nearly as zealous as the Scots) in the cause of preserving the reformed religion and opposing 'popery' and 'prelacy' (i.e., the bishops) throughout the three kingdoms of England, Ireland and Scotland. In fact however, it was an expedient device for the English parliament to enlist the Scottish armies in their struggle against Charles and his faction of noble supporters. Many of the Covenanters had vainly seen this alliance as one that would lead to a humbled King Charles administering his kingdoms through a unified Presbyterian Church, and were sorely disappointed to see Charles beheaded by the English parliament, and their own country subsequently pacified by Cromwell's army.

The covenanting tradition continued after the Cromwellian interregnum (1650–60), and some of the best remembered folk heroes of the covenanting period come from the latter half of the seventeenth century. But by this time it was a substantially transformed phenomenon. The last band of Covenanters still fighting against the English in 1649, called the Remonstrants, was a kind of extremist sect with its own church and army, committed to struggle against all odds while royalist sympathisers and defeated Covenanters adjusted to the new political reality. The Restoration under Charles II after 1660 brought with it new attempts to impose religious conformity on Scotland, often under harsh military discipline, but though outlawed, dissenting followers of the covenanting tradition carried on in secret, particularly in the south-west of Scotland. The later covenanting uprisings of 1666 and 1679, responding to these pressures, had a decidedly populist base of marginalised and sectarian groups from the most disempowered segments of society, which often engaged in conflicts not just with the state but with their more immediate social superiors (Stevenson 1988: 59–69; Kiernan 1989).

The striking feature of the classic covenants is the way in which allegiances to church and crown, God and king, were played off against one another, and the way the covenants were used to assert the authority of religion, church, and God over the king, while at the same time trying to forswear rebellion. The space and voice for the sovereignty of the developing kirk-based Scottish elite, representing (for better or worse) a Scottish populace, was created and opened up by exploiting the tensions between notions of divine and royal sovereignty. It is this pattern of asserting a bond that is at once social, political, religious, and moral, while by the same stroke rendering it problematic and in need of re-negotiation, that is so characteristic of the covenant.

– ON DEVIL'S PACTS –

There is a darker side to these religious transformations of the bonding idiom. Along with the growing concern with covenants between God, king, and people, there developed a preoccupation with witches' pacts with the devil. The later sixteenth and seventeenth centuries were punctuated by periodic and extremely virulent witch-hunts with major peaks or 'national panics' in 1591, 1597, 1629, 1649–50, and 1661–2, and with a rate of execution ten times higher than in England. Although there is some correspondence to other upheavals of the time – plague, famine, war – there is no simple correlation. The period was one of constant dislocation, and the hunts, for the most part, appear not to have been predictable reactions to specific social stimuli, but rather a part of the ongoing political processes and the general atmosphere of anxiety and unrest (Larner 1981: 60–79).

The variety of confessions suggests that those accused of being witches, about 80 per cent women, included hapless village marginals scapegoated for the misfortunes of others, active practitioners of folk-medicine/magic, and some who may have been involved in an ideology that was consciously oppositional to the kirk and crown. In any case, all were caught up in the Scottish legal mechanism which, because of its heritage from Roman law of provisions for extracting confessions and further accusations through torture, was particularly prone to oppressive brutality when placed in the hands of the king and the kirk elders in their efforts to consolidate their respective power bases. James VI/I gave this process a major boost with his book *Daemonologie* (1597), a scholarly proof of the existence of witches. In addition, *Newes From Scotland* (1591, authorship uncertain), offered a glorifying account of the King's brush with death, along with his new bride, on board a ship in a storm called forth by a conspiratorial coven of witches at North Berwick in 1590. This seems to have functioned as propaganda to help justify his often strong-armed political tactics. The North Berwick witch trial stimulated the first major panic in 1591, and lent legitimacy to the Kirk's intensified efforts to seek out witches in subsequent decades (Wormald 1991: 168-9; Smout 1972: 184-92).

Christine Larner points out that the demonic pact early on was regarded by the Scottish judiciary as the single most essential element in indictment. In the confessions, repeatedly, it is the making of the pact, and the naming of other members of the pact, that is central (Larner 1981: 145). Thus one indictment from 1661 of five women and one man reads:

> ilk and ane of you have shaken off all fear of God, Reverence and regard to the Lawes of this kingdome, hes betaken yourselves to the service of Satan, the enimie of your salvations entered in a Covenant and paction with him whairby you renounced you baptismes and interest in jesus Christ engadged yourselves to be the devills servants, and suffered your bodies quilke aught to have been temples to the Holie ghost to be polluted defiled by suffering him to have carnall copulation with you. (Larner 1981: 146-7)

As this passage suggests, there was often a mixing of the idioms of covenants and pacts, and Larner points out that

> [a] feature of the witch-beliefs that was particularly strong in Calvinism was the idea of Covenant. Scottish theology which was strongly rooted in the Old Testament made the idea of a covenanted people peculiarly its own. It was reflected elsewhere in Europe in the rising secular concept of the social compact, but in Scottish hands it was firmly theocratic. The covenanted people were God's people, firmly bound to him in a special relationship by a special promise . . . The Demonic Pact was therefore, for the Scots, a particularly horrific inversion. The term 'covenant' was frequently used in the final indictments and the confessions as a synonym for the Pact. (ibid.: 172)

I would suggest that if popular conceptions of the covenant were indebted to popular conceptions of bonds, and conceptions of covenants and demonic pacts were also interrelated, at least as promulgated by the Kirk, then it is likely that the demonic pact also, at least implicitly, resonated with the notion of bonding (cf. ibid.: 148). Apart from whatever threat, real or imagined, that witches may have posed for the authority of kirk and crown, they were portrayed as people involved in a subaltern version of bonding (normally a male preserve) entering into contracts with the devil, rendering services to him in exchange for relief from chronic conditions of poverty and want, in exchange, that is, for 'maintenance'.

– THE CLAIMS OF RIGHT –

The Claim of Right of 1689 stated the terms under which the 'estates of the kingdom of Scotland' would accept William (of Orange) and Mary, already made King and Queen of England in the 'Glorious Revolution', as Scottish monarchs. Much of the document is taken up with listing the faults of the recently deposed Catholic King James VII, concluding that

> Therefore the Estates of the Kingdom of Scotland, Find and Declare that King James the Seventh being a professed Papist, did assume the Regal power, and acted as King, without ever taking the oath required by law, and hath by the advice of evil and wicked counsellors, invaded the fundamental constitution of the Kingdom, and altered it from a legal limited Monarchy, to an arbitrary despotick Power, and hath exercised the same, to the subversion of the Protestant religion, and the violation of the laws and liberties of the Kingdom, inverting all the ends of Government, whereby he hath forefaulted the right to the Crown, and the Throne is become vacant. (Donaldson 1970: 255)

The rest of the document states what the Scots require of their king: that he be Protestant, that he cannot impose taxes without the parliament's consent, that the royal powers are not absolute but limited, and that 'for the redress of all grievances, and for the amending and preserving of the laws, Parliaments ought to be frequently called, and allowed to sit, and the freedom of speech and debate secured to the members' (ibid.: 257). These conditions being met, the Claim of 1689 resolves that William and Mary be declared king and queen of Scotland.

The Claim of Right of 1842 was an episode in the Great Disruption that split the Church of Scotland in two. As related in Chapter 6, this Claim was drafted by the General Assembly of the Kirk, then dominated by the Evangelical faction, and was addressed to parliament. The immediate spur to the Claim was the Court of Session's overturning of the General Assembly's Veto Act of 1834, which had given the adult male members of the congregations the right to reject ministers appointed by local patrons, who were usually landlords. The Kirk then appealed to the House of Lords, which declared the Veto Act illegal. This issue had been a point of conflict since the Union of 1707, and before that between the Scottish parliament and several kings. At the base of the conflict was the right of the state to interfere in church affairs, a Church which I have argued functioned very much as the domestic wing of the state in Scotland. The Claim, which obviously harked back to the Claim of Right of 1689, was 'an intemperate document' (Checkland and Checkland 1989: 121) and 'a tremendous denunciation of patronage and the actions of Parliament and the Court of Sessions . . . [which] demanded in effect that the General Assembly and not the civil courts be the arbiter of the terms on which the Kirk held her rights and property' (Mitchison 1970: 385). This was more than the British state could concede, and instead led to the dividing and political weakening of the Kirk when the most ardent Evangelicals made the dramatic gesture of withdrawing from the established Kirk and setting up the Free Church of Scotland in 1843.

– MODERN NATIONALISM –

The Scottish Covenant, drafted in 1949, came out of ex-SNP leader John MacCormick's efforts to organise a national, non-party political movement in favour of the establishment of a Scottish parliament. In other words, he and the others involved in this effort sought both to broaden the consensus around the issue of constitutional change, and to create a testament to that consensus. The full text of the Scottish Covenant read:

> We the people of Scotland who subscribe this Engagement, declare our belief that reform in the constitution of our country is necessary to secure good government in accordance with our Scottish traditions and to promote the spiritual and economic welfare of our nation.
>
> We affirm that the desire for such reform is both deep and widespread through the whole community, transcending all political differences and sectional interests, and we undertake to continue united in purpose for this achievement.
>
> With that end in view we solemnly enter into this Covenant whereby we pledge ourselves, in all loyalty to the Crown and within the framework of the United Kingdom, to do everything within our power to secure for Scotland a Parliament with adequate legislative authority in Scottish affairs.

This effort was notable both for its broad appeal, and its minimal impact on Westminster politics. In a parliamentary system where the electoral success of a party organisation is the key to influence, the Covenant was easily ignored. More generally, the time was not ripe for such a radical alteration of the UK constitution. Still, it was a national affair well remembered by many of my informants, some of whom related vivid impressions of the drama and seriousness of the movement. What should be noted is that just as in the seventeenth-century covenants, the Scottish Covenant of 1949 stressed loyalty to the Crown and 'the framework of the United Kingdom' while also asserting the sovereignty of popular opinion in Scotland, and raising a challenge to the constitutional status quo.

In Chapter 3 we saw how the Campaign for a Scottish Assembly (CSA) organised the group of eminent Scots who drafted and published a report to the CSA called the Claim of Right in 1988, as a way of publicising and furthering the cause of a Scottish Constitutional Convention. In 1989 the document was published in an edited volume along with articles of commentary written from various perspectives on the issue.[1] Parts of the Claim were photocopied from that book and used as a focus of discussion in the Adult Learning Project's Democracy Group (see Chapter 4), and many of the basic arguments and debating points it sets out are heard frequently in movement circles. In other words it is a document which has been disseminated and I believe has had a significant influence on the discourse of the movement, or at least effectively summarises much of that discourse. The Claim is organised into three parts, the last two outlining the mechanics of setting up a constitutional convention and how it might work. The first part entitled 'The Need for Change in Scottish Government', carries the main thrust of the document's argument justifying the entire pro-parliamentary project. It is worth examining in some detail.

In the Introduction the authors point out that they 'frequently use the word "English" where the word "British" is conventionally used' (Constitutional Steering Committee 1989: 13), precisely to highlight the English bias of the UK constitution, so easily obscured by the term British. Section Two discusses the 'essential facts of Scottish history' (ibid.), asserting the unambiguous continuity of Scottish nationhood and culture from before the time of Union down to the present. But the Treaty of Union of 1707 is seen as inherently flawed:

> 2.6 The matters on which the Treaty guaranteed the Scots their own institutions and policies represented the bulk of civil life and government at the time; the Church, the Law and Education. However, there was never any mechanism for enforcing respect for the terms of the Treaty of Union. Many of its major provisions have been violated, and its spirit has never affected the huge areas of government which have evolved since. The say of Scotland in its own government has diminished, is diminishing and ought to be increased. (Constitutional Steering Committee 1989: 15)

Anticipating the counter-argument that Scotland has an entire governmental office and a Secretary of State devoted to it, they suggest that:

2.7 . . . The Secretary of State may be either Scotland's man in the Cabinet or the Cabinet's man in Scotland, but in the last resort, he is invariably the latter. Today, he can be little else, since he must impose on Scotland policies against which an overwhelming majority have voted. (ibid.)

Having shifted to the present situation in the third section, they argue that the various offices and procedures designed to deal with Scottish business via Westminster are ineffective. The most fundamental issue here is that if they want to have any input into Westminster, Scots are obliged to vote for political parties whose agendas are framed by British rather than Scottish concerns. Furthermore,

3.2 . . . the political arithmetic of the United Kingdom means that Scots are constantly exposed to the risk of having matters of concern only to them prescribed by a government against which they have voted not narrowly but overwhelmingly. (ibid.: 16)
[. . .]
3.8 We are not aware of any other instance, at least in what is regarded as the democratic world, of a territory which has a distinctive corpus of law and an acknowledged right to distinctive policies but yet has no body expressly elected to safeguard and supervise these. The existing machinery of Scottish government is an attempt either to create an illusion or to achieve the impossible. (ibid.: 17)

The fourth section moves from Scotland's political frustrations to the root of the problem: 'The English Constitution – An Illusion of Democracy'. Here the widely held view that the English/British constitution is dangerously antiquated and backward is trenchantly expressed in the opening paragraphs:

4.1 The English constitution provides for only one source of power; the Crown-in-Parliament. That one source is now mainly embodied in the Prime Minister, who has appropriated almost all the royal prerogatives. She/he appoints Ministers who, with rare exceptions, can be dismissed at will, and has further formidable powers of patronage. Because of party discipline and the personal ambition of members the consequence is that, so far from Parliament controlling the Executive (which is the constitutional theory) it is the Prime Minister as head of the Executive who controls Parliament.

4.2 Historically, the power of Parliament evolved as a means of curbing the arbitrary power of Monarchs. We have now reached the point where the Prime Minister has in practice a degree of arbitrary power few, if any, English and no

Scottish Monarchs have rivalled. Yet he or she still hides behind the fiction of royal sanction and the pretence of deference to Parliament to give legitimacy to a concentration of power without parallel in western society. The American constitution was framed largely with a view to making such a development impossible. Even the centralised and Executive biased French constitution distributes power, demonstrated by the recent balance between the President and the Prime Minister there. (ibid.: 18)

Section Five confronts the most fundamental objections that are often raised to the idea of an assembly/parliament. To the standard complaint that an assembly would put Scotland, like it or not, on a slippery-slope toward independence, the authors reply that this line of reasoning is an insult to the Scots, who will be perfectly able to decide democratically once they have a parliament whether they want more, or are satisfied (ibid.: 20–1). The next point is perhaps the most serious, and too lightly dismissed by the authors (cf. Fry 1989: 96). It addresses the 'West Lothian Question', so named because first raised in parliament in the 1970s by the anti-devolutionist Labour MP for West Lothian (in Scotland), Tam Dalyell. In short, it points out the anomaly of a system where Scots would continue to have representation in the UK parliament, with Scottish MPs voting on matters affecting England, while the English MPs would have no input into the Scottish parliament. The only way to restore symmetry to the political system would be all-around federalism, for which there is little impetus in England. The authors' rejoinder:

5.3.3 The United Kingdom is a political artefact put together at English insistence. If it is to continue, it must work for its living and justify its existence. It is for the English to decide how to govern themselves, but they must allow the continuing improvement of Scottish government. If they dislike the Parliamentary anomaly created by a Scottish Assembly, the remedy is in their own hands – a federal system. But the anomaly would be of practical effect only occasionally and temporarily. The defects of Scottish government are fundamental and continuing. (Constitutional Steering Committee 1989: 21)

To the charges that a parliament would simply add another tier of government that would require more money from tax payers they counter that '[t]his is a misunderstanding. An Assembly would not add to government, it would transfer from London to Scotland that part of government affecting Scotland only' (ibid.: 22). They further point out that the organs and costs of an administration already exist in the Scottish Office.

5.5.6 . . . The purpose of an Assembly is to give this administration better and more thorough political supervision, and to create policies based on Scottish needs rather than cosmetically adapted from London dictates. Only the elected members and their immediate staff would be additional to present administrative costs. (ibid.: 23)

Regarding the more general effects of an assembly on the economy, the authors suggest that it would be more attuned to local economic conditions and needs that get submerged in the larger British economy. To the charge that such an assembly would drive away business (presumably because it would, in keeping with the social democratic bent in Scotland, impose higher taxes and more regulations) they counter that:

> 5.6.9 . . . [l]arger businesses will stay in Scotland if the conditions for a healthy economy prevail. Smaller businesses, with stronger roots in the local economy have a greater incentive to stay. (ibid.: 25).
> [. . .]
> 5.6.12 . . . In general, business congregates where it can find politicians to lend it an ear and fight its cause. Scottish Assembly Members would know that their prospects of re-election depended at least in part on what they were judged to have done for the Scottish economy. If the close propinquity of politicians frightened off business the City of London would have decamped long ago. (ibid.: 26)

This is possibly the least convincing section of the Claim, which seems to put a brave face on genuinely thorny matters. It would probably be more accurate to say that larger businesses will stay in Scotland if the conditions for realising profit prevail, and the health of smaller businesses tends to depend on the presence of larger ones. One could also argue that the Tory party is so resented in Scotland precisely because it has lent an ear and fought the cause of business. In short, given the current world economy, for a Scottish parliament to create an economic atmosphere that is 'business friendly' without simply echoing neoliberal policies, may be a serious challenge. Be that as it may, Part One of the Claim ends on a more philosophical note, making a keen point:

> 7.2 The Government claims to act in the name of freedom and choice [i.e., the free market]. There are two kinds of choice; choice from what is offered, and choice of what is to be offered. Only the latter is effective choice. The crucial question is, 'Who edits the choices that are to be offered?' The ordinary citizen's power to edit the choices that are to be offered can be exercised better through elective institutions than in any other way. (ibid.: 28, my insertion)

Part One concludes:

> 7.5 There is a profound hypocrisy in saying that the Scots should stand on their own two feet [a reference to Conservative accusations of a 'dependency culture' in

Scotland] while simultaneously denying them the management of their own political affairs, and that denial is clear deprivation of choice for Scots. Scots can stand on their own feet only by refusing to accept the constitution which denies them the power to do so. (ibid.: 29; my insertion)

I have discussed this portion of the Claim at length because it is one of the most comprehensive statements on the whole subject. Unlike the Scottish Covenant, which was more a general statement of dissent, this was an elaborated yet succinct critique of the situation, including a detailed list of grievances.

As we can see, all three Claims of Right explicitly address basic constitutional issues, with varying degrees of success. In contrast to the Covenants discussed above, they do not seek so much to constitute a religious and/or political community as to speak and negotiate for one that is unambiguously established. But their assertion of rights for those communities (Scotland, the Kirk) takes place in a framework which assumes a larger community (Britain, the UK) in which the former are embedded. Taken together, chronologically (1638, 1643, 1689, 1842, 1949, 1988), these covenants and claims also highlight the shift of focus in conflicts over sovereignty, from one between Kirk and crown, to one between the modern managerial elite, ensconced in Scottish local government and civil society, and the UK parliament, dominated by the Prime Minister and the ruling party.

Obviously the referential links between recent events and those in a more distant past help produce a rhetoric of historical continuity, giving modern grievances a sense of historical depth and weight. But it is important not to infer that rhetoric replaces reality. There really is a history of ongoing, episodic conflicts and negotiations between Scotland and England, or Scotland and Britain – one that has been recurrently expressed in culturally patterned ways. Before elaborating this point in the next chapter, I will consider one last example in the covenant tradition.

As we have seen, the text which was signed and invoked at the Rally to Recall Scotland's Parliament was based upon an earlier one, called the 'Democracy Declaration of Scotland on the Occasion of the Holding of the European Summit at Edinburgh'. Drafted by the group Common Cause, it was read at a rally held in Edinburgh, scheduled to coincide with the presence of representatives from the EU member states attending the European Summit on 11 and 12 December 1992. The Democracy Declaration briefly outlines the argument of the 1988 Claim of Right, but is addressed to the European visitors:

A warm welcome to Scotland, one of Europe's oldest nations. The Edinburgh Summit is the latest in a long history binding Scotland to its European neighbours

. . . We recognise that on the Summit Agenda is the issue of the definition and implementation of the principle of subsidiarity. Let it be brought to your attention that subsidiarity – decision-making at the level closest to the people concerned – is being denied to the people of Scotland by the British state. It limits subsidiarity to relations between London and Brussels and seeks to remain the most centralised state in the European Community
[. . .]
Therefore, we call upon the people of Europe and the Government leaders at the Summit to recognise Scotland's right to national self-determination – the right to our own Parliament. We have voted for this right, we have asked for a referendum – now we appeal to you to raise our claim with the British Government as a matter of principle.

We have now an historic opportunity of a peaceful and democratic assertion of our national right. There is no issue of violence or ethnicity. For us rights are a means as well as an end in itself. The recognition of our right causes no harm to any other nation or people. We invite the President of the European Council to consider our case by meeting a representative delegation from Scotland.

At the heart of our nation's history, at the centre of Europe's future, lies rule by consent of the people. The call of our times is that of democratic renewal. When the eyes of the world are upon our capital, Edinburgh, we are confident that the peoples and governments of Europe will recognise the appeal of its host nation. We therefore raise our demand without fear or favour – SCOTLAND DEMANDS DEMOCRACY.

The striking aspect here is that this statement operates within a still larger framework than the Claims of Right. It attempts an 'end run' around UK level politics by taking the complaint to the European Union, as a kind of higher court of appeals. It does this by stressing a sense of shared history and community throughout Europe. Once again it both 'imagines' the community while at the same time articulating grievances within that community. The Coalition for Scottish Democracy reinforced this declaration by delivering a petition to the European parliament that made the same request for recognition. But as I have already suggested, both the Declaration and the petition have had little effect, member states being reluctant to interfere in each other's internal politics, and the European parliament being a relatively weak body in relation to the Council of Ministers. Nonetheless, the symbolism deployed in this event indicates the growing tendency to think about and address the problem of Scottish autonomy in a European framework, as not simply detaching from Britain, but 'getting on board' Europe.[2]

While the term 'declaration' is certainly less distinctive than either the Covenants or the Claims of Right, I believe that the famous Declaration of Arbroath is being invoked here, at least implicitly. The intriguing parallel between these two Declarations is in the appeal to a higher authority to mediate in the conflicts between Scotland and England/Westminster. The Declaration of Arbroath appealed to the authority of the Pope under the common rubric of medieval Christendom. The Democracy Declaration appeals to the parliament of the European Union, as members of that Union, and as fellow Europeans in a more abstract sense.

– DISCUSSION –

What comes through in all of this is a long historical trajectory of struggles over sovereignty, sometimes quiescent, sometimes not, but always punctuated by strikingly similar covenant events. Let us briefly review the chronology:

1320   The Declaration of Arbroath
c.1400–1600   The major period of Bonding
1638   The National Covenant
1643   The Solemn League and Covenant
1689   The Claim of Right (I)

1707   The Treaty of Union

1842   The Claim of Right (II)
1949   The Scottish Covenant
1988   The Claim of Right (III)
1992   The Democracy Declaration

The last three are unambiguously a part of the twentieth-century nationalist movement. The second Claim of Right of 1842 is the first instance which obviously refers back to an earlier one. This event is sometimes viewed as a forerunner of the current movement, a kind of proto-nationalism of the nineteenth century. But whatever the intentions, it actually led to the political weakening of what had been the core national institution since the Reformation – the Kirk (Paterson 1994: 56). And this in turn helps explain the conspicuous absence of major covenant examples between the Claims of Right of 1689 and 1842. During these years the Scottish political elites, for whom the Kirk was a bulwark, sought to consolidate rather than challenge the most central 'covenant' of all – the Treaty of Union of 1707. The Treaty of Union was created through two Acts of Parliament: the Articles of Union, and the Act of Security for the Church of Scotland. Both are detailed expositions of the terms of treaty, and are devoid of the strident language of protest and covenant that we have been examining. This is why I have set it apart in the list above.

This of course is not to say that there were no conflicts over the form and legitimacy of the state in eighteenth-century Scotland – the Jacobite rebellions were clearly just that. Furthermore, while less was produced along the lines of the major historic documents we have been examining, the idea of the covenant and the memory of the Covenanters remained strong. After the Union of 1707 the Moderate faction controlled the General Assembly of the Kirk and generally supported and sought to accommodate the Union, downplaying conflicts between church and state. But meanwhile the dissenting Evangelical faction was a major voice in Scottish public life, deeply concerned with the continuing significance of the covenants and their political implications. Throughout the eighteenth century a voluminous pamphlet literature developed, reflecting lively debates about the nature of the covenants, the obligations of subsequent generations to reaffirm them, and their compatibility with the taking of oaths to secular authorities. In 1733, in protest at the practice of lay patronage, the Associate Presbytery was formed, setting up a Secession Church and attracting around 10 per cent of the population, thus anticipating the Great Disruption by more than a century. In 1742, for the centennial of the Solemn League and Covenant, amid an atmosphere of Jacobite unrest, the Seceders organised a reaffirmation of the Covenants, involving a day of fasting, prayer, and preaching, and public reading and collective avowal of the Covenants (Brims 1989: 51).

The appeal of the Covenant in the eighteenth century however, was basically conservative, resisting change and outside interference, and often divisive within Scotland, leading to several church schisms. Thus it is not surprising that the more politically progressive movements oriented toward parliamentary reform, such as the Radicals and the Friends of the People of the 1790s, avoided the sectarian and backward looking imagery of the covenant (ibid.: 58). Later on the Scottish Chartists of the 1830s and 1840s were concerned with increasing the representation of lower-middle, working, and artisan classes in parliament, not with challenging its constitutional authority. These moderate goals of reform were shared with English Chartists, and thus the obvious parallel between covenant and charter did not come into play. It was not until the labour movement early in this century, epitomised by the Red Clydesiders, that the image of the Covenanters was reconnected to a progressive politics, being sufficiently 'historical' by this time to constitute a kind of non-literal symbol, evocative, but no longer a part of lively controversy (Brotherstone 1989b: 1; Harvie 1990; Knox 1989: 92–5). It is by the same token that the presbyterian/covenanting language has continued to be deployed in the discourse of Scottish nationalism, able to do its historicising work because of its relatively de-historicised context. How this rhetorical process works is the subject of the following chapter.

– NOTES –

1. This volume was published by Polygon Press, which as I observed earlier, has played a significant role in the publication of movement discourse. In 1991 Polygon published *A Woman's Claim of Right in Scotland: Women, Representation and Politics* (Woman's Claim of Right Group 1991), edited by a group of women involved in Scottish politics and concerned with demonstrating and analysing the serious gender inequality there. This further illustrates the presence of this idiom in the Scottish political vernacular.
2. In the field I attended a talk given by Winnie Ewing, the Grande Dame of the SNP (especially its centre-right), and MEP for the Highlands and Islands at the time, in which she likened Europe to a train leaving the station, and Scots as eager passengers being held back by a foot-dragging British government.

CHAPTER 10

Covenant, Contract, Convention

This chapter offers some ways of understanding the covenant tradition discussed in Chapter 9, in an effort to better comprehend its enduring rhetorical force. Three main approaches are taken. First, the covenant is considered as a form of historical metaphor, and as a possible example of what has been called 'the invention of tradition' (Hobsbawm and Ranger 1984). Then I explore the connections between the covenant tradition and that of social contract theory, although with a continuing emphasis on the importance of the metaphorical aspect. Finally, I address the implications of this focus on metaphor for the tension between contractual versus conventional justifications of the social and political orders.

– THE COVENANT AS HISTORICAL METAPHOR –

Let us take a closer look at how the events discussed in the last chapter have become symbolically interconnected. The chain of explicit historical references that we find evoked in this tradition suggests metaphorical and/or analogical processes whereby new events and situations are made sense of, articulated, and engaged, by emphasising parallels with earlier events.[1] This is a complex and obscure process which I think must be considered in at least two dimensions. On the one hand, perception is always prefigured by our expectations, causing past and present events to appear to 'fit together' in a more or less coherent way (cf. Guthrie 1995: 39–61; Lakoff and Johnson 1980: 3–6; Miller 1993). On the other hand, metaphor and analogy are used consciously, deliberately, and rhetorically to frame situations and achieve particular ends (Fernandez 1986: 3–70; Schön 1993). In the actual social process of the covenant tradition I have been describing it would be extremely difficult to say exactly where the one dimension picks up and the other leaves off, but both are undoubtedly at work. In covenant events of the twentieth-century nationalist movement, it is clear that leaders deliberately use historical references to add potency to their messages, likening struggles of the present to those of the past. These historical references are not cryptic however, but blatant. They do not do their rhetorical work by guile, appealing to some collective subconscious, but rather by evoking and reinforcing a certain common sense. These messages and metaphors make sense to those for whom it is already evident that Scotland has a long legacy of struggling with Britain/England over sovereignty, a struggle that is still going on. They lend weight to an argument that is already partially won.

The force of these metaphors lies in the fact that they provide not just striking and inspiring images, but compelling analogies, rich with parallels. They 'make' sense. It must be allowed that the sensitivity to these parallels depends on the degree of historical literacy one commands, and clearly there is a gradient here between a more highly educated and history-immersed intelligentsia and a broader public. But the very persistence of this idiomatic tradition implies that the messages being generated by those employing these metaphors are not falling on deaf ears, and my own experience in the field indicates that there is a rather high level of interest in history among movement activists, and more generally, there is a widespread respect for historical literacy about Scotland in Scotland (recall the ALP History Group), even if people do not all have the same command of that history, let alone the same opinions in regard to it. The richness of meaning may be 'thicker' for some and 'thinner' for others, but these degrees of understanding are in contact with one another, and influence one another.

Let me try to elaborate what I mean by 'analogical parallels' that tie together the various instances in this covenant tradition. I have already outlined the most basic parallels in the twofold definition of covenants we began with, that is, as the act of a community asserting its terms of membership within a larger community. These terms appear especially in the form of the assertion of two kinds of rights: 1. the right of Scots to choose their own leaders; and 2. the right of Scots to control their own domestic policies.

Regarding the first, we have seen that during the years of Conservative government many Scots came to view the power of Westminster to govern Scotland without a Scottish electoral mandate as illegitimate.[2] This situation was only exacerbated by the direct administration by a Secretary of State appointed by an unelected ruling party, under the Tories, leading to the frequent comparison of the Secretary of State to a colonial governor in Scottish nationalist discourse (cf. Hearn 1996: 59). The complaint resonates strongly with that of the Scottish barons asserting their right to choose their own king in 1320, and with the Covenanters' objections to the imposition of bishops on the presbyterian system. In the same fashion, the purpose of the original Claim of Right in 1689 was to establish the terms under which the incoming monarch would be acceptable. Finally, the conflict over church patronage that provoked the 1842 Claim of Right again deals with the right to appoint one's leaders, namely parish ministers, though on a more local level.

Regarding control over domestic policies, we have seen how the current preference in Scotland for a more social democratic approach diverges substantially from the policies imposed by London in recent years. The kinds of economic and infrastructural matters that are the focus of modern conflicts simply did not exist in the seventeenth century. But the religious conflicts of that time revolved around control over one of the major domestic issues of the day – forms of worship in Scotland. Remember that the initial trigger of these conflicts was the ill-considered imposition of a prayer book modelled on episcopalian liturgical forms. Again, the terms of the original Claim of Right set out the boundaries between monarchical versus parliamentary and church power in Scotland, and the conflict over patronage in the nineteenth century clearly combines issues of responsiveness to community by kirk ministers and the General Assembly's control over this domestic concern.

Finally, there is another aspect that is important here – the appeal to higher authority. I have pointed out the peculiar parallels between the Declaration of Arbroath and the Democracy Declaration in their appeals to pan-European levels of authority. In 1320 Scotland and England were separate warring kingdoms (albeit with their nobilities intertwined via a patchwork of overlordships that ranged across both kingdoms). The Pope was the only higher level available to appeal to. In contrast, appealing to the European parliament in 1992 meant attempting to circumvent a hierarchy of embedded levels of political sovereignty in which the British state is the middle term. More interesting, however, is the appeal not to concrete persons and institutions, but to supernatural or transcendental authority. After the Reformation (1560–7) and the Union of Crowns (1603) there developed a complex process of 'triangulation' of authority, wherein the Scottish elites repeatedly tried to frame the political situation so that while the king's authority was affirmed it was clearly subordinated to that of God, and the Kirk had a privileged position in articulating the will of God (Mitchison and Leneman 1989: 25–6). This classic device of Reformation politics (cf. Walzer 1985: 71–98), this particular way of addressing matters of sovereignty, held sway in Scotland right down to the Great Disruption. Modern nationalists rarely make appeals to the authority of God, but as we have seen, they often invoke a certain ideal conception of constitutional democracy, which the British system is seen as having betrayed, or at least having failed to live up to. Thus there is still a transcendent realm against which London leadership is measured, a higher authority that rests not in Brussels, but in the popular imagination of citizens of liberal democracies.

Over the period we have covered, conceptions of leadership, of what constitutes domestic policy, and of what constitutes the largest relevant arena of politics, have changed profoundly. But as I attempted to show in Part Two, there has been a remarkable underlying continuity of institutions in Scotland, that have evolved into the twentieth-century civil society that undergirds the nationalist movement today. The agencies involved have shifted, from popes, kings and the Godly elect, to civil society and parliaments at both the UK and European level; and the dominant conceptions of legitimate government have shifted, from a relatively decentralised feudalism, to a theocratic state, to laissez faire liberalism, to a Scandinavian style social democracy. But the cultural form of the covenant remains remarkably constant. In short, I am arguing that the present conflict over the strained union between Scotland and England that expresses itself in nationalism, and which I have argued is intimately bound up with the current retrenchment of the welfare state, is the latest permutation in a long history of varied and historically situated conflicts over Scottish sovereignty. The metaphor of the covenant has endured, and remains salient, because Scotland has retained a significant degree of structural and cultural autonomy, and its elites are still called upon to re-negotiate Scotland's position in a changing world.

– THE COVENANT AS INVENTED TRADITION –

At this point one might want to ask: what has become of the Jacobites and the Highlands? Surely no discussion of the traditions surrounding Scottish nationalism can be complete without them? Perhaps not, but I would like to argue that the importance of this tradition has been exaggerated. Hugh Trevor-Roper began his well known essay on the 'Highland Tradition of Scotland' thus:

> Today, whenever Scotchmen [sic] gather together to celebrate their national identity, they assert it openly by certain distinctive national apparatus. They wear the kilt, woven in tartan whose colour and pattern indicates their 'clan'; and if they indulge in music, their instrument is the bagpipe. This apparatus, to which they ascribe great antiquity, is in fact largely modern. (1984: 15)

This assertion is seriously misleading, and borders on crude stereotype. Most people I encountered in the nationalist movement are not heavily invested in tartan imagery, and indeed, view it with some ambivalence, or even hostility. The major significance of the kilt for most modern Scots is as a kind of standard male formal wear, at weddings for example, and as a culturally marked option for special occasions, such as ceilidhs. Scots tend to have a sophisticated and ironic understanding of the meanings surrounding tartanry, as both a symbol of national and cultural defiance, and as a fabrication for tourists. They are not nearly as 'taken in' by their own symbolism as Trevor-Roper would have us believe.

Trevor-Roper's tartan essay does an adequate job of outlining the development in the Lowlands in the eighteenth and nineteenth centuries of a romantic Highland tradition, including the modern kilt and system of clan tartans, and their putative antiquity. Yet he misleadingly casts the Highlands as a kind of cultural backwater: 'simply the overflow of Ireland' (ibid.). Although it is true that there were strong cultural and political connections linking the northern part of Ireland and the Scottish Highlands across the Irish Sea up to the seventeenth century, the Highlands and Lowlands within Scotland were, despite their linguistic divide, also interdependent. The Highland economy was largely based on cattle, which were sold to the Lowlands, and Scottish political history often hinged on feudal lords who constantly played both ends against the middle, as Highland clan chiefs in one situation, and as Lowland nobles in another. In short, Trevor-Roper's account is marred by an essentialist view of nationality and culture, which cannot confront the peculiar interstitial nature of the Gaidhealtachd on its own terms.[3]

Be that as it may, the cultural history of the Highlands as a whole is largely a separate issue from the history of Scottish nationalism. More relevant to the latter is the specific lore of the Stuarts and the Jacobites. Murray Pittock (1991) has offered a lengthy analysis of the 'Stuart Myth'. The crux of his argument is that the loss of the Stuart dynasty in 1688 has come to stand symbolically for the loss of independence and national agency in 1707. From the eighteenth century on the mythology/ideology of the Stuarts, as 'mythic deliverers', has become a 'protest history' in Scotland (1991: 2–5). The bulk of the text analyses, through literature, songs and poems, the development of the Jacobite myth, its co-optation and romanticisation in the Victorian period, and finally, its relevance to twentieth-century nationalism. He stresses the fact that the Jacobite myth took alternative forms: left/radical, and right/conservative, along with the more politically neutral popular stereotype. Towards the end he discusses the SNP, arguing that it has been too oriented toward single issues ('Scotland's Oil', fighting the Poll Tax, joining Europe), deploying a kind of pressure group politics. He suggests that they have neglected cultural and national identity, and should do more to cultivate the liberatory message of the Stuart mythology if they want to create the necessary unity of purpose.

Here again I take issue. First, it seems to me that it is the tragic-heroic struggles of the Jacobite Highlanders, more than the Stuarts themselves, that are fondly remembered. Support for monarchy as an element of government is weaker in Scotland than in England and as we have seen, nationalists are generally motivated by a vision of a more modern form of government. Secondly, while there is no doubt that Jacobite symbolism, in dress, songs and literature has an emotional appeal, it is a somewhat melancholy one. It is a story told in an 'elegiac mode' (McArthur 1994: 98), because the Jacobites lost their historical struggle, utterly. That is why it was possible in the later eighteenth and nineteenth centuries for them to become potent symbols of Scotland as a whole within the British Empire – because they no longer posed a real threat to the political system. It seems to me that Pittock seriously underplays the paradoxical unionist meanings of the 'Stuart Myth'. It is my argument that the covenant tradition, because of the strong analogical parallels it encodes, is of much deeper importance to modern Scottish nationalism and its links with the Scottish past than the trappings of tartanry. Although more obvious and symbolically loud, tartan symbols are perhaps by that same measure more superficial in regard to the actual complex of inherited meanings that are drawn upon to make sense of the present situation.

Probably the most influential attempt to relate the idea of tradition to nationalism and the nation-state remains Hobsbawm and Ranger's *The Invention of Tradition* (1984), where the Trevor-Roper essay just discussed first appeared. The contributors to this volume explored myriad ways in which national identity has been consolidated through the creation of rituals, iconographies, and practices that, while appearing to have great historical depth, were often of relatively recent invention (i.e., after the industrial revolution). As Hobsbawm points out in his introduction, these invented traditions

> seem to belong to three overlapping types: a) those establishing or symbolising social cohesion or the membership of groups, real or artificial communities, b) those establishing or legitimising institutions, status or relations of authority, and c) those whose main purpose was socialisation, the inculcation of beliefs, value systems and conventions of behaviour. (1984: 9)

The emphasis here is clearly on ways of consolidating a state-sanctioned social order in the interest of national elites. While I have no difficulty with this approach in principle, it is inadequate for the present purpose for two reasons. First, it simply fails to capture the double-edged quality of the covenant, which on the one hand consolidates political and ideological alliances, but on the other, has often been used to contest state-level authority. Secondly, the gravity and importance of the covenant in Scotland lies precisely in the fact that, no matter how changed over time, it is not a recent invention. The approach of Hobsbawm and Ranger is not suited to dealing with these dimensions.[4]

What is needed here is a somewhat less ironic notion of tradition. In an earlier attempt to develop a marxist conception, Raymond Williams suggested that:

> [w]hat we have to see is not just 'a tradition but a *selective tradition*: an intentionally selective version of a shaping past and a pre-shaped present, which is then powerfully operative in the process of social and cultural definition and identification. (1977: 115, emphasis in original)

It should be acknowledged that Williams was locating this more organic notion of tradition within a concern for processes of hegemony and cultural dominance similar to that of Hobsbawm and Ranger, and he primarily had in mind a broader sense of tradition as a way of life, or a set of norms, rather than as a specific historical chain of practice, which is my present concern. Still, this passage comes closer to capturing the process I have in mind in which an idiomatic, almost stylised way of doing something, manages to endure over a long period of time, even as it evolves to serve an array of historically situated purposes. A tradition in this sense connects the present with the past not simply through an evocation of the past, but through a continuing practical relevance. I see the covenant tradition as feeding into and reinforcing the present hegemony in Scotland of those who believe in the basic soundness of social democracy and the welfare state, while at the same time articulating dissent from the larger hegemony of neoliberal thinking in the UK and abroad. In the discourse of the Scottish movement, the covenant tradition helps define the friction between these two local versus larger hegemonies.

– THE COVENANT AS SOCIAL CONTRACT –

The idea of the covenant unavoidably evokes that of the social contract – a connection worth examining more closely. The notion of a social contract between ruler and ruled reaches back into medieval history (Lessnoff 1990: 5–6). In Scotland George Buchannan (1506–82), contributed to this line of thinking by arguing for the election of monarchs by the nobility, and the legitimacy of regicide in the case of tyrannical kings. None the less, as James VI's tutor, his ideas operated within the established genre of political advice to princes, as instructions toward good kingship, rather than as a fundamental challenge to the system of feudal monarchy. The concept took a new form, the one we most closely associate it with today, in the seventeenth- and eighteenth-century writings of Hobbes, Locke, Rousseau, and later Kant, who sought to provide new bases and justifications for the authority of the sovereign and the power of the state. The upheavals of that period saw a weakening of political legitimations based on notions of tradition and divine right. The arguments of the classic social contract thinkers deployed more universalising (and sometimes materialist) theories of human wills and motives, and the problems of aggregating them into the collective will of the polity. The details of the various and divergent conceptions of the social contract in this period need not detain us here. The crucial point is that this new emphasis on the consent of the governed helped lay the groundwork for modern conceptions of democratic politics.

The Scottish Covenants of the seventeenth and eighteenth centuries and the covenant-focused church controversies of the eighteenth century were part of this same trend of thought, carried on in terms at once both theological and national. Carefully considered, they reveal a specialised language for grappling with the problem of the foundations of political authority, and the relationship between what is ordained either by nature or God, and what is subject to human free will. The covenants themselves arose out of a background of what is known as federal theology, after the Latin word *feodus*, for 'pact' or 'contract'. In the late sixteenth and early seventeenth centuries networks of reformed scholastics and theologians in northern, Protestant Europe (especially the Netherlands), were developing the ideas of Luther and Calvin, with their emphasis on the individual's inner condition of faith as a sign of salvation. This heightened concern led to a new focus on the motif of the covenant in the Old and New Testaments, as a way of conceptualising the condition of being saved in both personal and social terms. During this period a key distinction developed between the Covenant of Works and the Covenant of Grace.[5] The Covenant of Works was that made between God and Adam, whereby in exchange for living according to God's laws, Adam and his descendants could enjoy a life of Edenic perfection. But Adam broke this original covenant. The Covenant of Grace refers to God's various offers to his people of chances to redeem themselves, despite their fallen state, through subsequent covenants with Noah, Abraham, Moses, David, and ultimately Jesus, the 'second Adam' and the only one truly capable of fulfilling the covenant. The Covenant of Works was also called a Covenant of Nature, or Creation, and was seen as constituting the fundamental order of the natural world, and binding on all humanity. The Covenant of Grace on the other hand, though offered to all people, was engaged by the reformed elect alone, and had to be actively entered into and maintained. This distinction provided a framework for relating secular and divine authority. The Covenant of Works was seen as establishing the natural laws on which the authority of the state was based, while the Covenant of Grace was the foundation of the Church and its authority. Thus the state was responsible for making all people accountable to Mosaic Law, and the Church was responsible for building the spiritual community of the elect who had entered into the Covenant of Grace.

This device of the two covenants justified the universal application of Christian morality by the civil magistrate, while at the same time allowing a distinction between the saved and the reprobate. Like all reformed theology it is also caught up in the dilemma of how to strike a balance between human free will, a necessary aspect of moral responsibility, and God's omnipotence. The problem: how to explain a world in which God is utterly sovereign, and yet people are morally responsible for their actions. As the faithful in eighteenth-century Scotland wrestled with this theological puzzle on the ground, in the context of church politics, it led to frequent disputes and schisms over whether those who emphasised the covenants, particularly the Covenant of Grace, had too voluntaristic a conception of their relationship to God, and whether religious covenants came into conflict with secular, civil covenants – whether one had priority over the other.

In the church debates and pamphlet literature of the time the doctrine of the two covenants was frequently applied. In essence, the more moderate view was that the Kirk was founded upon and responsible for administering both covenants, while the more evangelical wing, which had led the secession of 1733 around the patronage issue, saw the Kirk as specifically representing the elect of the Covenant of Grace. For them the tradition of covenanting was part of the necessary maintenance of the latter Covenant. Eventually the Secession Church experienced its own internal split when a hard-line faction, known as 'Anti-Burghers' argued that the covenants were incompatible with oaths to civil governments (e.g., to hold office in town councils, etc.). They claimed that such oaths involved a conflict of allegiance between divine and secular authority. A pamphlet of 1764 by John Goodlet, a member of the more moderate wing of the Secession Church, sought to counter this argument by explaining that while the Kirk is responsible for administering the Covenant of Grace among 'ecclesiastical society', through the Covenant of Works God had established natural law, which was the basis of 'civil' or 'political society'. In making this argument Goodlet explicitly refers to the work of John Locke, attempting to demonstrate that Locke's social compact and the Covenant of Works are, in effect, the same thing. It is a form of argument for the separation of church and state, which none the less maintains that the state's authority has Godly origins. Goodlet defends the moderate position against criticisms of the dissenters, and the even more hardline Reformed Presbytery, an offshoot of an older covenanting sect called the Cameronians, accusing them of collapsing the distinction between the two covenants when they claim that the authority of civil government can only be recognised when it is derived from that of ecclesiastical society.[6]

Scottish theology of this period, and these specific church controversies, are usually viewed today as enmeshed in arcane, legalistic hair-splitting, part of an intellectual backwater amid the achievements of the Enlightenment, which was allied with the moderate wing of the Kirk that eschewed such debates. My point here is to suggest that in fact major political discussions of the day regarding the contractual nature of political authority were being translated into theological terms that were at once also more populist. This was an important part of the context for the development of the classic social contract ideas, one that is largely neglected today. The crux of these conflicts is over sovereignty and authority, with God's Covenant of Grace serving as a conceptual device for challenging more remote loci of political power.

In the nineteenth and twentieth centuries social contract theories went out of fashion, displaced by a mixture of utilitarianism, utopianism, and realpolitik. But since the 1970s the model has been revived in political philosophy, once again in a new form, largely spurred by John Rawls's *A Theory of Justice* (1971).[7] These new formulations of the social contract are notable for their shift away from the basic legitimation of political authority and the state and toward arguments about distributive justice within the modern state, the authority of which, whether maximal or minimal, is now taken for granted. Most of this recent work tries to imagine what kind of political economic regime rational agents would agree to in a context free of coercion. In other words, they begin from basic liberal assumptions about the autonomous rational will of the individual, though not surprisingly, just as liberalism is highly varied along a left-right political spectrum, so are these new formulations. Rawls's work is very much a justification of the liberal welfare state, which takes an active role in guaranteeing equality of opportunity and basic well-being of its citizens. At the opposite end of the spectrum in a neo-Lockean mode, Robert Nozick (1974) defends the idea of a minimal state that primarily aims to preserve property rights, understood as somehow natural or pre-social. Still others have emphasised the idea of the social contract not simply as a way of protecting individual rights and autonomy, but as a necessary context for the formulation of shared conceptions of the common good. Thus Michael Walzer has suggested that:

> The social contract is an agreement to reach decisions together about what goods are necessary to our common life, and then to provide those goods for one another. The signers owe one another more than mutual aid, for that they owe or can owe anyone. They owe mutual provision for all those things for the sake of which they have separated themselves from mankind as a whole and joined forces in a particular community. (1983: 65)

Walzer's characterisation of the social contract highlights the centrality of matters of distributive justice within the political community for contemporary discussions. But as one reviews these various notions of the social contract it becomes clear that this is far from one clearly formulated idea – it is more a style of argument. The late Jean Hampton has argued, I think rightly, that

> even though theorists who call themselves 'contractarians' have all supposedly begun from the same reflective starting point, namely, what rational people could 'agree to', the many differences and disagreements among them show that although they are supposedly in the same philosophical camp, in fact they are united not by a common philosophical theory but by a common *image*. Philosophers hate to admit it, but sometimes they work from pictures rather than ideas. (1995: 379, emphasis in original)

Hampton's insight here points back to our discussion of historical metaphor. The social contract is an 'image' or a 'picture', because it arises out of a culturally embedded tradition of political thought, rather than being systematically designed, *de novo*, by philosophers. Moreover, the significance of the covenant as a particular cultural idiom of political practice lies in its connections to the broader idiom of the social contract metaphor. The metaphor of the covenant/contract in modern Scottish politics not only has a rich, concrete history, but it also has an array of current reference points, a set of variations on a theme. Of key importance are these three relationships: labour to capital; citizen to state; and Scotland to England. These dimensions are concretely historically interrelated, and the image of the contract tends to assimilate these tensions to one another in the political imagination.

It has become a commonplace to refer to the historical compromise between capital and labour framed in terms of Keynesian demand management as a kind of 'social contract'. Wisdom is not always abstruse, and sometimes the commonplace contains much insight. While the globalisation of capital is hardly as recent a process as is often suggested these days, it is readily apparent that changes in technology and capital mobility have weakened the bargaining position of organised labour since the 1960s. The capital-labour contract was a complex product of competition and bargaining by both parliamentary and extra-parliamentary means – of a particular concatenation of strikes and votes delivered and withheld. In turn, this contract was always superimposed upon a more classic conception of the social contract as one between citizens and the state. T. H. Marshall's (1983) conception of the progressive attainment of rights – civil, political and social – through the state, expresses this idea in abstract form. Ideas such as 'Homes fit for Heroes' after World War I in the UK, and the G. I. Bill in the US after World War II, express the role of the social contract metaphor as a rationale in the legitimation of the state. The citizen serves his country, upholding his end of the bargain, and the state owes him a certain standard of living in return.[8] Correspondingly, the critique of the welfare state from the right has emphasised the problem of ungovernability stemming from the constant expansion of rights and demands on resources from particular constituencies of the citizenry. In this view, the contract has got out of hand.

Across the globe the industrialised democracies of the 'West' have seen a general breakdown of this double contract between capital and labour, and the state and its citizens. And this breakdown is widely perceived as a result of intractable, natural processes of the world economy and market system, rather than the active decisions of capital interests with strategic advantages seeking to better their competitive positions. Thus we find ourselves in the situation addressed at the end of Chapter 7, that Habermas (1989b) has labelled 'the new obscurity', in which the utopian vision of a better world based on the mastery of the productive process has waned, to be replaced by a diffuse array of situated struggles, both progressive and reactionary.

But this breakdown is experienced in different ways in different places. In the US, for instance, due in part to the strength of anti-communism, there is a relatively weak sense in the popular imagination of the larger social contract as a product of strategic bargaining by labour, progressively entrenched in legislation. Instead post-war affluence is commonly understood as the natural outcome of superior morality and industriousness – with recent economic stagnation for the middle/working class frequently attributed to a decline in these same factors. Moreover, in common parlance in the US, the meaning of the word 'welfare' is restricted to poverty relief, the idea that the other limited entitlements in the US, such as social security and Medicare, are forms of welfare, would strike many in the US as strange. In short, US culture is relatively inarticulate when it comes to the larger two-fold contract between labour and capital, and citizens and the state, lacking the conceptual/metaphorical tools in popular discourse that could render the issues more concrete.

But, as Dickson has demurred, 'Scotland is different' (1989). According to my analysis, an important part of what makes Scotland different is that the 'larger' social contract of the post-war period is encoded through and made more tangible by a third dimension – the contracted unity of Scotland and England in the United Kingdom, and the grounding of this contract in an historical tradition of political conflict. In Scotland, objection to the breakdown of the larger social contract tends to get expressed in terms of nationalist politics. The opposition between capital and labour, between citizens and the state, gets metaphorically mapped onto the opposition between Scotland and England.

This happens for a variety of reasons deeply implicated in the north-south divide in the UK. If we regard this divide as simply a question of the divergence of voting behaviour, then perhaps it has become passé since Labour's return to power at Westminster. However, there is an important geography of power that lies deeper than voting behaviour. The actual centre of political power is in England, more specifically southern England, Westminster, and the 'City of London'. Both the major political institutions and the decisive weight of the popular vote are located there. Obviously the centralisation of power in the British constitution accentuates this. Further-more, to the extent that the recent weakening of the larger contract is a result of the growing importance of finance capital in relation to industrial capital, London is again a tangible centre of this process. The crucial point is that Scotland's history since at least 1603 has been one of complex negotiations, involving both resistance and assimilation, with London/England as the centre of political and economic power. As I have argued, current nationalist politics in Scotland is made possible by the fact that Scotland, through its institutions of civil society, has retained a significant degree of bargaining power in the contracted relations between Scotland and England. Moreover, in this century the elites controlling key Scottish institutions have primarily bargained for a better contract within the context of the welfare state – that is, the 'larger contract'. Though for much of the last three hundred years a notion of Scottish assimilation to England has been a dominant theme in British historiography (Beveridge and Turnbull 1989; Fry 1992; Kidd 1993), the underlying reality has not been so simple. The Scotland-England contract is encoded in the long history of Covenants, Claims of Right, and declarations, not to mention the Treaty of Union itself, that figure so prominently in the rhetoric of twentieth-century nationalist politics. The trust broken between capital and labour, between the welfare state and its citizens, is experienced and articulated as a breakdown in the contract between Scotland and England. In keeping with this, the central values that have underwritten the larger contract – egalitarianism, democracy, socialism or at least a certain version of distributive justice – have tended to become reappropriated as distinctively Scottish values. These are precisely the values that are seen as having been betrayed by capital/the state/England.

Let me stress that I am not arguing that nationalist politics in Scotland is a result of mystification in the form of metaphorical thought. I am arguing that metaphorical predication is an unavoidable aspect of social discourse, especially the political, and that therefore it should be engaged as consciously and wisely as possible. I am suggesting that the metaphor of the social contract provides a deep structure to Scottish politics that can be both helpful and a hindrance to that cause. On the one hand, it is important not to let the momentum of political rhetoric collapse the important distinctions on the other side of the contractual equation. The histories of capitalism, the modern state, and England are closely related, but they are not the same thing. On the other hand, if the contractual metaphor lends a certain concreteness to struggles over the larger contract, reducing Habermas's 'new obscurity' in Scottish public discourse, then so be it. In that case it is liable to endure, whatever our assessment of it. In this regard, much may depend on the new parliament and its perceived ability to bring the contract back into balance.

– THE COVENANT AS SOCIAL CONVENTION –

David Hume offered a classic critique of social contract theories in an essay first published in 1748 (Hume 1985a: 463–87). He argued that comparative historical evidence showed that political authority is generally founded upon 'conquest and usurpation' and adhered to out of established custom and habit, rather than rational principles. Although he considered the consent of the governed to be the best basis for government, he argued that mechanisms for eliciting consent were highly limited, and hardly the origin of political organisation. None the less, he was also a firm believer in the ultimate priority of public opinion and common sense over philosophy and ideology in shaping social life, and argued that the social order always rests on some sort of tacit consent, in the same way that speakers unconsciously consent to the system of rules that govern a shared language (cf. Gauthier 1998).

Hume's critique of contractarianism is a good example of his philosophical method as a whole, which was to sceptically question elaborate thought constructs, what he saw as overly 'refined' ideas, and reassert the conventional wisdom of everyday life. He would have agreed that the social contract is a metaphor, and would have argued that that is precisely where its danger lies – in taking one part of human social life, the making of promises and contracts, and trying to magnify it into an all-embracing explanation of political legitimacy. He saw the philosopher's task as one of informed social commentary, calling to account such overly ambitious ideological projects, and instead seeking to 'methodise and correct' the inherited body of collective opinion, in a limited, ad hoc manner (Livingston 1998). For Hume, social life was primarily a matter of inherited convention, rather than contractual agreement. In this respect Hume's views can be seen as akin to recent communitarian critiques of liberal theory, in particular John Rawls's contractarian liberalism (1971, 1996), that have argued against attempts to formulate universal criteria of justice and right, instead stressing the culturally and historically embedded nature of norms, values, and conceptions of the good life, and their incommensurability across cultures (MacIntyre 1984; Walzer 1983). Hume's often conservative cast of mind resonates with the communitarian's distrust of liberalism's pretensions to universal truths.

None the less, these supposed dichotomies between contractarianism and conventionalism, or liberalism and communitarianism, may be misleading. When Hume wrote, the social contract was still a novel idea, which as we have seen, permeated political discussions of the time. But today it has become more a part of the inherited stockpile of political ideas and assumptions, it has seeped down from the giddy heights of revolutionary ideology into the sedimentary layers of popular imagination, which is itself dependent on metaphorical modes of thought. This is part of the point being made in the previous sections. Consider Rawls's rather abstract thought experiment that provides the basis of his liberal theory of justice. He begins by asking us to imagine what kind of socio-political arrangements we would choose to live in if we had all the general knowledge about human nature and possibilities at our disposal, but were ignorant of what our own position in that chosen arrangement would be. This is his version of the social contract, which he calls the 'original position', in which judgements are made under a 'veil of ignorance'. Rawls assumes that under such a veil, all reasoning subjects would reach the same or similar choices. Moreover, he hypothesises that people deliberating from such a position would hedge their bets as to what position they might end up in by choosing an arrangement in which

> [a]ll social primary goods – liberty and opportunity, income and wealth, and the bases of self respect – are to be distributed equally unless an unequal distribution of any or all of these goods is to the advantage of the least favoured. (1971: 303)

The institutions and policies that Rawls argues would result from this process are: full employment, a social minimum income, equal education and cultural opportunities through subsidised public schools, regulation of capitalist firms, and the prevention of monopolies (ibid.: 275). Thus, while Rawls's method of justifying this vision of justice relies on a highly abstract heuristic model, the kind of society he sees as being justified is very familiar – some variation on the liberal welfare state that was the central tendency in all industrialised democracies through the middle of the twentieth century. Considering that *A Theory of Justice* was first published in 1971, we can see it as an attempt to justify what was thought by many at that time to be the inherent tendency of the modern democratic state. In this light it is worth remembering the importance for Rawls's theory of what he calls 'reflective equilibrium' – the principle that the worth of a moral theory lies in a balance between its internal coherence, and its concordance with the actual practice of making moral judgements (ibid.: 48–51). So in the light of Hume's critique, the question becomes: do we read Rawls as devising an implausible theory based on an over-extended metaphor, or as attempting to systematise the conventional assumptions of twentieth-century liberal culture? In fact, we can read Rawls in both these ways at the same time. His is an artificial thought project that arises out of a concrete historical and cultural milieu that sets the bounds of his thinking. In a similar fashion, the main thrust of this chapter has been that the covenant tradition and the metaphor of the social contract in Scottish nationalist discourse are at once both ideological and cultural, a shifting mixture of strategic invention and inherited convention.

Hume believed that the origins of government lay not in complex reasoning, but in feelings of trust and interdependence that arise naturally out of the family and kinship. These 'natural virtues' provide the model for the 'artificial virtues' of justice cultivated by the 'social artifices' of law and government (Hume 1978: 477–84; 1985b: 37–41; cf. Baier 1988). In a similar manner, the argument made in Chapter 1, that Scottish nationalist discourse draws on an implicit notion of a moral economy of the modern welfare state, seeks the roots of the Scottish movement in a diffuse moral sentiment, rather than an ideological program. As with all social movements, there is ideology in abundance here, but there is also a deeper social fabric of feelings of justice and injustice, righteousness and indignation, of trust gained and trust broken. I have tried to show through cumulative presentation that the sense of being wronged and treated unfairly found in the Scottish movement is not simply the outcome of deliberations about justice and good government, but also of a deeply felt threat to the basic ability to cultivate trust and co-operation at a communal and interpersonal level. There is a kind of wisdom encoded in these feelings – that there is such a thing as society, and it needs to be a caring society – which should be respected and taken seriously, even if at some levels it is intractable to reasoned analysis.

– NOTES –

1. For major collections of essays addressing various aspects of the theory of metaphor, see Ortony (1993) and Sacks (1979). For a collection of anthropological essays on the theory of metaphor, see Fernandez (1991). For anthropological case studies using the concept of metaphor, see Sahlins (1981) and Ohnuki-Tierney (1990). For a closely related collection of essays frequently addressing the subject of metaphor, see Holland and Quinn's *Cultural Models in Language and Thought* (1987).

2. Indeed, the present Labour Government does have a strong Scottish mandate, but that support was to some degree contingent upon the new government's commitment to constitutional reform.

3. For correctives one can begin with Hunter (1976); Smout (1972: 39–46); and Withers (1988, 1992).

4. The 'invention of tradition' idea has led to some complex ethical and epistemological debates in anthropology about how competing claims to authority are made and what happens when anthropologists seek to 'debunk' the histories/traditions of those they study. See Friedman (1992) and Briggs (1996).

5. This discussion draws especially on David A. Weir's *The Origin of the Federal Theology in Sixteenth-Century Reformation Thought* (1990), and also Burrell (1964), Henderson (1957: 61–74), Ferguson (1968: 102–32), and more generally, Skinner (1978: 235–8, 302–48).

6. See Goodlet (1764). This pamphlet can be found bound with others in the New College Library, Edinburgh, shelfmark: A.c.5.14/1–2. The argument in this section is based on a general survey of the religious pamphlet literature from this period, held in the New College Library.

7. For introductions to the long history of social contract theory and its recent revival, see Bobbio (1987: 118–37), Boucher and Kelly (1994), Hampton (1995; 1986: 256–84), and Lessnoff (1990).

8. It seems appropriate to preserve the sex bias in the language here both because of the specific subject, and because it reminds us that by and large the benefits of the welfare state have gone to (white, middle class) men.

Conclusion

'Convention' is a curious word – its ambiguities summing up much of what this book has been about. As in the last chapter, it can mean an habitual or customary way of doing things, but it can also mean an explicit agreement, or it can designate a social group reaching such agreements. Each of these meanings has been present in our exploration of Scotland's liberal nationalism, and their divergence relates to the paradoxical ring of the term liberal nationalism. Liberalism tends to argue that people everywhere are basically the same, governed by the same rational principles, which makes it possible to formulate universalist theories, both about how people behave, and about what is their common good. Liberals put their faith in our ability as individuals to reach agreements on how to live with each other, to establish conventions. Nationalism on the other hand, tends to be concerned with the inherited distinctiveness and particularity of cultural groups, and is inclined to defend norms, traditions, and conventional ways of doing things. We should expect that a liberal nationalism will evoke both these dimensions of convention at the same time.

As we have seen, these various senses of convention are present in the Scottish case. The egalitarian myths and moral economic language of the movement reinforce the conventionalised acceptance of social democratic values in Scottish culture, and the metaphor of the covenant symbolically links present values to a deeper history. Meanwhile, the modern democratic mechanisms of elections and referenda are seen as expressing, in John Smith's famous phrase, 'the settled will of the Scottish people'. Scotland's parliament is what the majority has agreed upon. And that majority has been in many ways represented and led in recent years by the Scottish Constitutional Convention, which came to embody these various strands of meaning. It is this complex interdependence of meanings that leads me to question the common theoretical dichotomisation of 'ethnic' and 'civic' forms of nationalism. While we can clearly distinguish ideologies that ground national identity in notions of biology and kinship, the term 'ethnic' usually has a much broader meaning, cognate to 'cultural', and what is culture if not the inherited and evolving body of rarely questioned social conventions? In the Scottish case, nationalism's civicness is culturally determined, it arises out of a stream of political traditions, and is hardly dreamt up *de novo* by a collection of rational subjects. This is not to say that it is irrational, but simply that its rationality, like all rationality, is culturally embedded, transmitted and sustained. The peaceful, democratic, and liberal cast of Scottish nationalism deserves credit and respect, but it is inseparable from the process of culture.

I have also tried to suggest a parallel between this problem of the ethnic-civic distinction in nationalism, and the debates between liberal and communitarian theorists. Liberalism, just as much as civic nationalism, is a culturally embedded process. Its claims to generality arise out of particular cultural traditions of thought. This is neither to deny that there are general truths about human nature and society, nor that most if not all cultures are inclined to generalise about humankind. It is simply to suggest that this process of speculative generalisation must invariably be fashioned out of a particular heritage of ideas (cf. MacIntyre 1990). Conversely, the communitarian's defence of value differences and tradition is somewhat prone toward the essentialisation and reification of cultures. As I have repeatedly argued, our appreciation of the organic integration of cultures needs to be balanced by an awareness of the way our general human capacity for culture means that particular cultures constantly influence each other, exchanging practices and ideas across shifting and permeable boundaries. The difference between a useful distinction and a misleading dichotomy can be difficult to discern, and this is so for both civic versus ethnic, and liberal versus communitarian constructions of reality. Minimally, we should bear in mind that what these conceptual pairs ultimately define is opposing styles of arguments about what nations are, and how social values are created, rather than actual types of nations, or societies.

Much of politics takes the form of, or at least can be construed as, a kind of clash of conventions, in the two senses we have been exploring. There is no denying the fact that established convention is a powerful force for political legitimacy. People are often loath to change political arrangements that work tolerably well, and need to be motivated either by deep dissatisfaction and crisis, or strong confidence in plans for improvement, or both. And when challenges to the political status quo are marshalled, at least in the Western tradition, they often take the form of an assembled group articulating and justifying the views of the aggrieved seeking change. This is part of the dynamic of how the Western political tradition develops –

old conventions being overturned by new conventions, which eventually become routinised and customary, as opposed to reformist or radical. I have tried to convey a sense of Scottish history as an accretion of institutions and cultural values laid down over the long term in this way.

Of crucial importance for this historical dynamic is the role of the middling ranks of society, interstitial classes that seek their livelihoods through core social institutions. Repeatedly it is members of this general sector of society that take the lead in critiquing the old conventions, and formulating the new ones, at the same time reclaiming history in terms conducive to the new moral vision. This was conspicuously the case in the Scottish Reformation and covenanting period, in which the developing class alliance of lairds, burghers, reformed ministers and lawyers led the push for new forms of church and confession with an integral relationship to the powers of the state. Similarly in our own period, the mobilisation of intellectuals and professionals ensconced in the institutions of contemporary civil society has been instrumental in advancing the cause of constitutional reform, and articulating unease with neoliberal trends. From Andrew Melville to Donald Dewar, ideological and institutional reform generally requires some sort of positioning within an institutional base, from which to act.

Historically, liberalism and nationalism arose together, in the wake of the Reformation, tied to the same evolution of political institutions. Both take root in the notion of the legitimacy of government resting on more direct and explicit forms of popular consent (Mosse 1975: 1–20). The covenant tradition is a peculiar local example of this process. Liberalism's attachment to the principle of the rule of law would be meaningless without a physical sphere of jurisdiction for that rule, a state to enforce it, and a population disposed to believe in the form and content of such laws. To some degree, liberalism needs the nation-state, though the nation may be construed in some cases as a sphere of common values consented to by a multi-ethnic population. Nationalism, for its part, is a doctrine of liberation, albeit couched in collective terms. Its claims for the recognition of cultural difference are akin to those made by multiculturalism, the difference being whether the cultural group and the polity need to be congruent. But liberal states do sometimes recognise limited forms of self-jurisdiction among the cultural (especially religious) groups they contain, and few nationalisms would claim absolute cultural homogeneity, instead recognising and even celebrating regional cultural variations.

The increase of freedom is the common and interlocking theme of both liberalism and nationalism, where they differ is in their respective emphases on the individual versus collective in their understandings of the nature of freedom. But the historical development of liberal thought alone has also wrestled with this question. As is well known, and amply demonstrated in the history of Scotland, the classical liberalism of the eighteenth and nineteenth centuries, with its emphasis on individual freedom, private property, and minimal government, was gradually displaced by a more modern, collectivist liberalism which sought to use the powers of the state to command the capitalist economy and improve the life chances of citizens (Ryan 1995). Neoliberalism, with its classical emphasis on the individual and hostility to the interventionist state, provides ideological arguments for the rejection of nationalism, but its current confluence with social conservatism has meant that it has often been bound to traditionalist defences of the particular nation-state in which it finds itself. Meanwhile, it is much harder for the modern liberal to formulate a coherent rejection of nationalism, because modern liberalism has sought a collective path to human emancipation, primarily through the development of the welfare state, which has been a quintessentially national project.

This tension between individualist and collectivist conceptions of how to enhance freedom is not simply a contrast between types of liberalism, or liberalism and nationalism. All the modern 'isms' – socialism, communism, even fascism – reflect varying attempts to master or resolve this basic tension. But nationalism, because of its fundamental connections to questions of territory, population and history, has tended to underwrite all other 'isms', because if they are to be more than utopian dreams, these political and ideological projects must be pursued in real time and real space – somewhere, sometime, somehow. As with nationalism, I think there is a common intuition that liberalism has a more ubiquitous significance for the modern period than these other ideologies. In this regard, it is perhaps useful to make a distinction between liberalism understood as a particular species of modern ideology, however variable, and liberalism understood as a general term for the epoch we live in, which is characterised by the dilemmas of how to balance individual and collective demands for freedom, and devise strategies for realising freedom, in highly complex forms of mass society with elaborate political and economic interdependencies among persons and groups (Bellamy 1992). Much of this book has been informed by a conception of modern history and society conforming to the latter conception of what liberalism is.

This study has also been concerned with the process of making political claims in general, the construction of arguments, and how they are shaped and constrained by the systems of thought, and material conditions in which they operate. David Hume once famously observed that it is impossible logically to derive prescriptions for right and wrong behaviour from our descriptive statements about the world (1978: 469–70). He believed that morality is best understood as the actual patterns of sentiments of approval and disapproval that manifestly accompany our social relations, and that rational moral systems could have little useful effect on this social fabric of feelings. Variously called the fact/value distinction, or the is/ought question (Hudson 1969), Hume posed an enduring dilemma for social and moral theory, which I doubt can be resolved. None the less, I think it is useful to ponder, because it is in the nature of social movements, and political and moral discourse, to try to bridge this gap, despite Hume's injunctions. Social movements such as nationalism that aim to promote a course of action, by definition generate arguments about what ought to be done. What is more, this 'ought' needs to be presented as possible, plausible, and capable of success if it is to motivate and guide social action. Only in the most desperate of political circumstances, with extremely limited options, will substantial numbers of people invest their energies in a program that seems unlikely to succeed. To give a political agenda a sense of viability, a rhetorical bridge must be created between a description of the world as it is, and a prescription for how it ought to be, along with a strategy for how to get from one to the other (Tarrow 1994: 118–34).

It is in this light that we should regard Scottish nationalism's rhetorical grounding in Scottish history. This happens because any argument for any future must do so by recourse to the past. It must both pose and address the questions: who are we? what do we want? and why? Moreover, people must come to believe that the past they know can cause the future they have chosen. An imaginary collectivity of liberal citizens agreeing a common future is not sufficient to generate political action – it is actual, historical, acculturated, situated subjects, facing concrete historical problems, that must be motivated. In practice, the 'ought' of social action must be derived from the 'is' of social circumstances, through whatever alchemy is available. Moreover, the very process of attempting to mobilise collective action, nationalist or otherwise, entails constructing a collective subject (a nation, a class, a race, a gender) whose will is to be realised. Thus what we have been examining is not simply a matter of Scotland making political claims, but of political claims making Scotland, over hundreds of years. The cause of the Scottish movement entails imagining a Scotland and its past, but the power and burden of such imaginings is not peculiar to nationalism, but rather falls on any political project, by the very nature of how we collectively think and act in this world.

References

This section includes only the books and articles cited in the text, and is not intended to be a comprehensive bibliography.

Aitken, K. (1992), 'The Economy', in M. Linklater and R. Denniston (eds), *The Anatomy of Scotland: How It Works*, Edinburgh and New York: Chambers, pp. 230–333.

Anderson, B. (1991), *Imagined Communities. Reflections on the Origin and Spread of Nationalism*, Second edition, London and New York: Verso.

Armstrong, J. (1982), *Nations Before Nationalism*, Chapel Hill: University of North Carolina Press.

Baier, A. (1988), 'Hume's Account of Social Artifice – Its Origins and Originality', *Ethics*, 98, pp. 757–78.

Barrow, G. W. S. (1989), *Kingship and Unity: Scotland 1000–1306*, Edinburgh: Edinburgh University Press.

Barry, B. (1996), *Justice as Impartiality. A Treatise of Social Justice, Volume 2*, Oxford: Clarendon Press.

Beiner, R. (ed.) (1999), *Theorizing Nationalism*, Albany: State Univerity of New York Press.

Bellamy, R. (1992), *Liberalism and Modern Society*, University Park, PA: Penn State Press.

Beveridge, C. and Turnbull, R. (1989), *The Eclipse of Scottish Culture: Inferiorism and the Intellectuals*, Edinburgh: Polygon.

Billig, M. (1995), *Banal Nationalism*, London: Sage.

Bobbio, N. (1987), *The Future of Democracy: A Defense of the Rules of the Game*, R. Bellamy (ed.), R. Griffin (trans.), Minneapolis: University of Minnesota Press.

Bobbio, N. (1989), *Democracy and Dictatorship: The Nature and Limits of State Power*, P. Kennealy (trans.), Minneapolis: University Minnesota Press.

Booth, W. J. (1994), 'On the Idea of the Moral Economy', *American Political Science Review*, 88(3), pp. 653–67.

Boucher, D. and Kelly, P. (eds) (1994), *The Social Contract from Hobbes to Rawls*, London and New York: Routledge.

Brand, J. (1978), *The National Movement in Scotland*, London: Routledge and Kegan Paul.

Breuilly, J. (1993), *Nationalism and the State*, Manchester and New York: Manchester University Press.

Briggs, C. L. (1996), 'The Politics of Discursive Authority in Research on the "Invention of Tradition"', *Cultural Anthropology*, 11(4), pp. 435–69.

Brims, J. (1989), 'The Covenanting Tradition and Scottish Radicalism in the 1790s', in T. Brotherstone (ed.), *Covenant, Charter, and Party. Traditions of Revolt and Protest in Modern Scottish History*, Aberdeen: Aberdeen University Press, pp. 50–62.

Brotherstone, T. (ed.) (1989a), *Covenant, Charter, and Party. Traditions of Revolt and Protest in Modern Scottish History*, Aberdeen: Aberdeen University Press.

Brotherstone, T. (1989b), 'Introduction', in T. Brotherstone (ed.), *Covenant, Charter, and Party. Traditions of Revolt and Protest in Modern Scottish History*, Aberdeen: Aberdeen University Press.

Brown, A., McCrone, D., Paterson, L. and Surridge, P. (1999), *The Scottish Electorate: The 1997 General Election and Beyond*, London: Macmillan.

Brown, A., McCrone, D. and Paterson, L. (1998), *Politics and Society in Scotland*, Second edition, London: Macmillan.

Brubaker, R. (1992), *Citizenship and Nationhood in France and Germany*, Cambridge, MA: Harvard University Press.

Brubaker, R. (1996), *Nationalism Reframed: Nationhood and the National Question in the New Europe*, Cambridge: Cambridge University Press.

Bryant, C. G. A. (1993), 'Social self-organisation, civility and sociology: a comment on Kumar's "Civil Society"', *British Journal of Sociology* 44(3), pp. 397–401.

Bryson, L. (1992), *Welfare and the State. Who Benefits?* London: Macmillan.

Burrell, S. A. (1964), 'The Apocalyptic Vision of the Early Covenanters', *The Scottish Historical Review*, 43(135), pp. 1–24.

Butterfield, H. (1978), *The Whig Interpretation of History*, New York: AMS Press.

Calhoun, C. (1997), *Nationalism*, Minneapolis: University of Minnesota Press.

Chatterjee, P. (1993), *The Nation and Its Fragments: Colonial and Postcolonial Histories*, Princeton, NJ: Princeton University Press.

Checkland, O. and Checkland, S. (1989), *Industry and Ethos. Scotland, 1832–1914*, Second edition, Edinburgh: Edinburgh University Press.

Cohen, A. (1996), 'Personal Nationalism: A Scottish View of Some Rites, Rights, and Wrongs', *American Ethnologist*, 23(4), pp. 802–15.

Cohen, J. L. and Arato, A. (1994), *Civil Society and Political Theory*, Cambridge, MA and London: MIT Press.

Colley, L. (1992), *Britons: Forging a Nation, 1707–1837*, London: Pimlico.

Connor, W. (1990), 'When is a nation?', *Ethnic and Racial Studies*, 13(1), pp. 92–103.

Connor, W. (1994), *Ethnonationalism: The Quest for Understanding*, Princeton, NJ: Princeton University Press.

Constitutional Steering Committee (1989), 'A Claim of Right for Scotland', in O. D. Edwards (ed.), *A Claim of Right for Scotland*, Edinburgh: Polygon, pp. 9–53.

Consultative Steering Group (1999), *Shaping Scotland's Parliament. Report of The Consultative Steering Group on the Scottish Parliament*, Edinburgh: The Stationery Office Limited.

Davie, G. E. (1961), *The Democratic Intellect: Scotland and Her Universities in the Nineteenth Century*, Edinburgh: Edinburgh University Press.

Desan, S. (1989), 'Crowds, Community, and Ritual in the Work of E. P. Thompson and Natalie Davis', in L. Hunt (ed.), *The New Cultural History*, Berkeley: University of California Press, pp. 47–71.

Deutsch, K. W. (1953), *Nationalism and Social Communication*, Second edition, Cambridge, MA: MIT Press.

Devine, T. M. (1988), 'Introduction', in T. M. Devine and R. Mitchison (eds), *People and Society in Scotland: Volume I, 1760–1830*, Edinburgh: John Donald, pp. 1–8.

Devine, T. M. (1990), 'The Tobacco Lords of Glasgow', *History Today*, 40, pp. 17–21.

Devine, T. M. and Finlay, R. J. (eds) (1996), *Scotland in the Twentieth Century*, Edinburgh: Edinburgh University Press.

Devine, T. M. and Mitchison, R. (eds) (1988), *People and Society in Scotland, Volume I, 1760–1830*, Edinburgh: John Donald.

Dickson, A. and Treble, J. H. (eds) (1992), *People and Society in Scotland, Volume III, 1914–1990*, Edinburgh: John Donald.

Dickson, M. (1994), 'Should Auld Acquaintance Be Forgot? A Comparison of the Scots and English in Scotland', *Scottish Affairs*, 7, pp. 112–34.

Dickson, T. (1989), 'Scotland is Different, OK?', in D. McCrone, S. Kendrick and P. Straw (eds), *The Making of Scotland: Nation, Culture and Social Change*, Edinburgh: Edinburgh University Press and The British Sociological Association, pp. 53–69.

Donaldson, G. (1970), *Scottish Historical Documents*, New York: Barnes and Noble.

Donnachie, I., Harvie, C. and Wood, I. S. (eds) (1989), *Forward! Labour Poitics in Scotland, 1888–1988*, Edinburgh: Polygon.

Donnachie, I. and Hewitt, G. (1989), *A Companion to Scottish History from the Reformation to the Present*, London: B. T. Batsford Ltd.

Duncan, A. A. M. (1991), 'The Making of the Kingdom', in R. Mitchison (ed.), *Why Scottish History Matters*, Edinburgh: Saltire Society, pp. 1–14.

Dworkin, R. (1978), 'Liberalism', in S. Hampshire (ed.), *Public and Private Morality*, Cambridge: Cambridge University Press, pp. 113–43.

Esping-Anderson, G. and Korpi, W. (1987), 'From Poor Relief to Institutional Welfare States: The Development of Scandanavian Social Policy', in R. Erikson et al. (eds), *The Scandanavian Model: Welfare States and Welfare Research*, Armonk, NY: Sharpe, pp. 39–74.

Esping-Anderson, G. and Kersbergen, K. van (1992), 'Contemporary Research on Social Democracy', *Annual Review of Sociology*, 18, pp. 187–208.

Ferguson, A. (1966 [1767]), *An Essay on the History of Civil Society 1767*, D. Forbes (ed.), Edinburgh: Edinburgh University Press.

Ferguson, W. (1968), *Scotland, 1689 to the Present*, Edinburgh: Oliver and Boyd.

Fergusson, J. (1970), *The Declaration of Arbroath*, J. Fergusson (trans.), Edinburgh: Edinburgh University Press.

Fernandez, J. (1986), *Persuasions and Performances: The Play of Tropes in Culture*, Bloomington: Indiana University Press.

Fernandez, J. (ed.) (1991), *Beyond Metaphor: The Theory of Tropes in Anthropology*, Stanford: Stanford University Press.

Finlay, R. J. (1994), *Independent and Free: Scottish Politics and the Origins of the Scottish National Party, 1918-1945*, Edinburgh: John Donald.

Finlay, R. J. (1996), 'Continuity and Change: Scottish Politics, 1900-45', in T. M. Devine and R. J. Finlay (eds), *Scotland in the Twentieth Century*, Edinburgh: Edinburgh University Press, pp. 64-84.

Forsythe, R. (1992), 'Sport', in M. Linklater and R. Denniston (eds), *The Anatomy of Scotland: How Scotland Works*, Edinburgh and New York: Chambers, pp. 334-53.

Foster, G. (1965), 'Peasant Society and the Image of Limited Good', *American Anthropologist*, 67, pp. 293-315.

Foster, J. (1989), 'Nationality, Social Change and Class: Transformations of National Identity in Scotland', in D. McCrone, S. Kendrick and P. Straw (eds), *The Making of Scotland: Nation, Culture and Social Change*, Edinburgh: Edinburgh University Press and The British Sociological Association, pp. 31-52.

Foster, J. (1991), 'The Common Market and the National Question', *Communist Review*, Spring, pp. 4-13, 27-8.

Freire, P. (1970), *Pedagogy of the Oppressed*, M. B. Ramos (trans.), New York: Continuum.

Friedman, J. (1992), 'The Past in the Future: History and the Politics of Identity', *American Anthropologist*, 95, pp. 837-59.

Fry, M. (1987), *Patronage and Principle*, Aberdeen: Aberdeen University Press.

Fry, M. (1989), 'Claim of Wrong', in O. D. Edwards (ed.), *A Claim of Right*, Edinburgh: Polygon, pp. 93-8.

Fry, M. (1992), 'The Whig Interpretation of Scottish History' in I. Donnachie and C. Whatley (eds), *The Manufacture of Scottish History*, Edinburgh: Polygon, pp. 72-89.

Frykman, J. and O. Löfgren (1987), *Culture Builders: A Historical Anthropology of Middle-Class Life*, New Brunswick, NJ and London: Rutgers University Press.

Gallagher, T. (ed.) (1991), *Nationalism in the Nineties*, Edinburgh: Polygon.

Gauthier, D. (1986), *Morals By Agreement*, Oxford: Oxford University Press.

Gauthier, D. (1998), 'David Hume, contractarian', in D. Boucher and P. Kelly (eds.), *Social Justice from Hume to Walzer*, London and New York: Routledge, pp. 17-44.

Geertz, C. (1963), 'The Integrative Revolution: Primordial Sentiments and Civil Politics in the New States', in C. Geertz (ed.), *Old Societies and New States*, New York: Free Press, pp. 105-57.

Geertz, C. (1973), *The Interpretation of Cultures*, New York: Basic Books.

Gellner, E. (1983), *Nations and Nationalism*, Ithaca, NY: Cornell University Press.

Gellner, E. (1996), 'Do nations have navels?', *Nations and Nationalism*, 2(3), pp. 366–70.

Gluckman, M. (1973), *Custom and Conflict in Africa*, New York: Barnes and Noble.

Goodin, R. E. and Le Grand, J. (1987), *Not Only the Poor: The Middle Classes and the Welfare State*, London: Allen and Unwin.

Goodlet, J. (1764), *A Vindication of the Associate Synod upon the Head of their Principles about the Present Civil Government*, Edinburgh: David Paterson.

Gough, I. (1979), *The Political Economy of the Welfare State*, London: Macmillan.

Gouldner, A. W. (1979), *The Future of Intellectuals and the Rise of the New Class*, London: Macmillan.

Gramsci, A. (1971), *Selections from the Prison Notebooks of Antonio Gramsci*, Q. Hoare and G. N Smith (eds and trans.), New York: International Publishers.

Gramsci, A. (1994), *Antonio Gramsci. Pre-Prison Writings*, R. Bellamy (ed.), Cambridge: Cambridge University Press.

Grant, A. (1991a), *Independence and Nationhood: Scotland 1306–1469*, Edinburgh: Edinburgh University Press.

Grant, A. (1991b), 'The Middle Ages: the Defence of Independence', in R. Mitchison (ed.), *Why Scottish History Matters*, Edinburgh: Saltire Society, pp. 15–25.

Gray, A. (1992), *Why Scots Should Rule Scotland*, Edinburgh: Canongate Press.

Gray, J. (1999), *False Dawn: The Delusions of Global Capitalism*, London: Granta.

Gray, M. (1988), 'The Social Impact of Agrarian Change in the Rural Lowlands', in T. M. Divine and R. Mitchison (eds), *People and Society in Scotland, Volume I, 1760–1830*, Edinburgh: John Donald, pp. 53–69.

Greenfeld, L. (1992), *Nationalism: Five Roads to Modernity*, Cambridge, MA: Harvard University Press.

Guthrie, S. E. (1995), *Faces in the Clouds: A New Theory of Religion*, New York and Oxford: Oxford University Press.

Habermas, J. (1989a), 'The Public Sphere', in S. Seidman (ed.), *Jürgen Habermas on Society and Politics: A Reader*, Boston: Beacon Press, pp. 231–6.

Habermas, J. (1989b), 'The Crisis of the Welfare State and the Exhuastion of Utopian Energies', in S. Seidman (ed.), *Jürgen Habermas on Society and Politics: A Reader*, Boston: Beacon Press, pp. 283–99.

Habermas, J. (1990), *Moral Consciousness and Communicative Action*, C. Lenhardt and S. W. Nicholsen (trans.), Cambridge Cambridge, MA: MIT Press.

Habermas, J. (1993), *Justification and Application: Remarks on Discourse Ethics*, C. P. Cronin (trans.), Cambridge, MA: MIT Press.

Habermas, J. (1996), 'The European Nation-State – Its Achievements and Its Limits. On the Past and Future of Sovereignty and Citizenship', in G. Balakrishnan (ed.), *Mapping the Nation*, London: Verso, pp. 281–94.

Hampton, J. (1986), 'How the Traditional Social Contract Argument Works', in J. Hampton, *Hobbes and the Social Contract Tradition*, Cambridge: Cambridge University Press, pp. 256–84.

Hampton, J. (1995), 'Contract and Consent', in R. Goodin and P. Pettit (eds), *A Companion to Contemporary Political Philosophy*, Cambridge, MA: Blackwell, pp. 379–93.

Harvie, C. (1981), *No Gods and Precious Few Heroes: Scotland Since 1914*, London: Edward Arnold.

Harvie, C. (1998), *Scotland and Nationalism*, Second edition, New York and London: Routledge.

Harvey, D. (1989), *The Condition of Postmodernity*, Cambridge, MA and Oxford: Blackwell.

Hasenfeld, Y., Rafferty, J. and Zald, M. (1987), 'The Welfare State, Citizenship, and Bureaucratic Encounters', *Annual Review of Sociology*, 13, pp. 387–415.

Hassan, G. (ed.) (1999), *A Guide to the Scottish Parliament*, Edinburgh: The Stationery Office Limited.

Hastings, A. (1997), *The Construction of Nationhood: Ethnicity, Religion, and Nationalism*, Cambridge: Cambridge University Press.

Hearn, J. (1996), 'The Colony at the Core: Scottish Nationalism and the Rhetoric of Colonialism', in A. Marcus (ed.), *Anthropology for a Small Planet: Culture and Community in a Global Environment*, St James, NY: Brandywine Press, pp. 50–63.

Hearn, J. (1998), 'The Social Contract: Re-Framing Scottish Nationalism', *Scottish Affairs*, 23, pp. 14–26.

Heclo, H. (1981), 'Towards a New Welfare State?', in P. Flora and A. Heidenheimer (eds), *The Development of Welfare States in Europe and North America*, London: Transaction, pp. 383–486.

Hegel, G. W. F. (1991), *Elements of the Philosophy of Right*, Cambridge: Cambridge University Press.

Henderson, G. D. (1957), *The Burning Bush: Studies in Scottish Church History*, Edinburgh: The Saint Andrew Press.

Henwood, D. (1998), *Wall Street: How it Works and for Whom*, London and New York: Verso.

Henderson, J. (1989), *The Globalisation of High Technology Production*, London and New York: Routledge.

Himsworth, C. M. G. and Munro, C. R. (1998), *Devolution and the Scotland Bill*, Edinburgh: W. Green.

HMSO (1993), *Scotland in the Union: A Partnership for Good*, London: HMSO Publications Centre.

Hobsbawm, E. (1992), *Nations and Nationalism Since 1780: Programme, Myth, Reality*, Second edition, Cambridge: Cambridge University Press.

Hobsbawm, E. (1984), 'Introduction: Inventing Traditions', in E. Hobsbawm and T. Ranger (eds), *The Invention of Tradition*, New York: Cambridge University Press, pp. 1–14.

Hobsbawm, E. and Ranger, T. (1984), *The Invention of Tradition*, New York: Cambridge University Press.

Holland, D. and Quinn, N. (eds) (1987), *Cultural Models in Language and Thought*, Cambridge: Cambridge University Press.

Hood, N. (1995), 'Inward Investment and Scottish Devolution: Towards a Balanced View', *Quarterly Economic Commentary*, 20(4), pp. 67–78.

Hroch. M. (1985), *Social Conditions of National Revival in Europe. A Comparative Analysis of the Social Composition of Patriotic Groups among the Smaller European Nations*, Cambridge: Cambridge University Press.

Hudson, W. D. (1969), *The Is/Ought Question*, New York: St. Martin's Press.

Hume, D. (1978 [1739–40]), *A Treatise of Human Nature*, Second edition, Oxford: Clarendon Press.

Hume, D. (1985a [1777]), 'Of The Original Contract', in *Essays: Moral, Political, and Literary*, Indianapolis: Liberty Fund, pp. 465–87.

Hume, D. (1985b [1777]), 'Of The Origin of Government', in *Essays: Moral, Political, and Literary*, Indianapolis: Liberty Fund, pp. 37–41.

Hunter, J. (1976), *The Making of the Crofting Community*, Edinburgh: John Donald.

Ignatieff, M. (1994), *Blood and Belonging*, London: Vintage.

Jedrej, C. and Nuttall, M. (1996), *White Settlers: The Impact of Rural Repopulation in Scotland*, Luxembourg: Harwood Academic Press.

Jones, P. (1992a), 'Politics', in M. Linklater and R. Denniston (eds), *Anatomy of Scotland: How Scotland Works*, Edinburgh and New York: Chambers. pp. 373–93.

Jones, P. (1992b), 'Local Government', in M. Linklater and R. Denniston (eds), *Anatomy of Scotland: How Scotland Works*, Edinburgh and New York: Chambers, pp. 180–203.

Jones, P. (1992c), 'Introduction', in M. Linklater and R. Denniston (eds), *Anatomy of Scotland: How Scotland Works*, Edinburgh and New York: Chambers, pp. 1–5.

Kay, B. (1993), *Scots: The Mither Tongue*, Revised edition, Hastings Square, Darvel, Scotland: Alloway Publishing Ltd.

Keane, J. (1984), 'Introduction', to C. Offe, *Contradictions of the Welfare State*, Cambridge, MA: MIT Press.

Keane, J. (ed.) (1988), *Civil Society and the State*, London: University of Westmintser Press.

Keating, M. (1996), *Nations Against the State: The New Politics of Nationalism in Quebec, Catalonia and Scotland*, London: Macmillan.

Keating, M., and Bleiman, D. (1979), *Labour and Scottish Nationalism*, London: Macmillan.

Kedourie, E. (1993), *Nationalism*, Fourth edition. Oxford: Blackwell.

Kellas, J. G. (1989), *The Scottish Political System*, Fourth edition, Cambridge: Cambridge University Press.

Kemp, A. (1993), *The Hollow Drum: Scotland Since the War*, Edinburgh: Mainstream.

Kidd, C. (1993), *Subverting Scotland's Past: Scottish Whig Historians and the Creation of an Anglo-British Identity, 1689–c. 1830*, Cambridge: Cambridge University Press.

Kiernan, V. G. (1989), 'A Banner with a Strange Device: The Later Covenanters', in T. Brotherstone (ed.), *Covenant, Charter, and Party: Traditions of Revolt and Protest in Modern Scottish History*, Aberdeen: Aberdeen University Press.

Kirkwood, G. and Kirkwood, C. (1989), *Living Adult Education: Freire in Scotland*, Buckingham: Open University Press.

Knox, W. (1988), 'Religion and the Scottish Labour Movement, c. 1900–39', *Journal of Contemporary History*, 23, pp. 609–30.

Kohn, H. (1967), *The Idea of Nationalism*, Toronto: Collier Books.

Kumar, K. (1993), 'Civil Society: An Inquiry Into the Usefulness of an Historical Term', *British Journal of Sociology*, 44(3), pp. 375–95.

Kymlicka, W. (1995), 'Misunderstanding Nationalism', *Dissent*, Winter 1995, pp. 130–7.

Lakoff, G. and Johnson, M. (1980), *Metaphors We Live By*, Chicago: University of Chicago Press.

Larner, C. (1981), *Enemies of God: The Witch-hunt in Scotland*, Baltimore: The Johns Hopkins University Press.

Lash, S. and Urry, C. (1987), *The End of Organized Capitalism*, Cambridge: Polity Press.

Lawson, A. (1991), 'Why This Final Issue', *Radical Scotland*, 51, p. 3.

Lenman, B. (1981), *Integration, Enlightenment, and Industrialization: Scotland 1746–1832*, Toronto: University of Toronto Press.

Lessnoff, M. (ed.) (1990), *Social Contract Theory*, New York: New York University Press.

Levy, C. (1987), 'Conclusion: Historiography and the New Class', in C. Levy (ed.), *Socialism and the Intelligentsia, 1880–1914*, London and New York: Routledge and Kegan Paul, pp. 271–90.

Linklater, M. (1992), 'The Media', in M. Linklater and R. Denniston (eds), *Anatomy of Scotland: How Scotland Works*, Edinburgh and New York: Chambers.

Linklater, M. and Denniston, R. (eds) (1992), *Anatomy of Scotland: How Scotland Works*, Edinburgh and New York: Chambers.

Livingston, D. W. (1998), *Philosophical Melancholy and Delirium: Hume's Pathology of Philosophy*, Chicago and London: The University of Chicago Press.

Llobera, J. R. (1994), *The God of Modernity: The Development of Nationalism in Western Europe*, Oxford and Washington, D.C.: Berg.

Lowie, R. H. (1947), *Primitive Society*, New York: Liveright.

Lynch, M. (1992), *Scotland: A New History*, London: Pimlico.

Lynch, M. (ed.) (1993), *Scotland, 1850–1979: Society, Politics and the Union*, London: The Historical Association Committee for Scotland and the Historical Association.

MacCormick, J. (1955), *The Flag in the Wind: The Story of the National Movement in Scotland*, London: Gollancz.

MacCormick, N. (1996), 'Liberalism, Nationalism and the Post-Sovereign State', *Political Studies*, XLIV, pp. 553–67.

Macdonald, M. (ed.) (1993), 'Democracy and Curriculum', *Edinburgh Review*, 90, Summer 1993, pp. 5–69.

Macinnes, A. I. (1988), 'Scottish Gaeldom, 1638–1651: The Vernacular Response to the Covenanting Dynamic', in J. Dwyer, R. A. Mason and A. Murdoch (eds),

New Perspectives on the Politics and Culture of Early Modern Scotland, Edinburgh: John Donald, pp. 59–94.

MacInnes, J. (1994), 'Rise and Be a Broadcaster Again?', *Scottish Affairs*, 7, pp. 135–41.

MacIntyre, A. (1984), *After Virtue*, Second edition, Notre Dame: University of Notre Dame Press.

MacIntyre, A. (1990), *Three Rival Versions of Moral Enquiry: Encyclopaedia, Genealogy, Tradition*, Notre Dame: University of Notre Dame Press.

Mackie, J. D. (1978), *A History of Scotland*, Second edition, New York and London: Penguin Books.

MacMillan, J. (1993a), 'State of the Unions Addresses Deeper Fears', *Scotland on Sunday*, 9 October, p. 18.

MacMillan, J. (1993b), 'Workers on a Tightrope Must Have a Safety Net', *Scotland on Sunday*, 21 November, p. 16.

MacMillan, J. (1994), 'Campaigns for Community are a Lot of Talk', *Scotland on Sunday*, 25 September, p. 16.

Makey, W. (1979), *The Church of the Covenant, 1637–1651: Revolution and Social Change in Scotland*, Edinburgh: John Donald.

Mann, M. (1993), *The Sources of Social Power, Volume II*, Cambridge: Cambridge University Press.

Mann, M. (1996), 'Nation-states in Europe and Other Continents: Diversifying, Developing, Not Dying', in G. Balakrishnan (ed.), *Mapping the Nation*, London: Verso, pp. 295–316.

Marr, A. (1992), *The Battle for Scotland*, New York and London: Penguin Books.

Marshall, G. (1992), *Presbyteries and Profits: Calvinism and the Development of Capitalism in Scotland 1560–1707*, Edinburgh: Edinburgh University Press.

Marshall, T. H. (1983), 'Citizenship and Social Class', in D. Held et al. (eds), *States and Societies*, New York and London: New York University Press.

Marx, K. (1967), *Capital, Volume I*, New York: International Publishers.

Mason, R. A. (1998), *Kingship and the Commonweal: Political Thought in Renaissance and Reformation Scotland*, East Linton, Scotland: Tuckwell Press.

Maxwell, S. (1976), 'Beyond Social Democracy', in G. Kennedy (ed.), *The Radical Approach: Papers on an Independent Scotland*, Edinburgh: Palingenisis Press Ltd, pp. 7–20.

McArthur, C. (1994), 'Culloden: A Pre-emptive Strike', *Scottish Affairs*, 9, pp. 97–126.

McCreadie, R. (1991), 'Scottish Identity and the Constitution', in B. Crick, (ed.), *National Identities: The Constitution of the United Kingdom*, Cambridge, MA and Oxford: Blackwell, pp. 38–56.

McCrone, D. (1992), *Understanding Scotland: The Sociology of a Stateless Nation*, London and New York: Routledge.

McCrone D. (1993), 'The Unstable Union: Scotland Since the 1920s', in M. Lynch, (ed.), *Scotland, 1850–1979: Society, Politics and the Union*, London: Historical Association Committee for Scotland and The Historical Association, pp. 43–9.

McCrone, D. (1998), *The Sociology of Nationalism*, London and New York: Routledge.

McCrone, D. and Bechhofer, F. (1993), 'The Scotland-England Divide: Politics and Locality in Britain', *Political Studies* 41, pp. 96–107.

McCrone, D., Bechhofer, F. and Kendrick, S. (1982), 'Egalitarianism and Social Inequality in Scotland,' in D. Robbins (ed.), *Rethinking Social Inequality*, Hampshire, England: Gower, pp. 127–48.

McCrone, D., Kendrick, S. and Straw, P. (1989), 'Introduction: Understanding Scotland', in D. McCrone, S. Kendrick and P. Straw (eds), *The Making of Scotland: Nation, Culture and Social Change*, Edinburgh: Edinburgh Univesity Press and The British Sociological Association, pp. 1–12.

McFadden, J. and Lazarowicz, M. (1999), *The Scottish Parliament: An Introduction*, Edinburgh: T. & T. Clark.

McGregor, P., Stevens, J., Swales, K. and Yin, Y. P. (1997), 'The Economics of the "Tartan Tax"', *Quarterly Economic Commentary*, 22(3), pp. 72–85.

McIlvanney, W. (1991), *Surviving the Shipwreck*, Edinburgh and London: Mainstream Publishing.

McKim, R. and McMahan, J. (eds) (1997), *The Morality of Nationalism*, New York and Oxford: Oxford Univeristy Press.

McLean, R. (1988a), *Labour and Scottish Home Rule, Part 1*, Whitburn, Scotland: Scottish Labour Action.

McLean, R. (1988b), *Labour and Scottish Home Rule, Part 2*, Whitburn, Scotland: Scottish Labour Action.

Midwinter, A., Keating, M. and Mitchell, J. (1991), *Politics and Public Policy in Scotland*, London: Macmillan.

Miller, D. (1995), *On Nationality*, Oxford: Clarendon Press.

Miller, G. A. (1993), 'Images and Models, Similies and Metaphors', in A. Ortony (ed.), *Metaphor and Thought*, Second edition, Cambridge: Cambridge University Press, pp. 375–400.

Mitchell, J. (1990), *Conservatives and the Union: A Study of Conservative Party Attitudes to Scotland*, Edinburgh: Edinburgh University Press.

Mitchell, J. (1997), *Strategies for Self-government: The Campaigns for a Scottish Parliament*, Edinburgh: Polygon.

Mitchison, R. (1970), *A History of Scotland*, London: Methuen and Co. Ltd.

Mitchison, R. (1990), *Lordship to Patronage: Scotland 1603–1745*, Edinburgh: Edinburgh University Press.

Mitchison, R. and Leneman, L. (1989), *Sexuality and Social Control: Scotland 1660–1780*, New York: Basil Blackwell.

Moore, C. and Booth, S. (1989), *Managing Competition: Meso-Corporatism, Pluralism, and the Negotiated Order in Scotland*, Oxford: Clarendon Press.

Morton, G. (1998), *Unionist-Nationalism: Governing Urban Scotland, 1830–1860*, East Linton, Scotland: Tuckwell.

Morton, G. (1996), 'Scottish Rights and "Centralisation" in the Mid-Nineteenth Century', *Nations and Nationalism*, 2(2), pp. 257–79.

Mosse, G. (1975), *The Nationalization of the Masses*, Ithaca and London: Cornell University Press.

Nairn, T. (1981), *The Break-Up of Britain*, Second edition, London: Verso.

Nairn, T. (1997), *Faces of Nationalism: Janus Revisited*, London: Verso.

Nielsen, K. (1999), 'Cultural Nationalism, Neither Ethnic nor Civic', in R. Beiner (ed.), *Theorizing Nationalism*, Albany: State University of New York Press.

Nozick, R. (1974), *Anarchy, State, and Utopia*, New York: Basic Books.

Offe, C. (1987), 'Democracy Against the Welfare State?', *Political Theory*, 15(4), pp. 501–37.

O'Leary, B. (ed.) (1996), 'Symposium on David Miller's *On Nationality*, *Nations and Nationalism*, 2(3), pp. 407–51.

Ohnuki-Tierney, E. (1990), 'The Monkey as Self in Japanese Culture', in E. Ohnuki-Tierney (ed.), *Culture Through Time: Anthropological Approaches*, Stanford: Stanford University Press.

Ortony, A. (ed.) (1993), *Metaphor and Thought*, Second edition, Cambridge: Cambridge University Press.

Paterson, L. (1991), 'Ane End of Ane Auld Sang: Sovereignty and the Re-Negotiation of the Union', in A. Brown and D. McCrone (eds), *The Scottish Government Yearbook, 1991*, Edinburgh: Edinburgh University Press.

Paterson, L. (1994), *The Autonomy of Modern Scotland*, Edinburgh: Edinburgh Univerisity Press.

Payne, P. L. (1996), 'The Economy', in T. M. Devine and R. J. Finlay (eds), *Scotland in the Twentieth Century*, Edinburgh: Edinburgh University Press, pp. 13–45.

Pierson, C. (1991), *Beyond the Welfare State? The New Political Economy of Welfare*, University Park, PA: University of Pennsylvania Press.

Pierson, C. (1995), *Socialism After Communism: The New Market Socialism*, University Park, PA: University of Pennsylvania Press.

Pittock, M. G. H. (1991), *The Invention of Scotland. The Stuart Myth and the Scottish Identity, 1638 to the Present*, London and New York: Routledge.

Polanyi, K. (1957), *The Great Transformation: The Political and Economic Origins of Our Time*, Boston: Beacon Press.

Rawls, J. (1971), *A Theory of Justice*, Cambridge, MA: Harvard University Press.

Rawls, J. (1996), *Political Liberalism*, New York: Columbia University Press.

Reid, J. M. (1960), *Kirk and Nation. The Story of the Reformed Church of Scotland*, London: Skeffington.

Roseberry, W. (1989), *Anthropologies and Histories: Essays in Culture, History, and Political Economy*, New Brunswick, NJ and London: Rutgers University Press.

Ryan, A. (1995), 'Liberalism', in R. E. Goodin and P. Pettit (eds), *A Companion to Contemporary Political Philosophy*, Oxford and Cambridge, MA: Blackwell.

Sacks, S. (ed.) (1979), *On Metaphor*, Chicago and London: University of Chicago Press.

Sahlins, M. (1981), *Historical Metaphors and Mythical Realities: Structure in the Early History of the Sandwich Island Kingdom*, Ann Arbor: The Univerisity of Michigan Press.

Sandel, M. (1982), *Liberalism and the Limits of Justice*, New York and Cambridge: Cambridge University Press.

Sandel, M. (ed.) (1984), *Liberalism and Its Critics*, New York: New York University Press.

Schön, D. A. (1993), 'Generative Metaphor: A Perspective on Problem-Setting in Social Policy', in A. Ortony (ed.), *Metaphor and Thought*, Second edition, Cambridge: Cambridge University Press.

Scott, A. M. and Macleay, I. (1990), *Britain's Secret War: Tartan Terrorism and the Anglo-American State*, Edinburgh: Mainstream.

Scott, J. (1976), *The Moral Economy of the Peasant*, New Haven: Yale University Press.

Scott, P. (1979), *1707, The Union of Scotland and England*, Edinburgh: Chambers.

Scottish Constitutional Convention (1990), *Towards Scotland's Parliament. A Report to the Scottish People by the Scottish Constitutional Convention*, Edinburgh: The Scottish Constitutional Convention.

Scottish Constitutional Convention (1995), *Scotland's Parliament. Scotland's Right*, Edinburgh: The Scottish Constitutional Convention.

Scottish National Party (1992a), *Independence in Europe: Make It Happen Now! The 1992 Manifesto of the Scottish National Party*, Edinburgh: Scottish National Party.

Scottish National Party (1992b), *Recovery in Scotland: Make It Happen Now! How We Will Rebuild the Scottish Economy*, Edinburgh: Scottish National Party.

Scottish National Party (1997a), *Yes We Can Win the Best for Scotland: The SNP General Election Manifesto 1997*, Edinburgh: Scottish National Party.

Scottish National Party (1997b), *Yes We Can Win the Best for Scotland: The SNP General Election Budget 1997*, Edinburgh: Scottish National Party.

Scottish Office (1997), *Scotland's Parliament*, Edinburgh: The Scottish Office.

Scottish Watch (1994), *The New Scottish Clearances*, Dumfries, Scotland: Scottish Watch.

Seligman, A. (1992), *The Idea of Civil Society*, New York: Free Press.

Seton-Watson, H. (1977), *Nations and States*, Boulder, CO: Westview Press.

Siol Nan Gaidheal (1990), 'Constitution', *Siol Nan Gaidheal News*, 4/5, p. 6.

Siol Nan Gaidheal (1993), 'Aims and Principles of Our Movement', *Siol*, 11, pp. 36–7.

Skinner, Q. (1978), *The Foundations of Modern Political Thought, Volume II, The Age of Reformation*, Cambridge: Cambridge University Press.

Smith, A. (1981 [1776]), *An Inquiry into the Nature and Causes of the Wealth of Nations, Volumes I and II*, R. H. Campbell and A. S. Skinner (eds), Indianapolis: Liberty Fund.

Smith, A. (1986), *The Ethnic Origins of Nations*, Oxford: Blackwell.

Smith, A. (1991), *National Identity*, London: Penguin.

Smith, A. (1996a), 'Nations and their pasts', *Nations and Nationalism*, 2(3), pp. 358–65.

Smith, A. (1996b), 'Memory and modernity: reflections on Ernest Gellner's theory of nationalism', *Nations and Nationalism*, 2(3), pp. 371–88.

Smout, T. C. (1972), *A History of the Scottish People, 1560–1830*, London: Fontana.

Smout, T. C. (1987), *A Century of the Scottish People, 1830–1950*, London: Fontana.

Smyth, A. P. (1989), *Warlords and Holy Men: Scotland AD 80–1000*, Edinburgh: Edinburgh University Press.

Stevens, J. (1997), 'The SNP Budget for Scotland – A Comment', *Quarterly Economic Commentary*, 22(3), pp. 44–56.

Stevenson, D. (1973), *The Scottish Revolution 1637–1644: The Triumph of the Covenanters*, Newton Abbot, Devon: David and Charles Ltd.

Stevenson, D. (1980), *Alasdair MacColla and the Highland Problem in the Seventeenth Century*, Edinburgh: John Donald.

Stevenson, D. (1988), *The Covenanters: The National Covenant and Scotland*, Edinburgh: The Saltire Society.

Steward, J. (1972), *Theory of Culture Change*, Urbana: University of Illinois Press.

Tamir, Y. (1993), *Liberal Nationalism*, Princeton Princeton University Press.

Tarrow, S. (1994), *Power in Movement: Social Movements, Collective Action and Politics*, Cambridge: Cambridge University Press.

Taylor, C. (1989), *Sources of the Self: The Making of Modern Identity*, Cambridge, MA: Cambridge University Press.

Thane, P. (1984), 'The Working Class and State "Welfare" in Britain, 1880–1914', *The Historical Journal*, 27(4), pp. 877–900.

Therborn, G. (1987), 'Welfare State and Capitalist Markets', *Acta Sociologica*, 30(3/4), pp. 237–54.

Thompson, E. P. (1971), 'The Moral Economy of the English Crowd in the Eighteenth Century', *Past and Present*, 50, pp. 76–136.

Thompson, E. P. (1993), 'The Moral Economy Reviewed', in E. P. Thompson, *Customs in Common: Studies in Traditional Popular Culture*, New York: The New Press, pp. 259–351.

Tilton, T. (1990), *The Political Theory of Swedish Social Democracy. Through the Welfare State to Socialism*, Oxford: Clarendon.

Trevor-Roper, H. (1984), 'The Invention of Tradition: The Highland Tradition of Scotland', in E. Hobsbawm and T. Ranger (eds), *The Invention of Tradition*, Cambridge: Cambridge University Press.

Viroli, M. (1997), *For Love of Country: An Essay on Patriotism and Nationalism*, Oxford: Clarendon Press.

Walker, G. and Gallagher, T. (1990), *Sermons and Battle Hymns: Protestant Popular Culture in Modern Scotland*, Edinburgh: Edinburgh University Press.

Walzer, M. (1983), *Spheres of Justice: A Defense of Pluralism and Equality*, New York: Basic Books.

Walzer, M. (1985), *Exodus and Revolution*, New York: Basic Books.

Weir, D. (1990), *The Origins of the Federal Theology in Sixteenth-Century Reformation Thought*, Oxford: Clarendon Press.

Wilensky, H. (1975), *The Welfare State and Equality: Structural and Ideological Roots of Public Expenditure*, Berkeley: University of California Press.

Williams, R. (1977), *Marxism and Literature*, Oxford and New York: Oxford University Press.

Wilson, A. J. (1997), 'Stuck on the Starting Blocks: A Response to Mr Steven's Comment on the SNP General Election Budget 1997', *Quarterly Economic Commentary*, 22(3), pp. 57–66.

Withers, C. W. J. (1988), *Gaelic Scotland: The Transformation of a Culture Region*, London and New York: Routledge.

Withers, C. W. J. (1992), 'The Historical Creation of the Scottish Highlands', in I. Donnachie and C. Whatley (eds), *The Manufacture of Scottish History*, Edinburgh: Polygon.

Wolf, E. R. (1999), *Envisioning Power: Ideologies of Dominance and Crisis*, Berkeley: University of California Press.

Woman's Claim of Right Group (1991), *A Woman's Claim of Right in Scotland: Women, Representation and Politics*, Edinburgh: Polygon.

Wood, E. M. (1986), 'The New "True" Socialism', in E. M. Wood, *The Retreat from Class*, London: Verso, pp. 1–11.

Wood, F. (1989), 'Scottish Labour in Government and Opposition, 1964–1979', in I. Donnachie, C. Harvie and I. S. Wood (eds), *Forward! Labour Politics in Scotland, 1888–1988*, Edinburgh: Polygon.

Wood, P. W. (1997), 'An Analysis of the Scottish National Party's 1997 Election Budget Proposals', *Quarterly Economic Commentary*, 22(3), pp. 68–71.

Woolf, S. (1996), 'Introduction', in S. Woolf (ed.), *Nationalism in Europe, 1815 to the Present: A Reader*, London and New York: Routledge.

Wormald, J. (1980), 'Bloodfeud, Kindred, and Government in Early Modern Scotland', *Past and Present*, 87, pp. 54–97.

Wormald, J. (1985), *Lords and Men in Scotland: Bonds of Manrent, 1442–1603*, Edinburgh: John Donald Publishers.

Wormald, J. (1991), *Court, Kirk and Community: Scotland 1470–1625*, Edinburgh: Edinburgh University Press.

Wuthnow, R. (1987), *Meaning and Moral Order: Explorations in Cultural Analysis*, Berkeley: University of California Press.

Yack, B. (1996), 'The Myth of the Civic Nation', *Critical Review*, 10(2), pp. 193–211.

Zald, M. N. and McCarthy, J. D. (eds) (1987), *Social Movements in an Organizational Society*, New Brunswick, NJ: Transaction Press.

Index

Page numbers in **bold** indicate a main reference to the subject.